CARING FOR YOUR COLLECTIONS

CARING FOR YOUR COLLECTIONS

The National Committee to Save America's Cultural Collections, Arthur W. Schultz, Chairman

Foreword by *Arthur W. Schultz*

Introduction by *The Honorable Robert McCormick Adams*

With essays by *Huntington T. Block*, *Brian Considine*, *Meg Craft*, *Terry Drayman-Weisser*, *Margaret Holben Ellis*, *Wilbur Faulk*, *Doris A. Hamburg*, *William R. Leisher*, *John L. Marion*, *Richard Newman*, *Debbie Hess Norris*, *J. Scott Odell*, *Carolyn L. Rose*, *Leonard L. Silverstein*, *Joyce Hill Stoner*, *Shelley G. Sturman*, *Steven Weintraub*, *George Segan Wheeler*, *Sara J. Wolf*

Harry N. Abrams, Inc., Publishers, New York

Editor: Harriet Whelchel
Designer: Darilyn Lowe Carnes
Rights and Permissions: Barbara Lyons

Library of Congress Cataloging-in-Publication Data
Caring for your collections: preserving and protecting your art and other collectibles / National Committee to Save America's Cultural Collections ; Arthur W. Schultz, chairman.
p. cm.
Includes bibliographical references and index.
ISBN 0-8109-3174-5
1. Collectibles—Private collections—United States—Conservation and restoration. 2. Collectibles—Private collections—United States—Protection. I. United States. National Committee to Save America's Cultural Collections. II. Schultz, Arthur W.
AM303.C37 1992
790.1'32'0973—dc20 91-30466
CIP

Published in 1992 by Harry N. Abrams, Incorporated, New York
A Times Mirror Company

Printed and bound in Japan

Page 2: Chester Harding. Thomas Abthorpe Cooper. c. 1822. Oil on canvas. Collection The Art Institute of Chicago

CONTENTS

FOREWORD

Arthur W. Schultz

Many collectors believe the art they have acquired will last forever—unless it is stolen, burned, or vandalized. This is not true. Everything ages, including paintings, photographs, books, textiles, even statuary. Most often, barring a sudden calamity, the deterioration is slow moving, subtle, and unnoticeable. It is only with the passage of time that we finally detect the damage that the environment and inattention on our part has caused to our most valuable possessions. Frequently it is then too late to restore the loss or even halt further decay. When this happens, we have lost forever something of great value.

The purpose of this book is to alert us as private collectors to the dangers our cultural treasures face and to explain how these dangers can be avoided. Experts in various fields of conservation will identify the causes of deterioration and outline the steps we may take to conserve and preserve our fine objects. After reading the section(s) that pertain to a particular collection, we should be able to begin immediately a program to conserve our art and other treasures. Attentive care of our cultural collections can be the finest investment we have ever made, adding immensely to their value as well as to our enjoyment.

The need for and design of the book evolved from a study Andrew Heiskell commissioned me to make in 1987. Andrew, then chairman of the President's Committee on the Arts and the Humanities, observed that our cultural treasures were disintegrating and disappearing at a distressing rate simply through neglect and unintended abuse. He called upon me to head a National Committee to Save America's Cultural Collections, whose mission was to study the problem and propose appropriate action. Carolyn Rose, then chairman of the National Institute for the Conservation of Cultural Property (NIC), loaned the NIC's resources to the project and joined the President's Committee as joint sponsor. This book is one result of our efforts.

Since most of our national treasures still reside in private residences rather than museums, it seemed obvious that an effort should be made to help each of us safeguard our own treasures. We discovered there was not a single volume written for the general public that explained, in easy-to-understand terms, how one could preserve one's own cultural possessions. We decided to develop this book because we wished to take the mystery out of the proper care of fine cultural objects. We hope you find the results of value.

Seventeenth-century Italian painter Evaristo Baschenis took artistic license in his placement of the musical instruments in this painting. Collectors should avoid such overly casual handling, which is a common source of easily prevented damage to historical instruments. Courtesy Cooper-Hewitt Museum of Decorative Arts and Design, Smithsonian Institution

Many have worked hard to give birth to this book. Donald Hall, current chairman of the President's Committee, has become an avid supporter. Diane Paton, executive director of the President's Committee, and Jane Sennett Long, past project director of the National Committee, were helpful throughout in the management of myriad details. They were aided at the NIC by Lawrence Reger, president; Polly Arenberg, editor; and Migs Grove, program director for communications and special projects, who supplied support that was absolutely necessary to the completion of the project.

Several people gave me direction and encouragement from beginning to end, and I would like to acknowledge them here: Frank Hodsoll, past chairman, National Endowment for the Arts (NEA); John Frohnmayer, chairman, NEA; Lynne V. Cheney, chairman, National Endowment for the Humanities (NEH); Daphne Wood Murray, past director, Institute of Museum Services (IMS); Robert McCormick Adams, The Secretary, Smithsonian Institution; J. Carter Brown, director, National Gallery of Art (NGA); Dr. Franklin Murphy, chairman, board of directors, NGA, and member, President's Committee; Harold Williams, president, The Getty Trust; Daniel J. Boorstin, former Librarian of Congress; Arthur Beale, director of research, Museum of Fine Arts Boston; Luis Monreal, director general, Fundación "la Caixa," Barcelona; James N. Wood, director, Art Institute of Chicago, and member, National Committee; Katherine C. Lee, deputy director, Art Institute of Chicago; Armand Deutsch, past co–vice-chairman, President's Committee; Lambertus van Zelst, director, Conservation Analytical Laboratory, Smithsonian Institution; Paul Himmelstein, president, American Institute for Conservation of Historic and Artistic Works (AIC); Lois Burke Shepard, past director, IMS; Sarah Z. Rosenberg, executive director, AIC and its Foundation; Jane Slate Siena of the Getty Conservation Institute; Paul Gottlieb, Abrams' publisher, whose initial encouragement gave us the impetus to move ahead; and Harriet Whelchel, our editor, who worked so patiently and tirelessly with the authors.

I must pay special thanks to Nancy Reagan and Barbara Bush. Both presidential wives, through their support of the President's Committee on the Arts and Humanities, encouraged us to undertake and complete this work.

And, of course, my deepest gratitude goes to the authors, the best in the land in their areas of expertise, who tackled their assignments with vigor, enthusiasm, and professionalism.

I am very grateful to all.

INTRODUCTION

The Honorable Robert McCormick Adams

That this book fills a need for practical, authoritative advice invaluable to anyone who collects is self-evident and requires little amplification on my part. As a collector of modest proportions myself, I have found it a treasure trove, not only of specific tips and insights, but also of orientations to the larger subject of collecting and conserving as steps toward the full and lasting enjoyment of things of value. Spanning a broadly representative range of concerns, materials, and challenges to their preservation, the book equips collectors not simply to recognize and deal with those challenges but also to find deeper, unanticipated pleasure in what they have brought together.

So much is simple and straightforward. But perhaps there is more to be said on a larger and vaguer subject, collecting as a creative act in the context of our times. My wife's and my collecting has been largely an outgrowth of many years of travel, in Latin America, Africa, and eastern Asia, and especially in the Middle East. What we acquired of course evokes memories. More importantly, objects become symbols that embody stages in our slowly emergent understanding of other traditions of representation and canons of craftsmanship, the awakening of a capacity to hold and respect different aesthetics and perspectives. In becoming symbols, they invest the travel itself with coherence and meaning.

Social critic and historian Michel Foucault has rightly called this an era of simultaneity. Historical continuities were long the privileged ones in Western ways of thought, largely constraining change within a framework of tradition and "civilization" or within still narrower political, cultural, or geographic boundaries. That is less and less so today. We are awash in "information," shallow, repetitive, and uncritical as it is so often, that circles the world virtually at the speed of light. Even our private spheres of attention and discourse are all too often ineluctably drawn toward an overlap with precisely those phenomena most suited to media treatment—body counts, the grotesque and infamous, everyone's fifteen minutes' worth of fame but with an emphasis on sports and screen personalities, and endlessly churning fads in consumption, adornment, and entertainment.

Collecting, for its part, has also gone free form; beer cans, matchbooks, and baseball cards all have traded at multiples of an average annual salary. But collections across some segment of a lifetime, I would like to think, can be a bulwark against the surrender of our individual memories and trajectories to the pursuit of the purely evanescent.

Nothing is forever. Even of our great museums, a recent article in *Artnews* (May 1990) inevitably asks, "How permanent is the permanent collection?" The ideal private collections I envision are not successive clusterings of personal memorabilia, cast up onto the walls and vitrines of uncomprehending, succeeding generations of one's descendants as onto deserted beaches after many seasons of storms. But neither is each decision by which a collection grows an independent act. Applied within a more or less restricted field of opportunity, to be sure, it is a demonstration of evolving qualities of taste and insight whose parameters are indeed uniquely and enduringly personal.

Taste is a word I recently heard independently applied by several knowledgeable colleagues to a distinguished physicist. Most readers of this book no doubt would associate it not with science but with connoisseurship; however, the connotations are the same in either case. Taste implies trained judgment, not limited to gross criteria but concentrating, in fact, on subtle characteristics that can be recognized only with much experience and analytical penetration. Yet it is also a product of more than just simple experience, which can only hone but not create a strong native talent and sense of attraction. Taste and collections evolve together, building upon one another.

How can taste, a passion for bringing into association with each other some previously unperceived likenesses or relationships, and an abiding concern for conserving that newly enhanced sense of the world's beauty and complexity not also evolve together? This, in fact, is the coherence of qualities that the contributors to this book all prize and seek to communicate.

PUBLISHER'S NOTE

The book is divided into chapters according to medium or type of collectible or along broad general themes, and each chapter has been written by an expert in that particular field. A number of chapters—those relating to environment, insurance, or security, for example—should be of interest to all collectors. On the other hand, someone who collects only ceramics will not necessarily read the chapter on metal objects; therefore, most chapters are designed to be more or less self-sufficient. Many collectibles, however, are made of a combination of materials—for example, ethnographic objects often combine textiles, wood, ceramic or metal beads, ivory, shell, and so on; silver utensils may incorporate ivory, ceramic, or wood; and wooden objects can be overlaid with paint or inlaid with mother-of-pearl or ivory. Readers are urged to refer freely to related chapters, making use of the index, the guide to resource organizations and materials, and the bibliography provided at the back of the book.

Because this book is aimed at the individual collector, technical guidelines are provided in the form most familiar to a lay audience. Hence, temperature is given in Fahrenheit degrees and light levels in footcandles.

THE MORTALITY OF THINGS

Joyce Hill Stoner

A conservator of works of art on paper at the Henry Francis du Pont Winterthur Museum in Wilmington, Delaware, takes light levels near a mezzotint.

". . . She cannot fade, though thou hast not thy bliss,
For ever wilt thou love and she be fair!"

—John Keats
"On a Grecian Urn"

Philosophy professors tell us that we believe ourselves to be immortal until we are almost thirty years old. At that point we become aware of our mortality and have more interest in the history of mankind. When do we realize the mortality of our things? Is it when we come across a scrapbook of our grade-school drawings and find the paper brittle, the Scotch tape or glue brown and nonfunctioning, and the scrapbook pages thinned by silverfish? The maiden on Keats's Grecian urn may at first seem forever young compared to the mortal observer, but on closer look we'll find the crazed glazes, cracks, and stains reflecting the course of her life; she too has a mortality.

A French conservator recently shocked curators into awareness of the mortality of works of art by a slide lecture about two polychrome carved

Opposite:
Resist the urge to use decorative greenery, which can catch fire readily, around candlesticks or near artworks.

wooden angels "separated at birth" to live in different museums. One angel went to a museum with climate control and was kept out of harsh lighting conditions on a safe pedestal. The other was put in unmonitored storage and underwent floods, rough handling, and resultant flaking of paint and loss of limbs. When the two "siblings" were at last reunited, the effect, of course, was stunning.

Our homes have many of the same problems that small museums do: erratic climates, variable light, inadequate storage, and, perhaps most of all, untrained personnel. We are the greatest assets or dangers to our personal collections. We decide where to place objects and paintings or how to store memorabilia. We choose the movers; we train (or act as) housekeeping staff; we decide how much to spend on heat, ventilation, air conditioning, or humidity control. We decided to move the turret-topped tea table with all the porcelain figurines still on it so the decorator could reach the valance. And now we must choose the decorative-arts conservator to treat the broken ones. Or will we let our neighbor's niece-who-is-doing-so-well-in-art-school do it? Or will we do it ourselves?

Our situation is complicated by our historical era; we live in what Arthur Miller called in his play *The Price* "the Disposable Age." If something falls apart, we assume we can buy another—perhaps an even better one. We are only recently discovering that this is not always so, and it is perhaps time to invest in the care of our collections. If you are reading this book, your collection already has a much better chance to be inherited than many. There are those who read books on various pursuits, from parenting to collecting, and those who rely on intuition and learn by trial and error. Probably none of us has so many possessions (or children) that we would wish intentionally to provide them with disadvantageous futures through experimentation. There are basic collection conservation principles that—while not foolproof—will at least reduce the risks and provide a reasonable chance your collection will be appreciated by succeeding generations. Just as doctors study the many factors that are likely to affect our own lifespans, practitioners in the field of conservation study the circumstances that may lengthen or shorten the life of art objects or other family treasures.

Defining "Conservation"

The restoration of damaged works of art can be traced to antiquity. Greek and Roman artisans were well versed in their craft and in the properties of the materials they used; the artisans themselves were the obvious choice to treat broken sculpture or scratched murals. The first documented treatment of Michelangelo's mural *The Last Judgment* took place in 1564, only twenty-four years after it was completed. Peter Paul Rubens and Charles Willson Peale not only painted works we admire today, but they also restored their own works and the works of others.

By the nineteenth century, artists could for the first time buy "off the shelf" products: tubed oil paints and stretched and primed canvases. No longer did they undergo long years of apprenticeship grinding colors and pleasing the master by careful preparation and knowledge of materials. The age of Lord Byron and Romanticism changed the artist's self-concept from that of a superb craftsperson to an inspired genius. The Industrial Revolution produced materials faster and more cheaply, but they were of variable permanence. The artist was no longer the best choice for treatment of his or her own works or the works of others.

The first scientific laboratory in a museum was established in 1888 at Berlin's Staatliche Museen; the British Museum followed suit in 1921; and in 1928 the Fogg Museum at Harvard University in Cambridge, Massachusetts, set up a laboratory that brought together under one roof—for the first time in the United States—art historians, scientists, and restorers to determine why works of art deteriorate and what could be done about it. Other conservation departments were established in the following decade at the Museum of Fine Arts, Boston; the Brooklyn Museum; the Walters Art Gallery, Baltimore; the Philadelphia Museum of Art; and the National Gallery in Canada.

Today the word conservation is meant to be an overarching term for a field that concerns not only the restoration of damaged works but also their preservation through an understanding of the requirements for best long-term care; scientific examination to determine the component materials before making judgments; and thorough documentation of the works themselves in addition to description of any treatment carried out to give a "leg up" to the next generation of caretakers.

Handling Works of Art

Caroline Keck, a pioneer American conservator and author, noted plainly, "A work of art lasts as long as its parts stay stuck together." Works of art and cultural property are often composed of highly incompatible materials that react differentially to moisture, temperature change, and strong light. These material concoctions are all seeking entropy—fervently attempting to return to the random state of disorder they enjoyed before a dedicated craftsman, artist, or artisan fashioned and assembled them. The recent graduate of a conservation program stands firmly with arms crossed and earnestly demands "50 percent relative humidity for all works!" Why is this? An ivory-handled knife in the Winterthur Museum collection demonstrates this readily. At humidities measured somewhat above 50 percent, the steel blade corrodes, rusts, and expands. At humidities measured somewhat below 50 percent, the ivory handle shrinks and splits. The knife disassembles itself unless we intervene.

On a more basic level, when we reach to pick up a silver teapot, a drop of perspiration or even the fingerprint from a fairly clean hand, if not wiped away, can cause marked corrosion in less than a month. Our thumbprints may inadvertently be bequeathed to our descendants through individualized corrosion patterns on the family silver. (Nineteenth-century butlers wore white gloves when handling the silver, which prevented this.) Careful handling of works must always be considered.

The most important advice for handling artworks is to use common sense. Before picking up a work—plan ahead. Do not lift the heavy frame from the wall if you have not chosen a place to put it that will not damage the scrollwork on every corner. Check for loose parts. Do not start to move something with one person when three will be needed midstream. Do not first take out the lower drawers from a heavy high chest, lest it fall over on you. Use two hands or more—possibly gloved. Do not pick up a chair from the top with one hand, which can leave you a disconnected chair rail in the one hand. Ditto candlesticks. Do not hurry. If the phone rings, let it ring. If someone is anxious to open the window—now—take the time to move all the breakables off the table in front before sliding the table out of the way. Many owners who arrive at a consultation day with a damaged piece are often chagrined when they realize how predictable, and preventable, a particular accident may have been.

People often move fine furniture across the country with no damage. To move only fourteen blocks, however, the movers might cut some corners. We are told that accidents to people often happen "close to home." This is no doubt analogous to accidents to possessions. Work with your movers to treat each piece with care, and discourage corner cutting; conservation treatment will cost more.

Effects of Moisture

As noted above, moisture can be damaging to metals, causing rusting and corrosion. Near the sea this is further complicated by salt-laden moisture, as used-car dealers well know. Severe moisture can cause wood to swell and paint to crack and flake off. Relative humidities above 70 percent can cause mold to grow nearly anywhere. Bookbindings, book paper, parchment diplomas, the canvas support of paintings, textiles, and photographs can all serve as host supports for mold growth. Mold spores are omnipresent in the atmosphere near or far from foodstuffs, and while fumigation kills fungus currently on an object, as soon as the humidity is high enough, new spores will produce new deteriorating agents that can cause nonremovable dark spotting and staining. Fluffy white growths can sometimes safely be brushed away, but the important step is to keep down the humidity and increase the air circulation. Remember too that

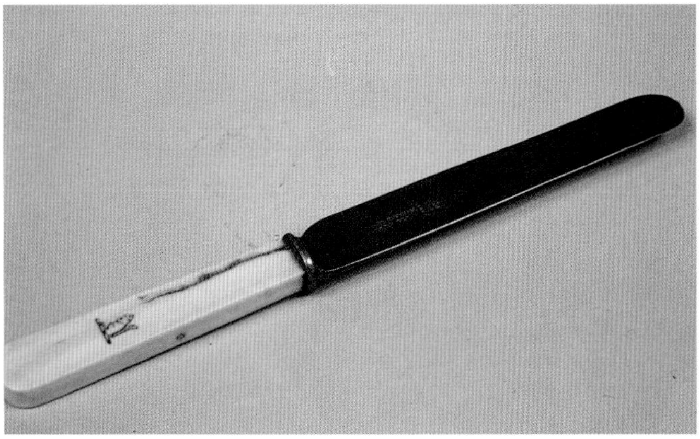

This knife demonstrates the difficulty of achieving an ideal environment for composite objects: Its ivory handle could crack at relative humidities below 50 percent, but its steel blade could rust at relative humidities above 50 percent.

while strong sunlight can kill fungus, it can also fade and damage textiles and paper.

Excessive dryness can be equally damaging, however. Wood and ivory shrink and split in low humidity, and the design layers of paintings tend to crack more severely in dry conditions. Your home has zones that tend toward dampness (basements and bathrooms) and zones that fluctuate more often (near doorways, chimneys, heating and air-conditioning vents, and outside walls). Panel paintings and pianos (a combination of both wood and ivory) should be kept away from severe fluctuations and extreme dryness. Organic materials—especially paper, textiles, parchment, and leather—should be kept away from the damp. Damp, dark areas are also often happy homes for an insect population. And while stone sculptures are perhaps the most resistant to the fluctuations in a hallway, they can be damaged by moisture, salt, or pollution. Overly moist or rapidly changing climates will speed the deterioration of most materials, especially heterogeneous combinations such as polychrome sculpture (made of wood *or* stone) or panel paintings.

Let There Not Be (Too Much) Light

When Henry Francis du Pont established the Winterthur Museum, he had an unusual awareness of the damage caused by exposure to light. He purchased enough period slipcovers and draperies to make possible four seasonal changes for many of the 196 period rooms in his museum in order that each would be exposed to light only one quarter of each year. When the museum opened to the public in 1952, du Pont put only half of the rooms on tour for the morning and the other half for the afternoon, and he arranged for shades to be drawn accordingly in the rooms off tour. He had also calculated which rooms were exposed more directly to morning sun and which to afternoon rays, and he designed the shades-up time to match the more gentle lighting conditions. Despite these precautions, many draperies faded and silks shattered beyond remedy. And by the 1970s, visitation demands no longer made possible the "down" time for room changeovers or shade pullings. The result is that the older textiles increasingly are replaced by reproduction fabrics.

All light is damaging and its effect is cumulative. Light exposure can transfer the design of a paper cutout work to its backing board. Anyone who has unframed an historic print or watercolor has found the stunning difference between the exposed area and the area protected by the frame. Oil paintings are generally more light stable, but Sir Joshua Reynolds and Vincent van Gogh were two artists who used "fugitive" pigments, which are now mere "ghosts" of their former hues. The Victoria and Albert Museum keeps its watercolors and ivory miniatures in a dark room, where the visitor is allowed to press a button for 120 seconds of light. Small sculpted wax figures in waxworks in eighteenth-century American collections have sagged toward the sources of light, slightly melted on the side near the window. Basket materials or other ethnographic works are readily damaged by light exposure. Even furniture woods can be bleached irrevocably by nearness to windows, and paintings lined with a wax adhesive can have a disattached "welt" raised where a sunbeam visits daily.

Remember that your home will have natural "zones" where there is more or less light. Once again, the organic materials—paper, textiles, baskets, wax—are most harmed by the exposure. Stone, metal, and ceramic works will be aged less in light rooms and hallways.

Nicotine, Foodstuffs, and Other Miscellaneous Culprits

Many of the activities that take place in your home will be recorded on the surfaces of your possessions. This author has removed varnishes from paintings exhibited in corporate boardrooms that were not nearly as yellowed as the thick film of nicotine from the "smoke-filled room" deliberations that had settled on the surfaces. A painting from an Italian restaurant gave off a tangible perfume of garlic and oregano. Another, from the dining room of a grand hotel, had received a generous splattering of chocolate mousse. Smoking or cooking will deposit films on works of art and anything else nearby—not as immediately discernible as the soot from a fire on another floor of your high rise, perhaps, but steadily accumulating nonetheless. Do not try to remove these films yourself; your assignment is to cut down the density of these activities near the works you wish to protect.

Holiday decorating seems to inspire many owners to hang greenery over their paintings or to swag the candlesticks over the mantel. At least half of the paintings treated by this author over two decades have had holly berries trapped between the frame and the stretcher, causing small bulges. An overmantel family portrait was burned severely across the bottom when the candles burned down to the mantel greenery, which then went up in flames.

If home renovations are taking place near your artworks, special precautions should be taken. The vibrations from jackhammers or lesser mechanical devices can cause pastel works to redesign themselves as powder in the bottom of the frame rabbet. Unseasoned paints (now liberally spiked with pesticides and antimildew agents) and other fresh plastering and building materials can exacerbate the corrosion of metals. Be sure that temporary art storage or shelter is secure. During renovation of a small museum in Canada, the contractors left a temporary roof covering that was not sufficient for the heavy rain over the weekend, and two floors of painting storage areas were flooded.

Pets and Pests

Foodstuffs in the kitchen are unavoidable. But holly berries in the parlor and cockatiel and guinea-pig food on the sun porch provide lures for additional inhabitants. Delightful holiday exhibits in historic houses complete with period food displays bring holiday mice and holiday carpet beetles into the collection. If the mice are eliminated through poison baits rather than traps, a mouse carcass inside the wall provides yet another welcoming site for a population of carpet beetles who will next move enthusiastically into the stored fur stoles, feather fans, or wool dinner jackets in a costume collection or a home. In order to learn if you have tiny carpet beetles pursuing their life cycles in your collection, an entomologist will suggest such enticing pursuits as checking the insect carcasses in your light fixtures and window sills to see if they are whole or partially missing. If parts are missing, another alien is there chomping away, and it would be best to immediately check any fur, feathers, or wool elsewhere in your home for holes or odd patterns of loss and disattachment. Hair from long-haired pets (or humans) can also accumulate in corners to form carpet-beetle breeding nests. Excellent housekeeping is the best defense here, along with keeping pet food on the balcony or in the garage (or microwaving it periodically) and thorough checking of organic treasures purchased in tropical climes before bringing them into your home.

The Importance of General Planning

Major museums have curatorial staff to decide on purchases and exhibition; conservation staff to advise on condition, storage, and priority for the time and the expense of treatment; registrars to count, categorize, track movement, and insure; and security officers to arrange protection. Unless you have a well-organized housekeeping staff (or unusually responsible teenage children), you must take on all or most of these functions for your own possessions.

As your own registrar, you should have lists of all your works, which should include materials, measurements, and other descriptive information. Keep a copy of this information in a safe place outside of the home, in case of loss. The written and photographic records provided by professional conservators after treatment of your works would be helpful additions to these records.

Consulting an Expert: A Brief Survey of the Field of Conservation

Each of the chapters of this book will be addressing this issue for a variety of possessions. The medical analogy is likely to appear often. There are steps you can take for a healthy life for both yourself and your artifacts, and there are times to consult a medical or art-conservation expert. There is rarely a good reason to "do it yourself." For example, a painting never needs cleaning for its survival—and yet this is an area where do-it-yourselfers abound. I have never seen a painting that actually benefited from such home care; some are lucky and survive with minimal discomfort from treatments such as the oddly ubiquitous clean-it-with-a-raw potato method (which leaves a delicious scum for cockroaches), and others suffer keenly after unwise oil coatings or enthusiastic water-based cleanings. If in doubt, hire a conservator to survey your possessions and let you know where the treatment priorities lie.

But where does this conservator come from? There were no formal graduate schools in art conservation in this country until the founding of the Conservation Center at New York University's Institute of Fine Arts in 1960. This program initially took only four students a year for a four-year, full-time program. In 1970 a second program was founded at Cooperstown Graduate Programs in Cooperstown, New York, where ten students a year were accepted, and the NYU program began admitting six students annually. A third program jointly sponsored by the University of Delaware and the Winterthur Museum was established in 1974; it admits ten applicants. (Respected but short-lived graduate programs were also established at Oberlin College and the Fogg Art Museum in the 1970s. These institutions now train advanced interns, and the Cooperstown Program has moved to Buffalo State College.) Each year the three current U.S. programs graduate about twenty-eight new conservation professionals, but additional trustworthy practitioners are trained in European programs or by apprenticeship. The required background is essentially a triple major in chemistry, art history, and studio art, and many students are almost thirty years old before they begin their formal training in the practice of conservation itself.

No national or state licensing program for conservators exists, but there are two national organizations, both in Washington, D.C.: the American Institute for Conservation of Historic and Artistic Works (AIC), whose membership is made up primarily of individual conservators, and the National Institute for the Conservation of Cultural Property (NIC), whose membership is composed of institutions who are concerned with conservation. Both offer publications, and the AIC has a new referral service to provide the names of conservators in your area. As a cross-check procedure, it might be best also to call a museum in your area and/or one that collects works similar to those you are concerned about. For instance, if you live in Los Angeles you might first telephone the AIC, then telephone the Los Angeles County Museum of Art and ask to speak with the Conservation Department, and if you have textiles with insect damage you could also call the Textile Museum in Washington. (A comprehensive listing of resource organizations is given at the back of this book.) If you keep hearing the same conservators' names, phone them. Unfortunately, seeking a conservator is one occasion when the Yellow Pages are not the best means. There you may find also listed a number of artists or framers who are eager for your business but who may not have the necessary training and skills, or who may treat a work only "cosmetically" when it acutely needs structural or preservative work.

Some museums or the training programs listed above may also offer a public consultation day

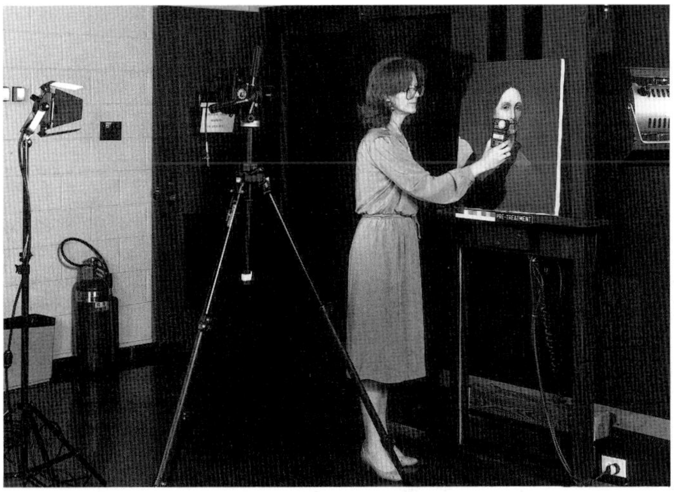

A painting conservator at Winterthur prepares documentary photographs during treatment of a portrait.

during which conservators may look at your work and offer advice about proper care and names of trained practitioners who work on similar items. There you may be able to learn the likely outcome of treatment; for instance, whether a large tear in a painting or work of art on paper probably can be mended invisibly, or whether treatment would be not only very expensive but also unlikely to yield an acceptable artwork at the end. Consultations of this sort may also give you an idea of parameters of time, materials, and cost.

There are also varying philosophies of treatment and changing techniques (as there are in medicine); do not hesitate to get several opinions about the treatment proposed. The field at large seems now to be moving toward a more conservative approach. Furniture conservators now often have an "additive" rather than a "subtractive" approach. In other words, if the bottom of the leg on a Windsor chair has heavy insect damage, rather than sawing off the end and replacing it with an entirely new foot, the conservator may carefully consolidate to save all original wood and tailor-fit the needed replacement part to the more ragged edge. Original finishes more often now are retained and protected. Slight discolorations in paper are sometimes considered acceptable in prints and drawings in order to avoid loss of integrity through bleaching; slight slackness or stretcher-bar marks are more often tolerated in paintings to avoid over-flattening, which often occurred during older backing or "lining" techniques.

Conservators who are members of the American Institute for Conservation abide by a *Code of Ethics and Standards of Practice;* copies of this publication may be obtained from the national office. According to those AIC guidelines, conservators should keep photographic and/or written *documentation* of the condition of the artifact before and after treatment, and materials used in any restoration or conservation treatment should be described. Owners are not to be kept in the dark and are to have approved the proposed procedures before they are carried out.

In addition, acceptable treatments should be *reversible;* that is, materials used during treatments, such as retouch paints and varnishes, should be removable without harm to the original materials. For example, undrained oil or alkyd paints are generally unwise choices for the retouching of a painting as they discolor rapidly and require potent solvents for removal, which can harm the original paint film. Some art or hobby stores sell over-the-counter treatment supplies that are able to dissolve away old coatings—and artists' signatures—in untrained hands. Fragile feather, hair, basket, or bone materials could be compromised beyond retrieval by aggressive coatings or adhesives. Much of the cost of many treatments involves the laborious removal of intractable substances unwisely applied during past restorations or do-it-yourself efforts; with paintings this may be excessive and insoluble oil repaint; with porcelain, dime-store glues; with furniture, polyurethane finishes.

Not to worry too much, all may not yet be lost. In the following chapters, experts will explain all of the foregoing in detail and in the context of specific types of artworks of which you may be a proud possessor. The authors of this compendium are spending their professional lives taking care of the materials of art and culture and offer the information and advice herein to aid those who have similar responsibilities for their personal possessions but must carry them out on a part-time basis. Depending on the care taken by their guardians, things of beauty as well as cultural or historical value may last for one or two more generations at most—or may be joys nearly forever.

CREATING AND MAINTAINING THE RIGHT ENVIRONMENT

Steven Weintraub

In today's art market, enormous sums of money are spent on works of art. For many collectors, the purpose of such an acquisition is to own an original masterwork. However, as a result of environmentally induced damage, certain colors will fade, and cracks and losses will alter the appearance of the surface. In the end, the object may be only a distant memory of the artist's original intent. For example, important to Mark Rothko's paintings were the precise choice of colors and the manner in which he interlaced these colors and shapes. Once these colors faded, the balance of hues altered the essence of the painting and the artist's original intention forever.

Independent of issues regarding market value, some precious and important aspect has been lost when these environmentally induced alterations take place. And they make us realize that the purpose of environmental protection is to preserve something far more precious than market value; the goal is the preservation of the artist's original image in all its beauty and subtlety.

Causes of Environmental Damage

Museums spend a great deal of time and money to provide safe environmental conditions to protect their collections. Few residential structures are designed to maintain museum-quality levels of relative humidity and light. The cost of maintaining levels is very high, and the controlled conditions of museums impose restrictions that are at odds with the use of the collector's home as a residential space. The inability to achieve proper museum conditions should not be used as an

The Chinese Parlor at the Henry Francis du Pont Winterthur Museum

excuse to do nothing, however. There are many steps that private collectors can take to provide environmental protection for their objects. First it is important to know something about the agents of environmental damage in order to control them. The principal causes of environmentally induced damage are light, temperature, relative humidity, air pollutants, and pests.

Light

Light is a form of energy. When an art object is exposed to light, it absorbs energy that can induce chemical change. Both natural and artificial light can cause cumulative and irreversible damage to organic material. Typical symptoms of light damage include fading of colors, yellowing of varnish films on paintings, bleaching of paper, and loss in physical properties such as the weakening of textiles. It is useful to think of very light-sensitive objects as having a finite life based on time, duration, and type of light exposure. While it may be inevitable that the life of the object will be used up over time, it is important to use light economically and wisely. There is no benefit to squandering the life of the artwork through excessive, unnecessary, or inefficient lighting, especially during those periods of the day when nobody is present to enjoy the collections on display.

Because good lighting is necessary in order to view art, a balance must be achieved between the necessity of light to see and the need to avoid damage. For the purposes of our discussion, light can be thought of as a continuous spectrum of energy divided into three categories based on wavelength:

Ultraviolet light (UV) is the shortest, most energetic form of radiation. It lies in the invisible part of the spectrum just below the blue portion of visible light. The high energy of UV causes significant alteration of organic materials; for example, sunburn is caused by the UV portion of sunlight. While skin can heal itself to some extent, the damage done to the organic components of a work of art is permanent and irreversible. Therefore, it is important to eliminate UV radiation entirely. This can be accomplished in three ways:

1. Use UV filters. These filters can be placed either on the source of light, such as a window or lighting fixture, or in front of the art object. UV-filtering solar-window films can be placed on window glass, and special UV filters are available for fluorescent lamps. UV-absorbing plastic and specially treated picture glass are available for protecting framed objects or objects in exhibition cases. Most plastic materials and glass reduce UV to some extent, but effective UV filtration can only be achieved with materials that are designated as UV filters.

2. If the light source is bounced off a painted surface, much of the UV component may be eliminated. The actual amount of UV energy absorbed depends on the type of painted surface reflecting the light. In general, most high-tinting white pigments have good UV-absorption characteristics.

3. Use light sources with a low component of UV, such as incandescent lamps. Tungsten halogen lamps and fluorescent tubes have a UV output higher than that of conventional incandescent lamps but far lower than that of daylight. For extremely light-sensitive materials, a UV-filtering lens is recommended for these type of lamps. Natural light is extremely rich in UV. For these UV-rich sources, UV filtration is a necessity.

Infrared light (IR) falls on the far end of the light spectrum, in the invisible region just beyond red. While the longer wavelengths are less damaging than short wavelengths because they are less energetic, IR causes damage because the absorbed energy heats up the surface of an object, thereby speeding up chemical deterioration processes and causing instability in relative humidity. Sunlight and incandescent lamps have a high IR component, while fluorescent lamps have a lower IR output.

For natural IR light, the primary method of minimizing heat buildup is to avoid direct sunlight. Various types of IR-reflecting solar glasses and plastic window films are available to reduce solar heat gain through glass. For incandescent sources, the lamp should be set at a sufficient distance to minimize the transfer of heat from the fixture to the object. The lamp should not be placed in an enclosed exhibition case directly with the object. Reflected light reduces the danger of direct exposure to infrared buildup. Finally, for extremely temperature-sensitive objects, there is a special class of dichroic lamps that reflects IR through the back of the lamp while visible light passes through the front lens.

Visible light lies between the UV and IR portions of the spectrum. The blue end of the visible spectrum contains the shorter (hence, the more energetic) wavelengths of light. Therefore, visible light sources that are rich in blue have more potential for damage than those rich in red light. Sunlight and full-spectrum fluorescent lamps have a high component of blue light. Warm fluorescent lamps have a lower amount of blue than cool fluorescent ones. Incandescent lamps have the lowest amount of blue light and are therefore the safest form of illumination for highly light-sensitive works of art. In fact, UV-filtered natural light can cause more than five times the amount of damage of an equivalent visible level of incandescent light.

The key to minimizing damage from visible light is to use light in an efficient manner. The human tendency to prefer high light levels must be weighed against conservation standards favoring lower ones. The standard unit for measuring the intensity of visible light is the footcandle or its metric equivalent, the lux (one footcandle equals about ten lux). While footcandle or lux meters range in price and quality, even the least expensive model will provide adequate information on the proper range of exposure. Museum standards for lighting works of art range from five to ten footcandles for extremely light-sensitive materials such as paper and textiles, to twenty to forty footcandles for moderately sensitive materials such as oil paintings and wood. Although it may not be possible to light an object satisfactorily at these recommended levels in a specific situation (a room may have hundreds of footcandles of light on a sunny day), these numbers should be considered a useful target for determining adequate lighting levels.

Light damage is cumulative and is actually the result of intensity multiplied by time, called footcandle hours. This means that ten hours of exposure at ten footcandles has the same cumulative damage as one hour at one hundred footcandles. Therefore, if a work of art will only be viewed for short periods of time, it is acceptable to light it at a higher footcandle level than that recommended for museums. By the same token, reduction of light during nonviewing periods will significantly reduce overall cumulative light damage. Methods for controlling visible light include:

1. Reduce daylight. Because natural light causes significantly more damage than an equivalent amount of incandescent light, light-sensitive artworks should be placed in a location that minimizes daylight exposure. If this is not possible, natural-light levels should be minimized with curtains, blinds, or tinted solar-reduction window films. Also, since people are more comfortable at lower light levels with warm, yellow incandescent light than an equivalent amount of cool, blue natural light, it is easier to achieve visually acceptable low lighting levels with incandescent rather than natural light.

2. Create efficient lighting situations. The eye adapts to a wide variety of illumination intensities. Within a room, the eye uses the brightest surface as a reference point; therefore, bright zones such as windows and highly reflective white walls make it difficult for the eye to adjust to the less reflective darker surfaces of artworks. Reduction in contrast between sources of illumination, wall surfaces, and the art permits lower levels of satisfactory illumination. For example, a dark painting viewed against a dark wall is easier to look at than if it were exhibited on a highly reflective white wall. Also, by reducing contrast between the work of art and the wall, less spotlighting and therefore fewer footcandles are required to achieve an acceptable level of illumination.

Glare from light reflecting off a glossy surface reduces the ability of the eye to view an object properly. Techniques for glare reduction, such as the use of indirect or angled light, help to use light in an efficient manner.

3. Rotate light-sensitive collections. Rather than display one object for an extended period and risk damaging that specific object, most museums prefer to slow the rate of damage to specific items by

The draperies and slipcovers at Winterthur are rotated on a regular basis in order to minimize the light exposure to the fabrics.

limiting its period of exhibition. For example, a museum might exhibit very light-sensitive materials, such as textiles and works of art on paper, for only two months per year.

Keep in mind that while paper and textiles generally are considered more sensitive than oil paintings or wood, many paintings or wooden objects may be equally vulnerable. Many contemporary paintings and sculpture, for example, are made from materials that are unstable and will alter with minimum light exposure over a short period of time.

Temperature

There is a general rule of thumb that the speed of a chemical reaction will double with an increase in temperature of about 20 degrees Fahrenheit. While the actual speed of reaction depends on a variety of conditions, the fact remains that the rate of chemical degradation is significantly affected by temperature. This is why chemically unstable materials, such as acidic twentieth-century paper or photographic color transparencies and negatives, benefit from storage at lower temperatures. In addition, the surface of objects will warm above room temperature as a result of absorbing infrared energy from direct sunlight or incandescent lamps. Dark surfaces absorb more energy than light surfaces. With temperature-sensitive materials, therefore, it is important to avoid direct exposure to these "heat" sources. (See suggestions in the section on light).

Relatively large changes in temperature (10 to 20 degrees Fahrenheit) will affect the dimensional stability of objects in two different ways. Many materials expand and contract as a direct result of a change in temperature. A mercury thermometer is a good example of this phenomenon: the mercury expands as the temperature rises. Some artistic materials, such as certain waxes and Plasticine, can soften and flow at a temperature around 100 degrees Fahrenheit. Thermally induced cracking can occur in objects consisting of layers of different materials that move at different rates with changes in temperature; cracks in the top layer of painted metal surfaces are examples of this type of damage.

Temperature is also important in the way that it affects relative humidity, which significantly affects the dimensional stability of organic materials.

The Relative-Humidity Problem

People are very sensitive to small changes in temperature but are hardly aware of large changes in relative humidity (RH). For this reason, residential and office spaces are controlled to maintain temperature in the human comfort range without consideration for humidity. The dimensional stability of art objects made from organic materials is just the opposite. While large changes in temperature have little direct dimensional effect, small changes in relative humidity can cause a significant change in dimension. Therefore, the control of relative humidity should be a primary objective for collectors.

It is important to understand some basic concepts about humidity in order to monitor and control it. Humidity refers to water vapor in air. Air can hold more moisture at a high temperature than at a low one. Absolute humidity refers to the actual amount of water in air independent of temperature. Relative humidity is based on the percentage of water vapor in air, compared to what air can hold at 100 percent (full saturation) at a given temperature. As a consequence, when the temperature increases, the relative humidity decreases for a fixed amount of absolute humidity; conversely, a decrease in temperature causes an increase in relative humidity.

Humidity-related damage is based on relative humidity, not on the absolute amount of water vapor in air. For example, organic materials will expand as their moisture content increases in direct response to an increase in relative humidity, regardless of whether the change was due to a reduction in temperature or an increase in absolute humidity. It is important to understand this concept since it will be a key element in deciding how to control relative humidity.

MONITORING RELATIVE HUMIDITY

The first step in solving the humidity problem is to monitor the environment. A wide range of temperature and humidity monitors, called *thermo-hygrometers*, are available. There are a number of inexpensive mechanical dial and electronic digital meters on the market for under one hundred dollars. Some of these units are excellent and some models are very inaccurate. If you are unsure of what to purchase, your local museum specialist or conservator can provide some suggestions. Recording devices called *hygrothermographs* are available for six hundred dollars and up. Here too, the quality varies from model to model. Although expensive, these recording units maintain a continuous record of temperature and humidity.

Both types of units need to have their accuracy or calibration checked periodically, at least once and preferably twice a year, after the summer and winter seasons. Generally, a unit called a *psychrometer* is used for this purpose. A psychrometer consists of two thermometers, one to measure room temperature and one to measure the cooling effect of water as it evaporates from the tip of the thermometer. These units are considered accurate because they actually take a direct measurement of relative humidity, as opposed to the other units, which measure the expansion and contraction of an organic material or an electronic signal and convert it into an equivalent humidity reading. Sling and electric-fan psychrometers are relatively inexpensive (ranging from fifty to two hundred fifty dollars) but are inconvenient for spot RH readings, which is why they are used primarily as calibration devices. Without periodic calibration checks, it is possible for thermo-hygrometers and hygrothermographs to show errors of 20 percent RH or more over time. However, it should be noted that a good-quality monitoring unit, even when its accuracy shifts over time, should still provide valuable information on the rate and extent of RH change on a daily and seasonal basis.

The location of a humidity monitor is important. It should be placed in proximity to the art object of concern. Also, taking into account uneven temperature and humidity conditions within a room, it is important to locate humidity-sensitive collections away from dangerous zones. For example, a heat source such as a radiator or fireplace may create a drier climate within its immediate area in the winter than in other parts of the room. Often, the space immediately surrounding the interior surface of an exterior wall that has poor thermal insulation will have a higher RH than warmer interior walls. If the building has no winter humidification, this may be an ideal location for a painting. If there is some level of humidification, this area may actually exhibit excessively high humidity conditions for the winter.

To analyze your individual humidity needs, some sort of ongoing monitoring program, over a full year in order to examine seasonal performance, is recommended. This can be accomplished with a recording unit or through careful manual records of daily meter readings. Different parts of the house may have different results, so it is important to monitor the room or rooms that will contain the most important and humidity-sensitive objects in the collection. In compiling such records, remember to maintain some record of outdoor conditions in order to correlate interior and exterior conditions. Local newspapers publish daily and weekly weather summaries. Frequently, the local newspapers publish an annual summary of outdoor temperature and humidity conditions. It is also important to monitor the condition of the collection and note the kind of damage that occurs under specific seasonal humidity conditions.

Although we understand how individual art objects are damaged by humidity in a general way, it is difficult to provide one rule about a safe and appropriate level of relative humidity that holds true for a wide variety of climatic regions or for collections made up of a variety of materials. Even collections made up of similar materials can have different individual needs based on the type of construction or prior climatic history of the object. For example, some wooden furniture may sustain large swings in humidity without obvious signs of damage; other furniture pieces, such as those decorated with fine wooden inlays, can exhibit extensive surface damage as a result of small changes in RH. What follows is a breakdown of the effects of extreme humidity levels on various objects.

1. High relative humidity: Small increases in RH above 70 percent can cause large increases in damage, as described below:

- Rusting iron and "bronze disease" only become significant above 50 percent RH. As the RH level increases, the rate and extent of corrosion becomes much worse. Metallic corrosion is significantly reduced or stopped at lower RH levels. For this reason, it is important to have some level of humidity control for metals, even if an "ideal" low RH level cannot be maintained.
- Chemical deterioration of organic materials is accelerated in conditions of high humidity. Materials that are particularly prone to chemical damage, such as alum sized 20th Century paper, will deteriorate at a far more rapid rate at a high RH level than at a low one.
- Chemical attack from air pollutants is significantly increased at higher levels of RH.
- Permanent dimensional distortion of organic materials occurs at the higher RH range. Since the cellular structure of many organic materials such as wood and canvas absorbs more moisture at the high RH range than at the mid RH range, they tend to swell to a far greater extent at the high RH range. Permanent warpage of wooden panels as a result of crushed cellular structures and cracked paint layers are symptoms of such conditions of exposure to high RH.
- Biological problems from pests and microorganisms occur at the high RH range. Generally, RH below 70 percent is recommended for avoiding problems of mold. As the humidity increases above this level, the extent of microbiological attack will multiply with each small increase in RH.

2. Low relative humidity: A range of RH below 30 percent will also damage organic materials. While low RH conditions are recommended for metallic objects, many objects are made of both wood and metal, as for example the wood stock of a rifle. Therefore, it is important to determine if the object is a composite of several types of materials before determining optimal RH conditions.

- Many artifacts composed of organic materials can sustain some level of shrinkage without significant damage. However, if the object is subject to periods of low RH well beyond the normal bounds of tolerance, cracks, cupping of the paint layer, shrinkage in textiles and paper, and other types of dimensional damage will occur.

- Physical properties of organic materials are affected by RH. For example, at the low RH range, paper loses flexibility and becomes more brittle. Such objects are more subject to damage from handling at the lower end than at the mid-range of RH.

3. Drastic changes in relative humidity: Frequent and large shifts in RH will result in a large amount of dimensional movement and are a major cause of humidity-induced damage.

- Keep short-term fluctuations to a minimum. If an object is made from a variety of materials, such as a canvas painting or a book, each material will respond to RH changes at a different rate. This causes physical stress that results in structural damage to the object. Examples of dangerous short-term shifts in RH occur when winter heat or summer air conditioning is turned off at night, causing a large daily fluctuation in RH that can result in extensive damage to the collection.
- Long-term swings in RH typically occur between the winter and summer. Gradual long-term swings in RH create less stress than the large short-term shifts described above. However, the range of change in RH should be minimized to reduce the extent of overall dimensional movement in the object, thereby reducing the risk of damage from such movement.

In summary, it is important to keep within an RH range of 30 to 70 percent. For very sensitive objects, such as parchment, panel paintings, and inlaid furniture, even this range is excessively large. Therefore, it is necessary to have some idea about the sensitivity of the different types of objects within the collection, as explained in the following chapters.

Finally, it is important to choose an RH range based on what is practical to maintain given the exterior conditions within your geographical region and the limitations of humidification control within your house or apartment. In a hot and dry region of the southwest United States, it makes sense to maintain a range that errs on the low side, such as 25 to 40 percent RH. In a semitropical climate, a range of 55 to 75 percent may be a practical goal. For areas that experience humid summers and cold winters, even the wide range of 30 to 70 percent RH may be difficult to achieve. The important point is to minimize short- and long-term fluctuations by choosing a realistic RH range, even if it means exceeding the recommended RH limits to some extent. It is especially important to avoid long-term seasonal exposure to extreme RH values.

CONTROLLING HUMIDITY

Approaches to Seasonal RH Problems

Summer Many regions of the United States experience very humid conditions throughout much of the summer. An effective strategy for removing excess humidity is necessary throughout the entire high humidity season.

Standard refrigerant air conditioners in their normal mode of operation will take some moisture out of the air. In terms of RH, however, some of the advantages to vapor removal are minimized since the colder room air can result in a high RH even after some moisture has been removed. A standard air conditioner cannot be used to control RH with any precision since it is regulated on the basis of temperature, not relative humidity, but its dehumidification performance can be improved in several ways:

1. Set the central air-conditioning unit so that it takes in minimum humid outside air. If the entire house contains humidity-sensitive materials, some type of reheat coil should be installed on the air conditioner. The idea is to overcool the air to extract as much moisture as possible and then heat the air to human comfort. Although it uses a great deal of energy, this approach may be necessary in very humid climates and is a common design for museums.

2. If only certain rooms contain humidity-sensitive collections, a local, room-scale solution can be achieved by using a standard dehumidifier or a local air conditioner, or a combination of both, in conjunction with the central air conditioner.

Room dehumidifiers are basically air-conditioning units that use their own waste heat to reheat the air instead of exhausting it to the outside. As the air passes over the cold coil, moisture is extracted. As the air is reheated, the relative humidity is reduced because of both the moisture that has been removed and the heat that is pumped back into the air. These dehumidifiers work best in warm, humid climates. At colder temperatures, the coils may ice, so it is important to purchase a unit that has an automatic deicing cycle. While a properly sized dehumidifier works well at the room scale, it actually heats the room above ambient room temperature. Therefore, in hot regions, a dehumidifier has limited applications in terms of human comfort.

When using a local dehumidifier, it is important to make sure that the container that collects the condensate works properly. Normally, the unit should shut off when the container is filled; otherwise the container will overflow and cause flooding. The container should be emptied regularly or be connected directly to a drain following the manufacturer's recommendation.

There are two ways of converting a window air conditioner into an efficient dehumidifier while maintaining some comfortable level of temperature. First, the unit should be set to close off outside exhaust so the unit is only circulating room air. Then, set the air conditioner at its coldest setting (assuming some excess capacity) and use a space heater to heat the room back to human comfort. The disadvantage to this approach is that it uses lots of electricity.

Alternatively, a room dehumidifier can be used in conjunction with either a central or window air conditioner for specific spaces that require special humidity control. The humidistat on the dehumidifier should be set to turn on only when it is reading a high RH level (above 65 to 70 percent RH). If the unit is used in conjunction with central air conditioning, the amount of air entering the room should be set to a minimum.

Winter When maintaining an indoor temperature significantly above outdoor conditions, the interior relative humidity drops dramatically due to the effect of heating a fixed amount of absolute humidity. It is not unusual throughout much of the United States to have indoor winter RH conditions of 15 percent or below during the major heating season.

The simplest method of increasing winter RH is to reduce indoor temperatures. Generally, however, in cold climates the higher level of relative humidity achieved by reducing temperature (while still maintaining a level of human comfort) is still too low for many organic materials. Another option is to add humidity. For houses with forced-air centralized heating, a humidifier can be added to the central ductwork. For houses or apartments without ductwork, a room-by-room approach is necessary. The combination of shutting off or reducing the heat in parts of the house to keep temperature cooler in conjunction with humidification is the best approach for protecting your collection.

If you choose to operate an automatic system at the room level, consultation with a mechanical engineer or reliable air-conditioning contractor is advisable. Automatic systems on the room level are difficult to install and operate properly. Attention must be given to water quality and the pattern of distribution, and the unit must be sized carefully to avoid excessive on-off cycling. If a spray (aspirating) unit is chosen, demineralized water must be used.

Alternatively, free-standing, high-maintenance humidifiers (where one must manually fill the tank with water) can be utilized. There are three types typically available; ultrasonic humidifiers, steam-vaporizing humidifiers, and evaporating drum humidifiers. Each type has its advantages and disadvantages. All require frequent water refills depending on the tank capacity. Vaporizing units require the most energy but provide the cleanest and safest form of humidity. Evaporative and ultrasonic units can develop microbiological contamination and should be cleaned on a weekly basis to avoid this. With the ultrasonic humidifier, it is important to remove mineral content either with the use of special filters or by filling with demineralized or distilled water.

There is a risk of condensation and damage to the house when adding humidity in the winter. Many internal surfaces within the house are much colder than average room conditions. For example, at an outdoor temperature of 30 degrees Fahrenheit, the room temperature may be 70 degrees. However, the inside surface of a single pane of glass window may be 40 degrees. If you maintain the house at an artificially high 40 percent RH, condensation would form on the cold glass surfaces. Potential damage to a house maintained at such artificially high humidity conditions in the winter includes corrosion of cold metal structural elements, saturation and deterioration of foam insulation materials, surface flaking on exterior stonework from freeze/thaw cycling, and wood rot on saturated surfaces such as window sills. Therefore, one must find a balance between the level of humidity that can be maintained in the house and the type of damage that can be done to the structure at a given interior level of humidity. This is a complex issue and the individual solution varies with the type of house construction involved, as well as regional climatic differences. Advice on the installation of automatic humidification and the risks involved (as explained above) should be sought from a mechanical engineer specializing in climate control. In general, mechanical engineers are more familiar with and more knowledgeable to advise on this type of problem than contractors.

Spring and Fall The strategies discussed above assume a long season of low or high humidity. The transitional seasons often provide rapid and unpredictable shifts in outdoor conditions, resulting in large interior swings in RH. While the average spring or autumn day usually maintains a safe, mid-range RH at a moderate temperature, one must prepare for either extreme, often within days of each other, and adjust the humidity-control system accordingly.

Humidistats and Controls

The operation of all of the humidity-control units described is based on the use of humidistats. Most home-unit humidistats are not very accurate and settings are not very precise. While it is possible to upgrade controls, this is expensive, technically difficult, and not often done. If the goal is to simply maintain a general "safe" range of RH, these simple humidistatic controls do provide a minimal level of acceptable performance.

Since many built-in humidistats are not marked with actual humidity settings, some actual relative-humidity set points should be marked on the unit. This can be accomplished as follows: Read the room humidity with a reasonably accurate hygrometer. Power up the unit and turn the humidistat knob until the unit starts to humidify or dehumidify. Mark that set point with the humidity read from the hygrometer. Repeat this procedure under various humidity conditions to develop several set-point marks on the humidistat. To supplement these inaccurate controls, it is absolutely necessary to monitor the environment with an accurate temperature/humidity meter or hygrothermograph. By tracking room humidity with these devices, it is easy to make corrections to the controlling humidistat to determine the proper humidity set point.

Microclimates

A microclimate is an enclosed space that is capable of providing an environment different from that of the surrounding space. We are surrounded by a multitude of microenvironments without realizing it. When a museum puts an object in a case for security reasons or to protect against dust, that sealed case creates a humidity microenvironment whether the museum intended it to be or not.

The concept of a microenvironment is as follows: A closed exhibition case has some level of air leakage to the room. If the case contains a large amount of organic material, the moisture content of the organic material will alter with the change in RH. This is because the object's moisture content tries to stay in equilibrium with a certain RH so that when the RH changes, the object's moisture content will also alter to find the new equilibrium. In a relatively sealed environment, the moisture given off or taken up by the object partially offsets the change in RH caused by case leakage; this is referred to as the buffering effect. To improve the buffering effect of case materials and reduce the danger of change in moisture content of the art object, museums often add silica gel to the case. The silica gel operates in a fashion similar to buffering material, except that on a pound-for-pound basis it is far more efficient. The construction of humidity-buffering microclimates requires special knowledge and skill, and a conservator should be consulted about the feasibility and technical aspects of construction of such cases.

Microclimates offer another option for humidity control that should be considered in the absence of or in conjunction with other means of RH control outlined above. For example, it may be possible to provide a sufficient level of RH control for moderately RH-sensitive objects using some of the simpler methods described. Specific, highly sensitive objects such as panel paintings could be protected in a more highly controlled microenvironmental display unit.

Air Pollution

Within a normal residential environment, it is very difficult to control particulate and gaseous pollutants, although these agents can cause a great deal of damage to collections. Accumulation of oily soot on decorative surfaces and formation of tarnish on silver are two examples familiar to everyone. While it is generally not possible to install a high-efficiency air-filtration system, certain steps can be taken to reduce the problem of air pollutants.

Particulate pollution comes in a variety of sizes and forms. It can be generated within the household or from the outdoors. Indoor-generated dust from fibrous materials like carpeting and clothing is best controlled by good housekeeping practices such as regular vacuuming. Other forms of particulate pollution come from tobacco smoke, fireplaces, oil-burning furnaces, and from kitchen cooking. These forms of pollution are especially dangerous because they tend to be greasy and difficult to remove. Once the sources of indoor pollution are understood, various protective strategies can be devised. Smoke from kitchen cooking, fireplaces, and furnaces should be well vented. Minimize tobacco smoking, or keep it away from areas where art is on display.

Dust from outdoors can be minimized by restricting and filtering outdoor air. Open windows and unfiltered window fans draw in a great deal of dust, as do window air conditioners set for ventilation and central air conditioners designed to take in some outside air. The best way to eliminate dust from these sources is to keep outside air from entering the house. However, human comfort and health require some level of fresh air. Therefore, the number of obvious points of outside air intake should be kept to a minimum and be properly filtered. Unfortunately, most filters used on residential air conditioners only remove large particles. Because high-efficiency filters impede the passage of air, the fans in these units may be too weak to push air through a fine-grade filter. A local air-conditioning contractor can provide information about possibilities for increasing filtration efficiency. For residential purposes, a grade of filtration around 65 to 85 percent Dust Spot Efficiency provides a reasonable level of protection. If the residence is located in a region with a lot of fine soot, as is typical for most urban areas, outside air should be kept out, especially in rooms containing art. In such cases, window air conditioners should be set for recirculation, rather than ventilation, to prevent the intake of highly polluted outside air.

Gaseous pollutants are generated from indoor and outdoor sources. Common sources of indoor pollution are fresh carpeting and newly applied oil-base paints. Often the materials used to make exhibition cases, including such components as wood and adhesives, may give off acidic gases that can cause corrosion and deterioration of art objects. One notorious example is oak. In the past, many museum cabinets were constructed from oak. Various types of metal artifacts, especially those containing lead, have seriously corroded as a result of exposure to the acid fumes given off by oak. A number of products available from archival supply companies are designed for the safe storage of sensitive materials. Given the wide choice and proprietary nature of products available in the marketplace, it is difficult to provide specific guidelines for the choice of safe materials. It is best to discuss with a conservator the choice of construction materials for sealed casework in order to avoid problems.

Outdoor gaseous pollutants are difficult to filter using conventional residential systems. Most air filters are capable of filtering particulate pollutants only, not gaseous pollutants. Again, therefore, the best strategy is to reduce the amount of outside air in highly polluted environments. However, there is a recent increase of interest and concern about indoor air quality, and various types of filtration systems are being developed for the residential market that are effective for both particulate and gaseous pollutants.

Pest Control

Pests cause a lot of damage to art collections. Once infestation occurs, damage can proceed rapidly. Protection against pest problems requires constant vigilance, careful monitoring, and good housekeeping.

The average household is beset by a wide variety of pests, ranging from small insects to rodents. As a result, we are careful to protect obvious food sources, such as pantry items. Unfortunately, many art objects are constructed of organic materials that also serve as excellent food sources for a wide variety of pests. The only way to protect vulnerable collections is to eliminate current pest populations and to prevent reinfestation.

Elimination can be a difficult problem and should be done in conjunction with a professional exterminator. If the art object itself is infested, such as termites in a wooden sculpture, some type of fumigation procedure will be required. Take care in handling delicate materials so as not to make the problem worse through mishandling. Also, caution should be used in deciding on a method of extermination, since the method itself may cause damage. For example, many bug sprays contain solvents that can blister paint if directed on the object. In the case of area fumigation, it is best to remove delicate art objects that could be affected adversely by the fumigant. If the extermination procedure requires direct handling or treatment of the object, a conservator should be consulted for advice about a safe approach.

The best solution to the pest problem is to prevent infiltration in the first place. Most museums now place a great deal of emphasis on preventive measures, referred to as "integrated pest management." This approach emphasizes two activities: monitoring for the presence of pests, and closing off points of access typically used by pests to infiltrate the building.

Monitoring for pests requires careful and regular inspection of the space and the collection. Make note of any evidence of activity, such as signs of insect damage and insect remains. Rather than using poison, it is best to use sticky traps since this provides visible evidence of insect activity.

Prevention of reinfestation requires careful detective work. It is necessary to determine where the pests are hiding within the house in order to assure total elimination. Since these locations are likely points for reinfestation, they are good places to locate sticky traps. It is also important to know how the pests entered the house in order to figure out how to deny them future access.

PAINTINGS

William R. Leisher

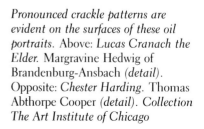

Paintings, like people, age at different rates and experience various physical changes over time. Colors may darken, become lighter, yellow, or even disappear. Paint layers become more brittle and crack. As oil paint dries, it becomes more transparent, allowing earlier designs to show through the final paint layers. Creases, bulges, and islands of ridged paint may form to distort the painting's surface. Dry, mat, chalky, or cloudy areas may disrupt the uniform gloss and transparency of a varnished painting. The velvet-like surface of a modern unvarnished painting may become disfigured by the accumulation of dust and the dark stains of oils transferred from one's hands and fingers. Some changes, such as color changes, cracking, and increased transparency of oil paint are inevitable. The bad news is that there is nothing we can do to prevent these changes from occurring.

While it is a natural inclination to resist change and to want to maintain the freshness or pristine quality of a painting, the fact is that our paintings would be better off if we could learn to accept and live with some of the changes wrought by time. Extreme caution must be advised regarding conservation treatments designed to compensate for the effects of the natural aging process or to return paintings to their former "new" condition. Premature and inappropriate treatments compromise the physical and visual integrity of the painting by creating a bad imitation, a caricature of the original work and the artist's intent. This danger is particularly true of twentieth-century works of art, which may display dramatic visual change because of the prevalent use of nontraditional materials, techniques, and unusual, frequently incompatible combinations of mediums and materials.

Although we may not be able to prevent some of the ravages of aging, the good news is that many of its effects can be at least delayed or mitigated, and damages caused by accident and careless neglect can be eliminated through informed and

Pronounced crackle patterns are evident on the surfaces of these oil portraits. Above: *Lucas Cranach the Elder.* Margravine Hedwig of Brandenburg-Ansbach *(detail).* Opposite: *Chester Harding.* Thomas Abthorpe Cooper *(detail). Collection The Art Institute of Chicago*

attentive care based on proven preventive maintenance techniques. By assuming the responsibilities of stewardship and placing an emphasis on preservation measures, the useful lifespan of your painting or paintings can be prolonged, thus insuring your enjoyment of them for many years.

Anatomy of a Painting

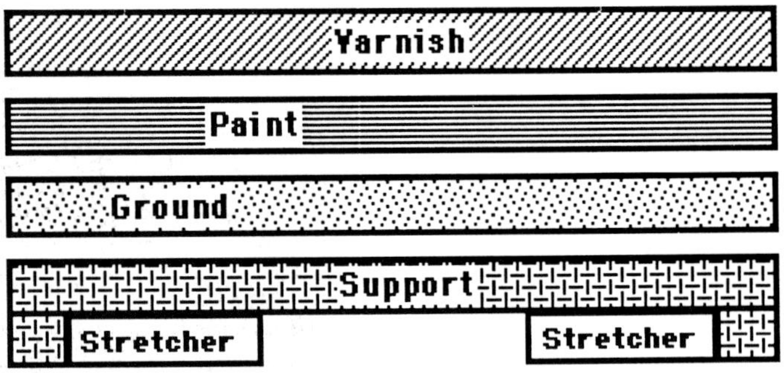

Diagram of the structure of a typical oil painting

Generally, paintings are categorized according to type of support and paint medium. Thus, one encounters designations such as oil on canvas, oil on panel, tempera on panel, oil on copper, acrylic on cotton, which are meant to convey the essential materials of a painting. The typical structure of a traditional easel painting resembles a multilayer cake. The bottom layer is the *support*. It is the surface upon which a painting is made. A variety of materials may be used as a painting support: wood (referred to as panel), fabric (linen, cotton, or hemp—often referred to in the generic as canvas), artist's board, all varieties of pressed board, metals, stone, plaster, leather, ivory, glass, plastics, and paper. The majority of collectible paintings are on either a fabric or wood support. The next element, called the *ground*, is a layer of material that is applied to the support to provide a smooth, uniform surface on which to paint. Typical ground materials include gesso (a plaster-like mixture), chalk, oil, and acrylic paints. The usual ground color is white, but it may be tinted in a broad range of colors depending on the final optical effects the artist desires. The design or *paint layers* may be multilayered or consist of a simple, single layer. The possibilities and range of painting materials are nearly unlimited in contemporary art. However, traditional painting materials usually include the following mediums: egg tempera, tempera (pigments bound in water and glue), oil, watercolor, gouache, and synthetic-based paints. *Varnish*, which is generally applied as the final layer, is a clear resin that may be either from natural sources such as damar and mastic (gums from trees) or copal (fossilized tree gum), or derived from synthetic manufacturing processes. Varnishes serve two functions: to form a protective barrier against airborne dirt and pollutants and to provide uniform gloss and color saturation for the paint layers. Under ideal circumstances, a conservator may remove and replace an aged varnish with fresh resins. Caution must be exercised by the conservator because the same natural resins used for varnishes may be mixed with the paint medium, creating a condition that makes varnish removal without harming the original paint surface impossible. It is also important to note that many late-nineteenth-century and twentieth-century paintings are not varnished and are intended by the artist to remain unvarnished.

Paintings on a canvas support usually have one more element, the wood frame, called the *stretcher*, to which the canvas is attached. The essential characteristic of a stretcher is that it can be expanded to maintain tension across a canvas to prevent bulges and creases caused by slackness of the support. The stretcher is expanded by adjusting keys or other apparatus located in each corner join of the stretcher. The process of adjusting the tension on the painting by expanding the stretcher is referred to by artists and conservators as *keying out* the stretcher. If the wood frame cannot be adjusted—that is, it is designed to be rigid—it is called a *strainer*.

Paintings on panel may also have an additional element on the back called a *cradle*. It is a lattice-like configuration of wood or metal battens attached to the back of a wood support to prevent warping. In theory, cradles were designed to allow movement of the wood in response to changing humidity while keeping the panel flat. In reality,

Stretcher with keys

Panel painting with cradle

the cradle locks the panel in place and puts tremendous pressures on the panel as it tries to respond to humidity changes in the surrounding environment. The traditional process of cradling wood-panel paintings is no longer practiced by experienced conservators. The problem of warping panels is best solved by maintaining a stable humidity. In addition to providing stable humidity, occasionally either a modified cradle or a very complex wood inlay technique is used to restore the flat plane of a panel.

Many combinations and variants in choice of materials and sequence of application or layering are possible in painting. The artists' selection, method, and sequence of application of their painting materials can have a direct and profound influence on the aging characteristics and longevity of their work.

The Benefits of an Optimum Environment

Most paintings consist of a complex layering of materials. Each layer may have its own characteristic dimensional response to changes of temperature and humidity in its surrounding environment. As the layers of the painting swell and shrink and expand and contract with frequent fluctuations in humidity and temperature, the adhesion between layers gradually becomes weakened. The loss of adhesive strength can eventually occur to the extent that the paint and ground may be loosened and fall away from the support.

Extreme temperatures and humidities must be avoided. At low humidities organic materials shrink, compressing the brittle paint layers, and wood supports may crack and split. At high humidities and temperatures the rate of chemical reactions increases and the painting becomes a fertile host for mold activity and insect infestation. Generally, the optimum relative humidity and temperature recommended for paintings are 50 percent RH and 68 degrees Fahrenheit. For various reasons it may not be possible or advisable to maintain the optimum humidity and temperature in your home. But you can improve considerably the environment for your paintings by trying to maintain stable conditions in moderate temperature and humidity ranges. In addition, the reduction of light levels and the elimination of ultraviolet light will help to retard fading and deterioration of varnishes and paint mediums caused by photochemical reactions. Exposure of paintings to direct sunlight should always be avoided. By providing a stable environment and controlled lighting you can do much to reduce the rate of deterioration and increase the longevity of your paintings.

Correct way to carry a painting, with one hand supporting the bottom and the other holding one of the sides

Rules for Safe Housekeeping

1. Do not touch painting and frame surfaces with any cleaning solutions, cleaning cloths, sponges, feather dusters, vacuum brushes, or hand-held vacuum cleaners.
2. If dust becomes a problem, a light dusting may be carried out with a soft badger or sable brush. Check first for loose frame elements or lifting paint.
3. Any cleaning attempt on a painting or gilded frame other than light dusting described above must be undertaken by an experienced conservator.
4. Do not use aerosols, sprays, insecticides, or oil-based pesticides near a painting.
5. Do not hang paintings on freshly painted or plastered walls. Wait until the walls are fully dry.
6. Do not use tools or work above or beside a painting.
7. Do not attach stickers or labels to the back of a painting. Do not write on the painting's back. Over time stickers and writing on the back can damage the paint layers on the front.

Handling Paintings

The greatest risk of damage to paintings occurs when they are handled and moved. Careless handling techniques have caused far more damage to works of art than have the effects of time and unstable environments. It is in your best interest and that of the painting's to handle and move it as little as possible. However, on those occasions when you must handle or move your paintings, the following guidelines will be useful in reducing the risk of damage.

1. Avoid touching the front and backs of paintings. Oils from fingers and hands can disfigure the paint and varnish surface, and pressures on the back of a fabric support can promote spiral (sigmoid) crack patterns in the paint layers.
2. Always check the painting and frame for damage and loose pieces before picking it up. Make sure the frame and hardware are secure.
3. Carry or handle only one painting at a time. Two people are required to handle large paintings safely.
4. Carry framed paintings with one hand supporting the bottom and the other the side. The painted side should be facing you. Do not carry the painting either by the top of the frame or the stretcher.

Panel painting properly attached in its frame

5. Paintings that are unframed should be handled carefully by the edges.

6. Never insert your fingers between the canvas and the stretcher bars.

7. Modern paintings that are either unvarnished or unprimed (the raw canvas is part of the design) and/or have paint around the exposed edges should be handled with clean cotton gloves.

8. Before you carry the painting, make sure the way is well lighted and clear and that there is a place prepared to receive it.

Frames and Framing

In addition to its obvious aesthetic function, the frame is there to protect the edges of the painting. Its presence on a painting allows for greater ease in safe handling and storage. Unfortunately, frames original to the painting, antique frames, and frames selected or designed by the artist are too frequently removed and discarded in favor of ones matching current tastes. Frames can be important visual and historical documents that are either essential to the successful presentation of the artist's concept and work or reflect the prevalent aesthetic view contemporary to the date of the painting. The primary rule to follow for nineteenth- and twentieth- century paintings as well as Old Masters is to leave the frame be until its significance and condition have been assessed.

The same care taken in selecting a conservator should be exercised in your selection of a framer. A good framer should have a sound historical knowledge of frames and a thorough understanding of conservation principles, in addition to his/her demonstrated abilities in the craft of frame making.

Guidelines for Framing

1. A margin of space should be present between the edge of the painting and the inner edge of the frame's *rabbet* (the groove cut in the edge of the frame to hold the painting). The space allows the stretcher to be keyed out when necessary and allows for the movement of wood panels in response to humidity changes. Cork or balsa spacers on which to rest the painting can be inserted along the bottom space.

2. The painting should be held secure in the frame with brass mending plates. The mending plates should be screwed into the thick area of the frame but *not* screwed into the stretcher or panel support. The end of the mending plate must hold the painting in place by pressure only. Paintings must not be nailed into frames.

3. The mending plates securing a wood panel in place should be attached only on the sides of the frame opposite the end grains of the panel. This location of the plates avoids locking the panel in place and allows it to respond more freely to temperature and humidity changes.

4. Stretcher keys should be secured with wire or string so they cannot fall out and slip between the canvas and stretcher bars. Several words of caution: the hole in the key for running the wire through should be made with the key removed from the

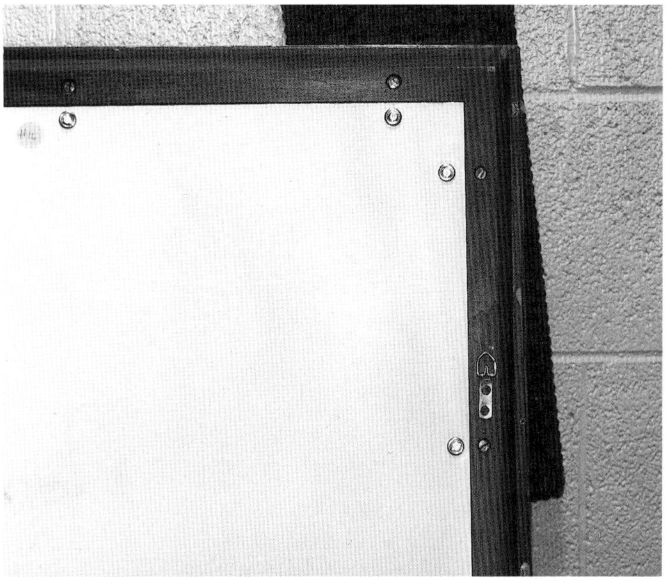

Reverse of framed canvas painting showing hardware

Paintings properly stacked with protective interleaves

stretcher. When tapping the key back into place with a hammer, protect the canvas from an accidental hit from the hammer by placing a piece of cardboard between the key and the canvas.

5. A backing board should be attached to the frame to protect the back of the painting from dust, pollutants, and mechanical shock.

6. If the painting is to be glazed, the glass or Plexiglas should be prevented from touching the painting's surface by the inclusion of an appropriate spacer between the glass and the painting surface.

7. For conservation reasons, picture lights are not advisable. They cause hot spots on the painting's surface, which could lead to accelerated aging in the area covered by the light. *Never* attach picture lights to the frame of a painting.

Hanging Paintings

When you hang your painting you should carefully consider location, hardware, and wall anchors. Remember that you want a safe environment for your painting. Think about the potential activities that may occur in the room or near the wall you have selected to hang the painting. Will those activities pose a threat? Should the painting be glazed to protect it from the residues of cigarette, pipe, or cigar smoke? Will the painting hang in a crowded area or narrow passage that is heavily traveled? Are the light levels appropriate? Does sunlight periodically sweep across the wall you have chosen? As a general rule, you should not hang paintings over radiators or walls with hot pipes running behind them, above fireplaces, or above tables and buffets where hot, steaming food may be placed or spattered. Bathrooms are particularly problematic, as are all of the locations just cited, because they produce moisture and/or heat, which will weaken the adhesion of paint layers and eventually cause loss of paint.

Sturdy screw eyes appropriate to the thickness and weight of the framed painting should be mounted on the thickest part of the frame. Screw eyes may be mounted to the side members of the stretcher if the painting is intended to be hung without a frame. If picture wire is necessary, you should select the appropriate weight of woven "picture" wire (it is usually identified by the weight it will support)—not string or cord. The picture wire should be looped through the screw eyes so that the painting hangs from a double strand of wire, and the ends of the wire should be secured so that they do not poke into the back of the canvas or panel. The wall hooks should also be sturdy and matched to the weight of the painting and frame. Do not hang paintings by their top element (stretcher bar or frame) directly on nails driven into walls. Hooks that are adhered by tape to the wall should also be avoided. For heavy paintings, make sure to drive the picture hooks into the wall studs, and consider mounting a bracket at the bottom of the picture to help bear the weight.

Storage

Occasionally, it is necessary to store paintings. Perhaps a room is being redecorated, or seasonal decorations displace some of your paintings, or you have more paintings than you can display at a given time. Your selection of an appropriate storage area should be guided by considerations of stability and safety. The extreme heat of an uninsulated attic and the extreme dampness of many basements make both locations quite inappropriate for storage. Try to locate a space that is moderate in temperature and humidity and that is relatively dust free. If you can designate a small room for art storage, keep it reasonably uncluttered, pull the shades down, and draw the curtains over the windows. Hang your paintings one above the other on the room's walls. Try to avoid stacking your paintings one against the other on the floor.

Perhaps you have only a few paintings and have only an empty corner or a closet to spare for temporary storage. If that is the case, you may have to stack paintings. Stack no more than two or three paintings together. Protect each painting and frame with a cardboard interleaf between the paintings. Use rolled towels as pads on which to set the paintings. Frames and paintings should not be placed directly on uncarpeted floors. Do not store paintings under windows, near radiators, furnaces, boilers, and water pipes. If you use a closet for storage, try to use it only for painting storage in order to avoid the risk of dropping things being removed or placed in the closet above the paintings.

Transporting Paintings

Paintings keep best when left alone to hang on the wall. The risk of damage is great when they must be transported to locations away from home. Even when museum professionals are handling, packing, and overseeing the painting you have loaned to them for exhibition, the risk of damage or loss exists. Professional training and experience may minimize the risks, but absolute guarantees eliminating the possibilities of damage cannot be given. However, the necessities of moving, selling, acquiring, conserving, and lending to important exhibitions may leave you no alternative—the painting must be moved.

If you find you must move a painting, always try to work with a fine-art transport company or a moving company with a fine arts department. Your local museum or a conservator should be able to refer you to a reliable company. Do not transport your painting in car trunks (uncontrolled temperatures) or by leaning it on car seats. If you must hand carry the painting and use automobile passenger compartments, make sure fragile frame elements are padded and that the painting and frame are well wrapped with protective paper, which should not touch the painting surface. Do not tape directly to the frame or painting surface. Identify the front and back of the package. The package should be well secured in the seat or on the floor of the car. Use the rear floor of a station wagon or minivan if possible. Jumping in and out of cabs with a painting is extremely foolish. Hand carrying a painting on an airplane must be discouraged altogether. Even with prearrangements and/or the purchase of an extra seat, you are courting disaster.

In most if not all situations, packing for shipment should be left to the experts. The following observations will help you to evaluate the quality of your packer's work:

1. Generally, paintings should be packed in a box (package) within a box.

2. The outer box should be sealed against dust and weather. The inner box or package should

protect from rubs, punctures, and dirt and should be cushioned on all sides.

3. All parts of the frame, hardware, and painting should be secure, with nothing loose in the package.

4. Screws should be used to attach the lid. The shipping container should not be subjected to hammering while the painting is in it.

5. Packing materials should consist of a variety of synthetic foam. Excelsior, dried moss, shredded paper, felt, hair, and crumpled tissue paper—while having a long history in packing—are all inappropriate by today's standards.

6. Glass glazing should be either removed or replaced with Plexiglas.

Documentation

One of the most important safeguards you can make is to keep a *dated* record of the condition of your painting from the time you acquire it. The record should consist of a written description and photograph. Valuable paintings should include high-quality photographs as part of their documentation. Your written record should briefly describe the painting by artist, title, date, dimensions, inscriptions, mediums, and support. In the condition description, note surface irregularities, scratches, scuff marks, bulges, significant cracks, loose or lifting pieces, dirt accumulations, and anything else that might be interpreted as damage or a change in condition at a later date. Don't forget the frame. Make diagrams or draw directly on a photocopy of the painting's photograph—anything to make it easier. Your condition record will become an invaluable reference point against which you can periodically determine if changes are occurring in your painting or if it has been damaged during a loan. It is also an important insurance document.

When a Conservator Is Needed

You should consult a conservator for any problems or needs beyond superficial dusting. Any uncertainty you have regarding the condition of your painting should be discussed with a conservator. Conditions such as lifting paint; loose or missing pieces; unexplainable new cracks, creases, and bulges; recent splits and checks in panel supports; punctures, tears, and holes; disfiguring discolorations; yellowed, darkened, and dull varnishes; stains; dirt buildup, called *accretion;* smoke damage; and water and food splashes are potential problems for a conservator. An experienced conservator should be able to determine whether or not the condition you have identified requires treatment.

As the result of past experience or training, you may feel familiar enough with painting materials and techniques to attempt treating the painting yourself. *Do not*, if you value your painting. The treatment of works of art is an extremely complex and serious matter. The issue is not one of simple mending or patching damages and breaks. All treatments have the potential for causing damage (sometimes irreversible) to the work if the proposed treatment and/or materials are inappropriate, unnecessary, or badly executed.

Even with professional conservators, treatment should be thought of as a last resort, and preventive measures should be emphasized to postpone cosmetic treatments if possible. Every effort should be made to increase the time between restoration/treatment. For example, you may choose to restrict the movement of a fragile painting by not allowing it to be loaned rather than have a conservator line (attach a reinforcement canvas) and clean the painting to make it secure for loan and exhibition activities. To a degree, one should accept the minor disfigurement of slightly yellowed varnished and minimally uneven surfaces of untreated canvases. As stated at the beginning of this chapter, to insist that all art look as if it were made yesterday carries the high risk of disfigurement or damage from the very treatment intended to restore and preserve the work.

Obviously there are legitimate reasons for treatment. Responsible, appropriate, and necessary treatments of works of art are carried out daily by conservators. But certain safeguards and precautions should be in place prior to initiating or authorizing treatment. The conservator is obligated to provide the client or owner with a fully

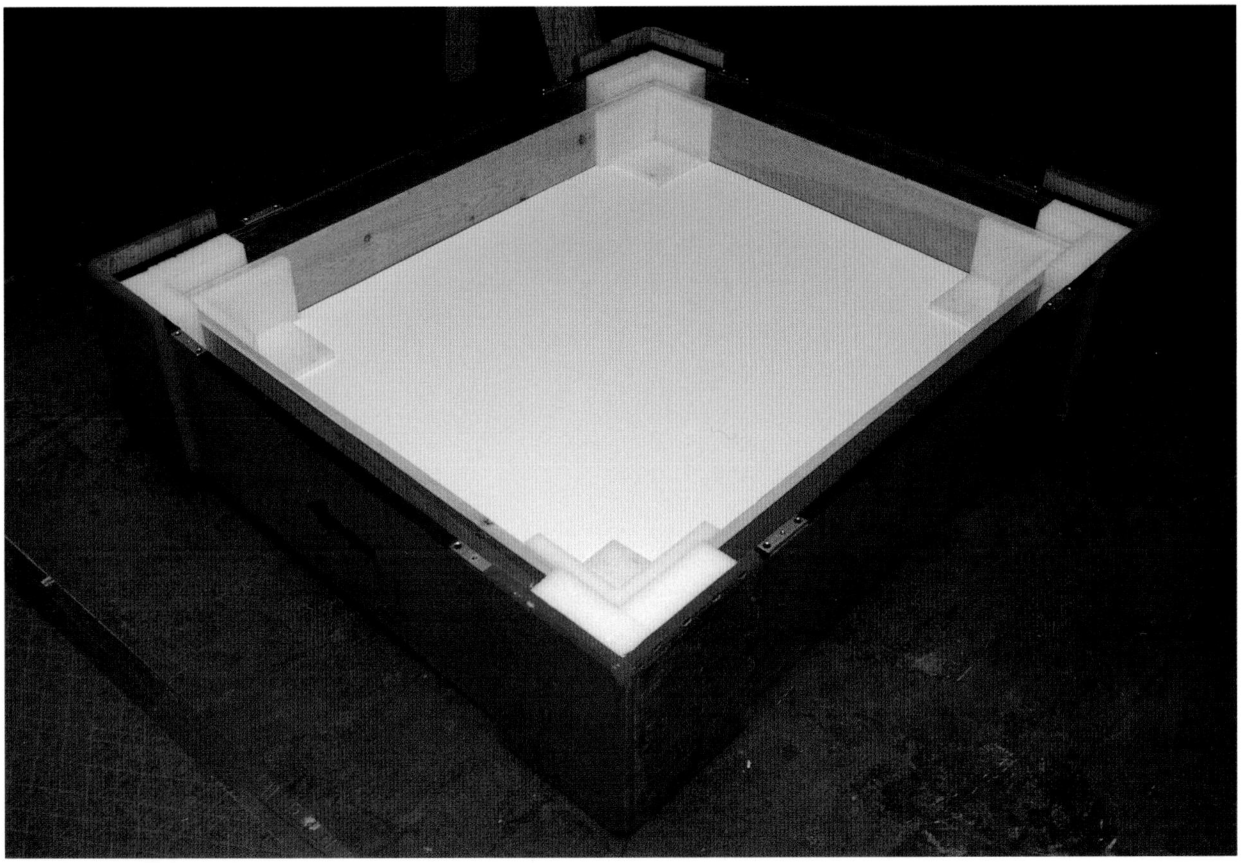

Packing-crate interior showing well-cushioned inner box

documented condition assessment and a treatment proposal based on the condition assessment. The condition assessment should describe the materials and construction of the painting and identify and locate condition problems such as discolorations, delaminations, breaks, disjoins, bulges, surface accretions, or lifting and flaking paint. Judgments regarding extent and degree of each condition problem should also be stated. The proposal for treatment should flow logically from the information in the condition assessment. All techniques and materials to be used in the treatment should be fully disclosed. As the client, you should thoroughly review and demand a satisfactory explanation of both condition assessment and treatment proposal. You should fully understand the rationale behind the materials and techniques proposed by the conservator. Furthermore, you should feel free to exercise your right to a second opinion. Consult your local museum or the AIC's Conservation Services Referral System in Washington, D.C., to locate conservators for a second opinion.

It should be stressed that there are many alternatives to treatment involving noninterventive methods for preserving works of art. There are also options regarding choice of treatments and conservators. All of these avenues should be explored thoroughly before taking any action that will affect permanently the condition of your artwork.

R MARSH 1929
Reginald Marsh
Rush hour - L.I.R.R. Station

WORKS OF ART ON PAPER

Margaret Holben Ellis

Works of art on paper—a very broad category ranging from Old Master drawings to fluorescent silkscreen prints of Marilyn Monroe to monetarily worthless but sentimentally priceless valentines or children's scribbles—are found in almost everyone's "collection." Requirements for inclusion in this category are vague and have more to do with an item's present-day function than its financial value or artistic imprimatur. Documents, maps, stamps, books, posters, ephemera, and photographs are close cousins of prints and drawings and, quite arguably, often are works of art in their own right; readers are encouraged to consult the accompanying chapters on these related paper-based items.

The Nature of Paper

Works of art on paper include prints; watercolors; collages; pencil, charcoal, chalk, and pastel drawings; and a host of other artistic creations that can be made in many different ways but have in common the paper on which, or of which, their images are composed. The determinant factor in their preservation is, therefore, paper, an invention more than two thousand years old and of enormous, if underappreciated, consequence to us all. While space precludes an explanation of paper's fascinating history or details of its manufacture, it can be said that, in general, the life span of a sheet of paper and, by extension, a work of art on paper, is determined by two factors—the way it was made to begin with and the way it is subsequently cared for. An understanding of the nature of paper is the first step, then, for the conscientious collector wishing to provide optimum care for a small or large collection.

Conservation problems that arise due to one or both of the above factors are often said to be either

The rectangular band of discoloration following the contours of this print is called a mat burn *and results from prolonged contact with poor-quality mat board used in framing. Reginald Marsh.* Penn Station. *1929. Hand-colored lithograph. The Metropolitan Museum of Art, New York. Purchase Charles Z. Offin Fund and the Mr. and Mrs. Dave H. Williams Gift, 1991.*

internally or *externally* caused. Many conservation problems come about because of the way the paper or artwork was created; therefore, the cause of the problem is internal or inherent to the piece. For example, the substances frequently used by papermakers over the last century or two—unrefined wood pulp, chlorine bleaches, and unstable sizing agents—can induce typical conservation problems such as darkening and embrittlement of the paper. Almost everyone is familiar with the rapid yellowing of newspapers left in the sun or paper crumbling to dust when curled; these are internally generated reactions catalyzed by external forces.

Deacidification, also called acid neutralization or *buffering*, is often recommended for these kinds of rapidly deteriorating papers, especially those in our archives and libraries. The deacidification of individual works of art, however, is an entirely different matter, since these processes can alter the colors of both paper and pigments or can penetrate unevenly, changing subtle surface textures. Before resorting to deacidification, collectors must take into account the unique, often subjective qualities of works of art, a distinction already identified as difficult. Other, less interventive, procedures may be preferable for retarding the deterioration of acidic papers.

Materials and methods used by an artist can also be the unintentional cause of many conservation problems. Paints may be incompatible with each other or with the paper beneath them, leading to flaking or staining; pastels are naturally powdery and certain colors prone to fading. It is important for collectors to realize that the ongoing problems or negative effects of some artist's materials can be lessened *significantly* by proper climatic conditions, framing, storage, and exhibition.

Conservation problems in works of art on paper can also be caused by external factors. Even the best paper will absorb acidity from improper mounting, matting, framing, and pollution. Overexposure to light and drastic fluctuations in temperature and humidity can also damage paper. More obvious external causes are fires, floods, insects, rodents, and—most ominous of all—people.

These external sources of deterioration take a far greater toll on our prints and drawings than internally generated defects and are plainly easier for collectors to control. Furthermore, the perceptive reader will have noticed that these are the same factors that, when correctly monitored and maintained, will significantly extend the life expectancy of works of art having inherent conservation problems due to the materials from which they were originally created.

Mounting, Matting, and Framing

Without a doubt, the greatest damage to works of art on paper occurs in mounting, matting, and framing with such commonly used materials as inexpensive wood-pulp matboard, corrugated cardboard (cedar shingles made handy backboards for frames in the nineteenth century), rubber cement, animal glues, synthetic adhesives applied both wet and with heat (dry mounting), masking, transparent and double-faced adhesive tapes, and brown gummed tape, just to mention a few. These materials share one characteristic in addition to cheapness and convenience—chemical instability. As these materials deteriorate over time, they also damage the artwork with which they are in contact. This damage most often occurs through a process called *acid migration*. Paper is naturally absorbent; it will readily take in any gas or liquid that surrounds it, including the acidic emissions given off from poor-quality matting and framing materials. *(Note:* This also includes oils from dirty fingers; handle the works as little as possible and with *very* clean hands.) Within a print or drawing, acidity attacks the chemical bonds of the long flexible cellulose molecules that make up the complex structure of paper and break them into shorter and shorter segments. (Cellulose, the raw material for making paper, is found in cotton, wood pulp, and other plant fibers.) The visual symptoms of this process are darkening, yellowing, and embrittlement of the print or drawing wherever it is in contact with one of these substances. Characteristic brown striations caused by corrugated cardboard; shadowy knots of wood transferred onto the paper from a nearby shingle;

The characteristic brown striations on the verso of this print have resulted from the corrugated cardboard with which it was in direct contact. Anton Schutz. Hub of the World *(verso). Etching. Private Collection*

square patches of discoloration emerging through the design from an identification sticker on the reverse; yellow, even orange, cellophane tape and adhesive stains—all are evidence of contact with common, everyday substances that are harmful to paper. Too often these materials are hidden from view within deceptively attractive mats and frames so that by the time they make their presence known, the damage has been done. In order to prevent such damage, works of art on paper should be correctly matted before they are framed or put into storage.

Mats are used to both present and protect works of art on paper. They are constructed from two sheets of stiff paper board and are usually joined with cloth or paper tape along their longer edge so that they open and close like a file folder, either horizontally or vertically. The bottom sheet of mat board supports the print or drawing while the outer *window mat* has an opening in it through which the artwork is viewed.

The most widely available, inexpensive, and decorative mat board is, unfortunately, the type that should be avoided. Poor-quality wood-pulp mat board is a stiff, bonded sheet of what looks like sawdust (bleached unrefined wood pulp) compressed between two sheets of paper called *liners*. The outer liner may be colored, textured, or even of fine art paper. The inner liner, the side that is in contact with the artwork, is usually quite thin and smooth. At first glance, this type of mat board looks like conservation-quality mat board, especially when new. With time, however, the inner core of unrefined wood pulp darkens and the entire board becomes acidic and brittle. The thin inner liner does little to slow down the migration of acidity from the mat board to the work of art, causing staining of its margins. *Mat burns*—continuous bands of discoloration corresponding to the angled edge, or *bevel*, of the mat window—quickly form on the artwork. Eventually, the mat begins to damage the very thing it was intended to protect and enhance.

Paper boards suitable for matting works of art on paper are not automatically used by framers nor are they available at all art supply stores. It is necessary, therefore, to specifically request (and be prepared to pay for) conservation-quality mat board. Three kinds of mat board are suitable for matting prints and drawings—rag board, buffered rag board, and "conservation" board, all of which have a neutral or alkaline pH (a pH of 7 or above) at the time of their manufacture. As its name implies, rag board is made from cotton rags or linters. Usually it has a neutral pH, but if it has been improperly treated during manufacture or storage afterward, even 100-percent-rag board can become acidic. Buffered rag board is made alkaline by the addition of a calcium or magnesium carbonate reserve to neutralize acidity. Conservation board, also called *museum*, *archival*, or *acid-free* mat board, is made from wood pulp that has been both chemically purified and buffered. Buffered mat board can significantly retard the degradation of works of art done on acidic, poor-quality papers.

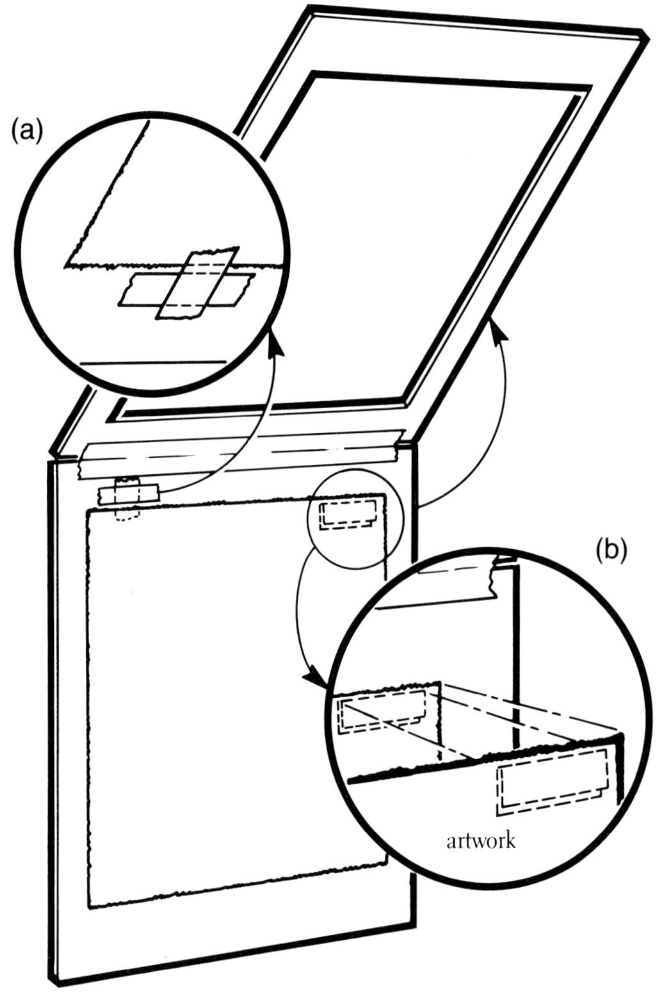

This diagram illustrates a mat and two hinging arrangements. If the edges of the artwork are to be covered by the window mat, the work can be attached with (a) hangers *of hinging tissue adhered to the mat with white gummed cloth and to the artwork with wheat-starch paste. If the edges are to be shown, a* (b) folding hinge *arrangement can be used. (The dotted lines indicate that the hinge lies between the verso of the work and the back mat.) In either case, be sure that the mat board is of archival quality. Diagram by Patrick J. O'Brien*

Conservation-quality boards are now available in a wide range of colors and thicknesses (measured in *plies*—the number of sheets laminated together to form the board, usually supplied in 2,4,6, or 8-ply).

The preferred method of securing prints and drawings into mats is with *hinges*, small strips of folded, long-fibered Japanese tissue adhered with purified starch paste. Typically, two hinges are applied to the top corners of the back of the artwork. Advantages to this hinge type and placement are many—they are strong, flexible, and lightweight, and their excellent aging characteristics have withstood the test of time. In addition, they allow the work of art on paper to expand and contract freely in response to shifts in temperature and humidity. Traditional hinges of this sort are not automatically used by commercial framers because of the greater labor and expense involved. In the long run, however, money invested in proper hinging and matting is well spent in comparison with the costs of restoration or loss in value of an artwork damaged by tapes, glues, and cheap mat board.

Photo corners made of *clear polyester film* (for example, DuPont Mylar Type D) or acid-free paper (*not* the small black ones found in family photo albums) are especially useful for attaching prints and drawings into mats and are often preferable because no adhesives are put directly onto the artwork, thus eliminating problems of staining or future hinge removal. These corners can be purchased or made at home.

While consumers must be aware that the descriptive phrases "acid-free," "museum quality," and "archival" are sometimes loosely used and not necessarily a *guarantee* of quality, it should be noted that the framing industry is clearly responding to the increased demand for materials that meet conservation standards. A new family of pressure-sensitive cloth or paper tapes with a tacky acrylic-based adhesive advertised as "archival" is quickly gaining popularity because of its convenience. A word of caution, however: while the chemical stability of this adhesive is vastly improved, with time these tapes become insoluble in water and require strong solvents for removal. Easy reversibility is normally considered an archival attribute.

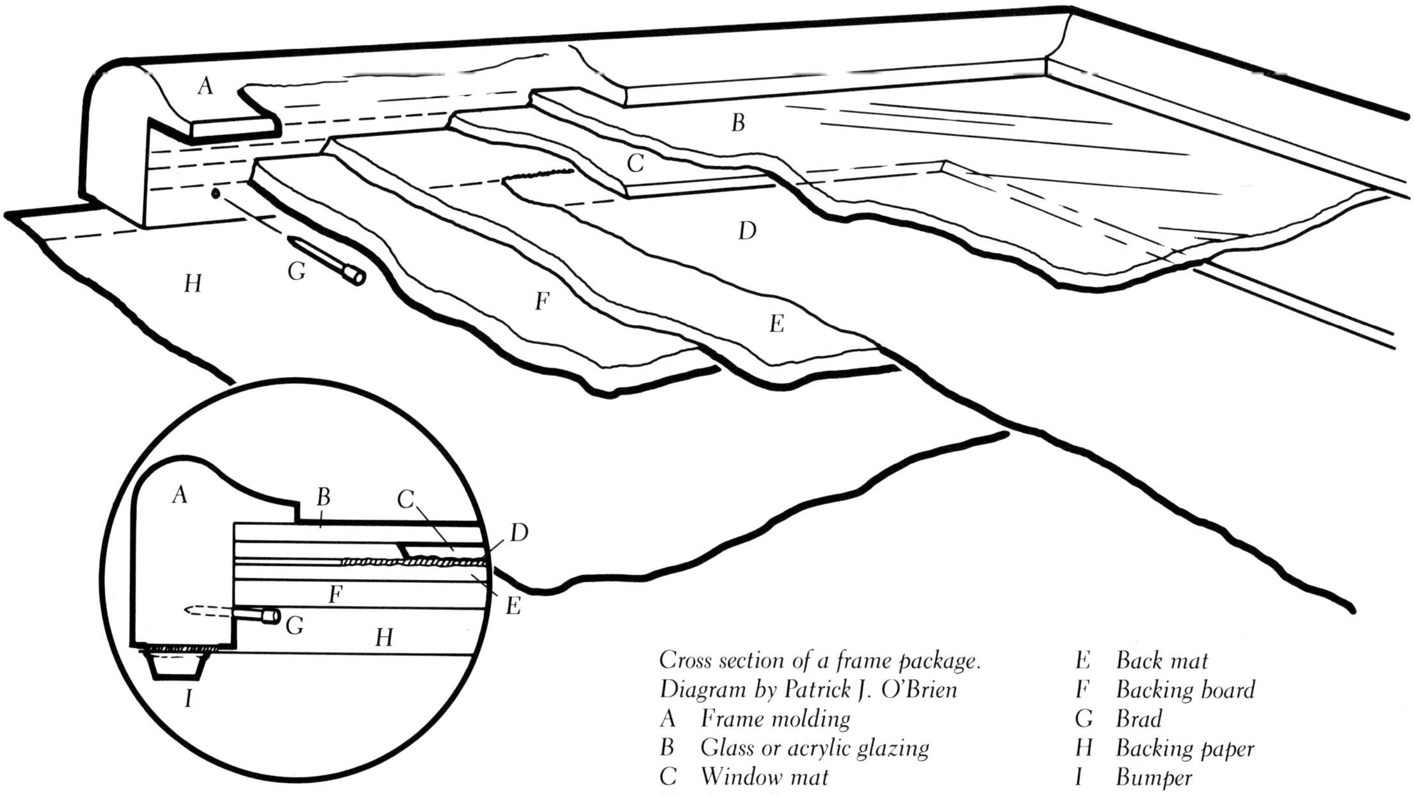

Cross section of a frame package. Diagram by Patrick J. O'Brien
A Frame molding
B Glass or acrylic glazing
C Window mat
D Artwork
E Back mat
F Backing board
G Brad
H Backing paper
I Bumper

If a matted artwork is not to be framed, the exposed surface of the print or drawing should be protected by a *slip sheet* of *neutral glassine* or *acid-free tissue* placed between the artwork and the window mat. Clear polyester film can be used except in proximity to flaking paints or powdery charcoal, chalk, or pastel; the film's static charge literally will pull pigment particles from paper.

If matting and framing a collection of works of art on paper is not feasible, at the very least they should be stored between *neutral glassine* or *acid-free tissue* or slipped into folders made of acid-free folder stock. These can then be put into sturdy *Solander* boxes or boxes constructed from acid-free cardboard, both specifically manufactured for storing prints and drawings. Artworks on paper should never be wrapped in cellophane, wax paper, brown paper bags, or newsprint; stored against wood or cardboard; or curled inside cardboard tubes.

Like mats, frames serve both to enhance and protect works of art on paper. A framed artwork is *not necessarily* a protected one unless a few further steps are taken to safeguard it. When selecting a frame, verify that the molding is sturdy and is securely fastened at each corner. *Miters* (joints) should be snug and properly aligned. The frame should be strong enough to carry the weight of the artwork and *glazing material,* whether glass or clear acrylic sheet, without bowing or spreading at the corners. The molding should be deep enough to accommodate glazing material, matted artwork, and backing materials.

After being properly hinged and matted, as described above, the artwork is fitted into the frame. Once in the frame, the work of art must not come into contact with the glazing material, which has been placed into the frame first. Wherever the two touch, moisture can condense and may result in mold growth. Indeed, this is one of the most important functions of a mat—to provide a "breathing space" that will accommodate the natural movement of the work of art on paper and dissipate any trapped humidity. Spacers or *fillets,* narrow strips of mat board or plastic inserted around the perimeter of the frame and hidden from view by the *rabbet,* the lip of the molding on which the glass rests, can also provide additional space for unmatted or particularly *cockled* (warped) papers.

Next, the remaining space behind the artwork is filled with acid-free corrugated cardboard or polystyrene cored board. Small stainless steel or brass nails called *brads* or *glazers' points* secure the sandwich firmly against the rabbet. The perimeter of the backboard should then be sealed with gummed paper tape or the entire back papered over to prevent dust penetration. All hardware used for hanging framed artworks should be sufficiently strong and properly attached. Replace rusty hanging wires with braided or twisted galvanized steel wire; do not put screws back into old holes in wooden frames.

The choice of glass or clear acrylic for glazing should also be made with conservation considerations in mind. Glass continues to be the usual choice because of its availability and lower price. It has disadvantages however: it breaks easily, is inflexible and so cannot withstand torsional stress, and is heavy; further, most kinds of glass provide no protection against harmful ultraviolet light emitted by all natural and many artificial light sources.

For these reasons many people prefer to use rigid clear acrylic *(polymethyl methacrylate)*, commonly called *Plexi* or *Plexiglas* (a registered trademark of one brand). Some types of acrylics can lessen, although *not eliminate*, damage caused by overexposure to light. Acrylic sheets are lightweight and are therefore preferable for framing large artworks. Because it is somewhat flexible and will not break, clear acrylic has also become the glazing material of choice for artworks that must travel. Acrylic does tend to scratch easily (more durable *polycarbonate* sheets can be used instead) and must always be cleaned gently.

As mentioned earlier, plastics can generate static electricity. Drawings done in powdery mediums such as pastel, charcoal, chalk, or even heavy graphite pencil are thus susceptible to the static charge built up when acrylic used as a glazing material is wiped clean. Loose pigment particles can be transferred from the paper to the acrylic and, needless to say, cannot be returned to the work of art. Works of art on paper done with paint that appears to be loosely adhered to the paper or actually flaking likewise should not be framed behind acrylic sheeting.

Note: If works of art framed behind glass *must* travel, the glass should be taped overall to prevent shattering in case of breakage on the road. Do not extend the tape onto the molding, however, as it will damage gilt or other finishes. Because it scratches so easily, Plexiglas should never be taped for travel.

Matting, hinging, and even framing can be done at home or at self-service framing establishments, but the process requires practice and special equipment and materials. Supplies are readily available to collectors from the sources listed at the end of this book. If a number of artworks are involved, the necessary time and money are well spent by the serious and capable do-it-yourselfer.

Minimizing Environmental Hazards

Light

A significant danger to works of art on paper is overexposure to light. The effect of light on prints and drawings is twofold—*visual* changes are usually the first hint of ongoing *structural* deterioration. Colors can fade or change hue completely. Light-sensitive substances used by artists include the paints used in hand-colored prints, the inks in Japanese woodblock prints, traditional brown iron gall inks and modern colored writing inks, pastels, watercolors, and felt-tip and ball-point pens. With prolonged exposure to light, papers can, depending upon their constituents, become dark brown or yellow—called *light staining* or, more discretely, *time toning*. In tandem with this phenomenon is a marked decrease in paper strength.

Damage to prints and drawings correlates with three specific and quite easily controllable lighting variables: the type of light, the intensity of light, and the duration of exposure to light.

While all light is dangerous, certain wavelengths are more harmful to paper and colorants than others. Ultraviolet light is invisible to humans but is especially destructive to both medium and paper because it supplies the energy needed to initiate chemical reactions. UV light is

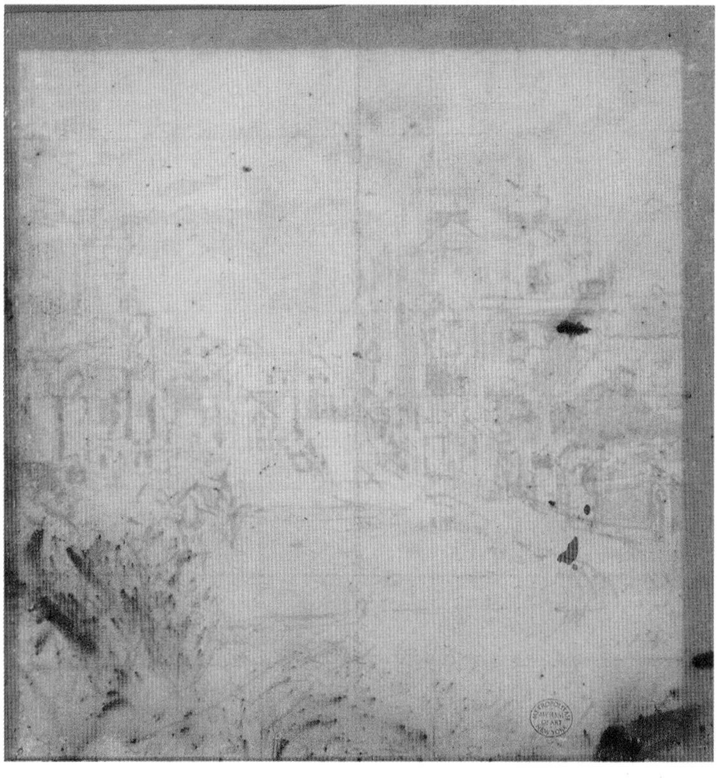

The recto (above) *and verso* (right) *of this watercolor, originally done on a bright purple paper, illustrate the harmful effects of prolonged exposure to light. Where protected by the window mat around the perimeter of the sheet, the paper and the watercolor retain their vibrant tonality. Walter Richard Sickert.* Entry Hill, Belvedere, Bath. *The Metropolitan Museum of Art, New York. Purchase Mr. and Mrs. Carl L. Seldan Gift, 1971*

found in high proportions in daylight (even on overcast days) and in significant amounts in fluorescent and tungsten halogen lighting. Ordinary incandescent (tungsten) lightbulbs do not produce appreciable amounts of UV light. They do, however, emit heat and should never be placed in proximity to works of art on paper; this includes fashionable gallery fixtures designed to be clipped onto frames.

Methods of reducing UV light in rooms where works of art on paper are displayed are straightforward. Blocking out all daylight with draperies and substituting incandescent for fluorescent fixtures are both effective. Filtration of UV is another versatile method, particularly for homeowners. Filtration is accomplished by the use of plastic filters, which are available in many forms. Exterior windows or skylights can be treated with colorless or slightly tinted UV-filtering film applied directly to the glass, or colorless or slightly tinted flexible blinds can be hung in windows (two methods often used for commercial display windows to prevent fading of valuable merchandise). Cylinders of similar filtering material can be slipped around fluorescent tubes. Finally, prints and drawings can be framed behind UV-filtering acrylic (UF-3, UF-4, OP-2), except in cases where powdery mediums make it inadvisable. Recently, however, a UV-blocking picture-framing glass has been introduced and should be widely available soon.

Many people inquire about the use of nonreflective glass to reduce disturbing glare, often a problem in private homes where lighting arrangements are not designed solely for viewing artworks. The most common type of nonreflective glass has been etched on one side to scatter light hitting it. To be effective, however, this glass must rest directly upon the artwork; it is not, therefore, a recommended framing product for works of art on paper. Two different optically coated nonreflective glasses are also available, one of which also filters out UV; both are significantly more expensive than ordinary picture-framing glass.

The intensity of the light source and the amount of exposure time should also be considered when displaying prints and drawings. While the proper level of illumination for works of art on paper has been much debated, it is generally agreed that 5 to 8 footcandles of light is acceptable for *limited* amounts of time. This figure represents an uneasy compromise between the need to exhibit an object and the desire to protect it.

The effects of exposure to light are cumulative—every day, month, and year takes its toll. For this reason, prints and drawings should never be permanently displayed. Three months of exposure time per year per artwork is a prudent policy adopted by many museums. For private collectors, some form of periodic rotation is advisable at the very least. Other methods of reducing intensity and exposure times include lowering wattage, putting in sheer draperies or, better, opaque ones, and, quite obviously, closing curtains and turning out the lights in little-used rooms or while absent on vacation. If these lighting restrictions seem excessive, it is for good reason—light damage is irreversible. When it is finally noticed, it is too late to lower the lights.

Temperature, Humidity, and Pollution

Although other aspects of environment are more thoroughly considered in other chapters of this book, brief mention should be made of the importance of maintaining proper climatic conditions for works of art on paper. Temperature and humidity levels should be as constant as possible; however, since daily and seasonal changes are to be expected in private houses, efforts should be made to allow them to shift more gradually. Although it is recognized that lower temperatures are better for preserving paper and lower humidity for certain kinds of paper, in a home a temperature average of 60 to 70 degrees Fahrenheit and a relative humidity range of 45 to 55 percent, plus or minus 5 points, are more reasonably maintained than one exact level. When relative humidity rises above 65 percent, action should be taken since the danger of mold growth is great. Watercolors in particular can easily become adhered to glass or foster mold growth due to the water-soluble gums and glycerine used in their manufacture. With high levels of humidity, these substances are reactivated and become sticky. Pastels also contain similar

The clusters of small browns spots that disfigure this print are called foxing *and usually indicate unsafe climatic conditions. André Durand.* Vieux Village et Son Environs *(detail). Lithograph. Private Collection*

gums that can provide nutrients for sustaining mold growth. Because these substances naturally attract and retain water longer, mold spores are given an even greater opportunity to grow. At the very least, fans can circulate the air, thus lowering the relative humidity. Because of the danger of mold growth, framed artworks on paper should not be hung on poorly insulated outside walls, stored in damp basements, or left for the season in unheated seaside homes.

At fairly frequent intervals, framed works of art on paper should be inspected closely for mold growth, which can take the form of an inconspicuous whitish haze, feathery strands, or small brown spots called *foxing*. If mold growth is found or suspected, the art should be unframed immediately and aired. This is usually sufficient to stop or prevent the growth since mold cannot survive in less than 65 percent relative humidity. Strips of paper soaked with fungicide such as *thymol* should never be inserted into framed prints and drawings as a preventive measure against mold; thymol damages many materials and, furthermore, it is toxic.

Rusty hanging wire and nails may indicate unsafe humidity levels. Flaking paint can also be an indication of frequent humidity changes; as the responsive paper expands and contracts below an inflexible paint layer, the attachment of medium to

Adhesion of this thickly applied and inflexible water-based paint to the paper has been disrupted due to desiccation of the paint's binder combined with movement of the smooth-surfaced paper below it.

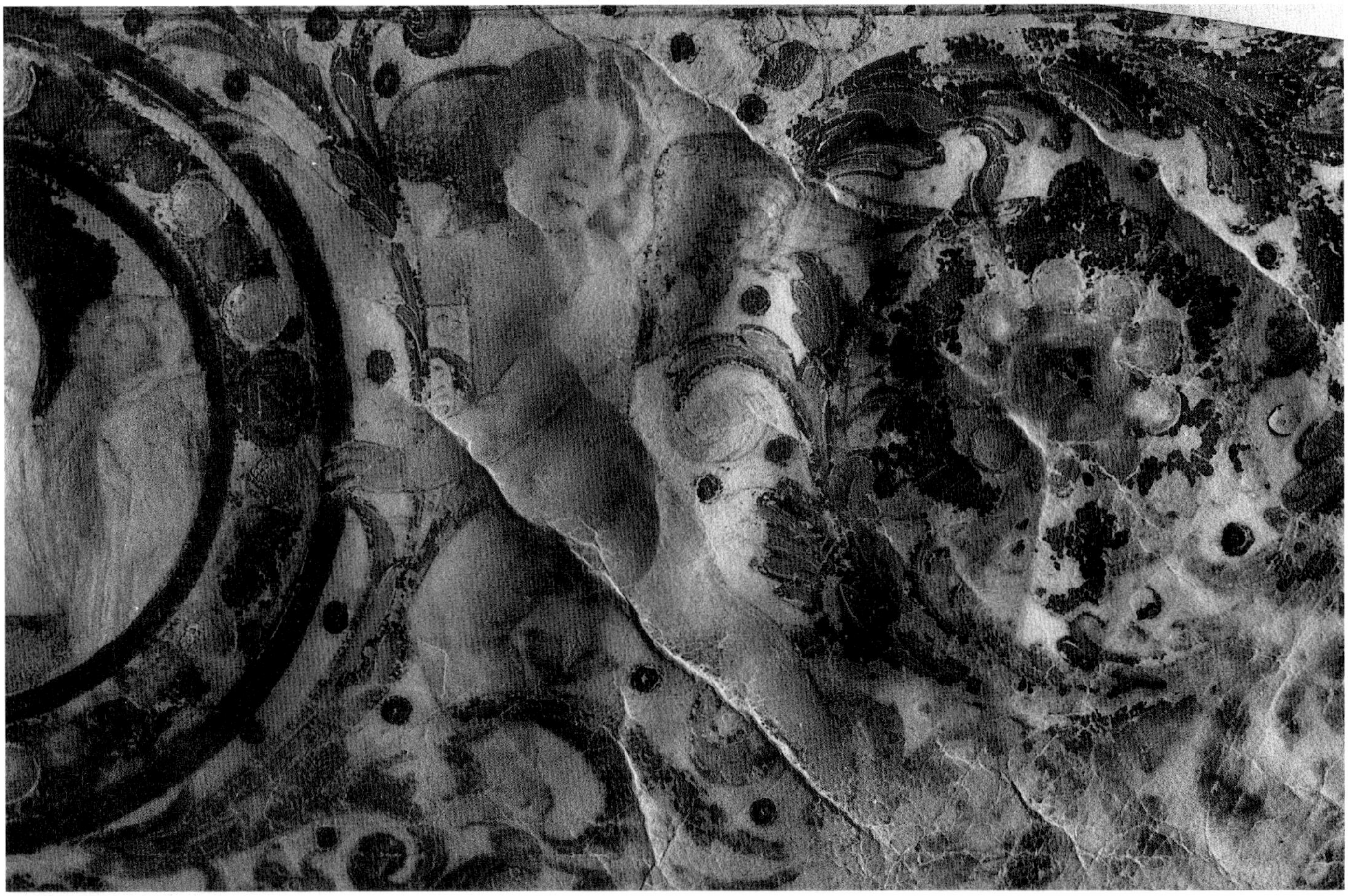

Parchment responds more drastically than paper to shifts in humidity, thus leading to the flaking of tempera paint as seen here. Italian. Private Collection

support becomes progressively weaker. Aggravating this development is the gradual embrittlement of paints due to desiccation of their *binders*, the natural gums and resins that invite the mold growth mentioned above. A conservator should be contacted at the first sign of flaking or weakening adhesion of pigment.

While collectors may feel helpless in fighting the pollution produced in urban areas, they should be aware that pollution—particulate and gaseous—can be produced in the home. Proper matting and framing is, once again, one of the most effective means of combating this danger, which can degrade paper and cause color changes in certain pigments.

A Word about Parchment and Vellum

Most prints and drawings usually encountered in North American collections are on paper. Parchment and vellum (a particularly fine grade of parchment) are mentioned briefly in response to frequent inquiries regarding decorative botanicals, pages cut from medieval antiphonals and illuminated manuscripts, as well as land deeds, indentures, and college diplomas, all popular collector's items found in many homes.

Often the same color and weight, parchment can be mistaken easily for sturdy paper; beyond an initial resemblance, however, parchment is nothing like paper. First of all, it is of animal not vegetable origin. Parchment, simply defined, is made from the cleaning and drying of an animal (usually goat, sheep, or calf) skin under tension. It is not tanned, which differentiates it from leather. Because of how and from what it is made, therefore, parchment requires slightly different care from that for works of art on paper.

Most collectors report that the most frequently observed conservation problem with parchment is buckling. Usually, the gentle undulations of parchment in response to fluctuations in temperature and relative humidity are not dangerous or visually disturbing. In fact, as with paper, some movement of parchment is absolutely normal. Standard conservation-quality matting and framing usually is quite adequate for protecting works of art or documents on parchment. Extreme buckling of parchment is, however, of concern if the resulting deformation is aesthetically displeasing or, more important, if the attachment of paint or ink to the parchment is disrupted. As the parchment moves below the inflexible paint layer, often the paint layer will simply crack or flake off. Items on parchment should be inspected periodically for this type of progressive problem. Drastic changes in temperature and relative humidity can cause the parchment to become permanently distorted, as the skin tissues relax from the directional orientation imposed upon them during manufacture. Extra care should be taken to maintain proper environmental conditions for parchment and vellum items during storage and exhibition.

Documentation

The importance of periodic inspections of works of art on paper accompanied by updated written and photographic documentation cannot be underestimated. By the time symptoms such as light staining, mold growth, or fading become apparent to the casual viewer, a great deal of damage, often irreversible, has occurred. Even the most devoted collector cannot remember every speck and wrinkle, which seem suddenly to appear overnight. In addition to easing such fears, examination reports are useful on a day-to-day basis for quick reference. For instance if an item is requested for loan, a look at its documentation will indicate any special requirements that would affect its travel or exhibition arrangements. These reports, including original sales receipts, and photographs, are also invaluable in resolving insurance adjustments whether for routine appraisal (certainly advisable in today's art market) or from claims arising from calamities such as fire or flood.

To be noted on an examination report is not only the overall condition of the artwork but also exactly how it is hinged, matted, and framed. Remember that once an artwork is in a frame it is very difficult to ascertain whether a mat is acid free or if the acrylic filters out ultraviolet light. Many collectors note these details on the back of the frame itself along with exhibition dates and places.

Documentation is also useful in deciding when professional conservation services are necessary. As a rule of thumb, any visual change (and some can be so gradual as to be barely perceptible) in either the paper or the medium indicates at the very least that the frame should be opened and the contents examined. Perhaps a hinge has slipped or excess cockling has caused the piece to come into contact with the glazing material—two situations which could lead to more serious damage. While unframing a print or drawing does not necessary require a conservator's expertise, a conservator will be able to quickly assess whether a serious conservation problem is in the making.

The final and most easily controllable factor ensuring the preservation of works of art on paper should be mentioned once again—people. It is our responsibility, as collectors, to treat the prints and drawings that delight us today as the cultural and artistic heritage of a much larger family.

Men Of Culpeper County In The Memorable War Of 1861-'65. Record Of Service By Sons Of Culpeper In War Between The States

[Below the Exponent prints the record of those gallant sons of Culpeper who, sixty odd years ago, served in the army of the Confederate States of America. In later issues will be published the muster roles of the several companies that were raised wholly in Culpeper. The names of the men belonging to these companies, do not appear below.]

Amiss, Carroll, enlisted 1862, at Culpeper; Captain Utterback's Company Artillery; served over two years; killed July 2, 1864, at Petersburg.

Apperson, G. F., enlisted 1863; Company F, 6th Virginia Cavalry, Wickham's Brigade, Fitz Lee's Division; served till close of war in ordinance department.

Banks, S. N., enlisted 1861, Co. D, 13th Virginia Infantry, Kemper's Brigade, Pickett's Division; discharged and re-enlisted 1862 in Stuart's Horse Artillery; wounded 1863 at Gettysburg; captured 1865 in North Carolina; held in hospital.

Battle, James Robert, enlisted April 17, 1861; Co. C, 13th Virginia Infantry, Pegram's Brigade, Early's Division; lost one eye at Petersburg.

Beckham, J. G., enlisted 1863; Mosby's Battalion; promoted lieutenant.

Beckham, J. M., enlisted 1861; Co. E, Wheat's Battalion, Taylor's Brigade, Ewell's Division; cadet Military Institute; promoted lieutenant.

Beckham, W. A., enlisted 1861; Co. termaster's department under A. M. Barbour.

Berlin, Sanford W., enlisted March 17, 1862, in Alexander's Battery at Fort Spottswood; served till May 2, 1862; then temporarily attached to the 5th Alabama Battalion; transferred June 26, 1862, Co. M, 55th Virginia Infantry, Walker's Brigade, Hill's Division, May 6, 1864, captured in the two days fight at Wilderness; held at Point Lookout till August 10, 1864; transferred to Elmira, New York; released July 1, 1865.

Borst, John B., enlisted March, 1861; Co. K, 10th Virginia Infantry, Stuart's Brigade, Jackson's old Division; promoted regimental commissary.

Bowers, S. Carson, enlisted April, 1861; Co. E, 4th Virginia Infantry, Stonewall Brigade; promoted captain.

Bowman, William B., enlisted September, 1864; Co. H, 10th Virginia Infantry, Terry's Brigade, Gordon's Division; captured April 6, 1865, near Appomattox; held at Point Lookout.

Bradford, H. C., enlisted April 18, 1861; Co. B, 6th Va. Cavalry, [illegible] Brigade, Fitz Lee's Division; [illegible] 1864 at Culpeper [illegible] tol and Point Lo[illegible]

Bragg, [illegible] Co. B [illegible]

[illegible] 1862; Mosby's command Cavalry; captured 1863 in Fauquier county; held at Fort Delaware.

Brown, George W., enlisted May 1, 1861; Co. F, 21st Virginia Infantry, Jones' Brigade, Johnston's Division; wounded May 5, 1864; died May 12, 1864.

Brown, James R., enlisted February, 1862, Co. F, 21st Virginia Infantry, Ewell's Brigade, Johnston's Division.

Brown, Joseph D., enlisted September, 1864; Co. F, Mosby's Command; detailed to supply the army with provisions, 1862; died November 27, 1879.

Brown, W. H., enlisted April 30, 1861, Co. B, 7th Virginia Infantry, Kemper's Brigade, Pickett Division; promoted second sergeant; wounded July 3, 1863, at Gettysburg.

Burdett, James B., enlisted October, 1864; Co. A, 7th Virginia Infantry, Pickett's Division.

Burke, George F., enlisted 1862; Co. B, 6th Virginia Cavalry, Fitz Lee's Brigade, Stuart's Division; wounded July 3, 1863, at Gettysburg; captured at Cold Harbor; held at Point Lookout and died there.

Burke, James E., enlisted January 1, 1863; Co. B, 6th Virginia Cavalry, Jones', Lomax's, Poague's Brigade, Fitz Lee's Division.

Burke, James Elias, enlisted July 15, 1861; Co. K, 49th Virginia Infantry, Early's Brigade, Ewell's Division; promoted orderly sergeant; wounded July, 1863, at Gettysburg; captured March 25, 1865, at Petersburg; held at Point Lookout; released June 23, 1865.

Burke, J. H., enlisted February 14, 1862; Co. B, 6th Virginia Cavalry, Fitz Lee's Brigade, Stuart's Division.

Burke, John M., enlisted 1861; Co. B, 6th Virginia Cavalry, Jones' Brigade, Hampton's Division; killed at Spotsylvania C. H.

Burke, M. N., enlisted October, 1864; Co. B, 6th Virginia Cavalry, Lomax's Brigade, Stuart's Division; wounded 1864 at Front Royal.

Burnley, Charles T., enlisted 1862; 2d Richmond Howitzer Artillery.

Burrows, H. C., enlisted April 16, 1861; Co. E, 1st Virginia Artillery; first sergeant; wounded July 18, 1861, at Blackburn's Ford; captured at Gettysburg, July 3, 1863; held at Fort Delaware and Point Lookout.

Burton, Arthur W., enlisted November, 1862; Co. L, 10th Virginia Infantry, Jackson's Brigade, Jackson's Division; wounded at second Manassas, August 27, 1862; at Chancellorsville May 2, '62; at Mine Run November 30, '63.

Bushong, Isaac A., enlisted July, 1861; Co. H, 52d Virginia Infantry, Johnston's Brigade; second lieutenant; discharged May, 1862.

Carrico, William H., enlisted March, 1862; Pelham's Artillery, Fitz Lee's Division.

Chadduck, John M., enlisted 1861, at Culpeper; Co. G, 12th Virginia Cavalry; wounded 1864 at Charles City; service four years.

Christian, John T., enlisted July, 1861; Co. E, 1st Virginia Cavalry, Wickham's Brigade, Fitz Lee's Division.

Collins, E. B., enlisted 1861; 7th Virginia Infantry, Pegram's Brigade, Pickett's Division; captured 1865 at Appomattox; held at Point Lookout.

Cooper, Alexander H., enlisted April, 1861; Co. I, 6th Virginia Cavalry, Fitz Lee's Brigade, Stuart's Division.

Corbin, Joseph R., 4th Cavalry.

Corbin, Lemuel A., enlisted 1864; Co. C, Mosby's Command Cavalry; wounded 1864 at Berryville.

Covington, Robert C., enlisted July 16, 1861, served in hospital department at Culpeper C. H., Virginia; afterwards acted as wagon master of the 7th Georgia till 1862, when discharged.

Covington, Thomas H., M. D., detailed as physician at home; captured January 1864, in Culpeper county; held at Point Lookout.

Covington, Thomas R., enlisted April, 1862; Co. F, 9th Virginia Cavalry, Beale's Brigade, Fitz Lee's Division; wounded December, 1864, near Reame's Station.

Creel, Matthew, enlisted 1861, in the Valley of Virginia; 52d Virginia Infantry, Early's Brigade, Ewell's Division; killed August 27, '62 at second Manassas.

Cunningham, John M., enlisted September, 1861; 1st Virginia Artillery, Jackson's Division; first lieutenant; promoted captain, captured at home 1863; held at Fort Warren.

Curtis, T. O., enlisted April 10, 1861; Co. E, 13th Virginia Infantry, Walker's Brigade, Early's Division; promoted first sergeant, wounded June 6, 1862, at Cross Keys; December 13, 1862, at Fredericksburg; May 19, 1864 at Spotsylvania C. H.; captured March 28, 1865, at Petersburg; held at Point Lookout.

Daniel, Samuel A., enlisted March 16, 1862; Purcell's Artillery, Hill's Division.

Davis, A., enlisted 1863; Co. F, Mosby's command; captured July 1863, at Falls Church; held at Old Capitol; Washington, D. C., two months.

Doggett, Basil, enlisted May, 1861; Co. A, Infantry, Kemper's Brigade, Pickett's Division; wounded at Fredericksburg and Gettysburg; captured March, 1865, at Richmond; held at Point Lookout.

Doggett, James, enlisted June 1861; Horse Artillery, Fitz Lee's Division.

Doggett, Meredith J., enlisted May 1861; Co. A, 4th Virginia Cavalry, Pegram's Brigade, Pickett's Division; [illegible] 1880.

[illegible] Francis B., enlisted April, [illegible] E, 7th Virginia Cavalry; [illegible] May 5, 1864, at Wilderness.

[illegible] John E., enlisted 1861; Co. [illegible]

[illegible] captured [illegible] county, Virginia [illegible] Division.

Duncan, R. R., enlisted August, 1861; Co. B, 6th Virginia Cavalry; promoted lieutenant and captain; wounded 1862 at second Manassas; 1864 at Trevillian's and in the Valley; captured '64 in the Valley; held at Fort Delaware.

Duncan, V. F., enlisted 1861; Co. B, 6th Virginia Cavalry, killed May 23, 1862, at Cedarville.

Embrey, L. J., enlisted April, 1861; Co. A, 9th Virginia Cavalry, Beale's Brigade, Fitz Lee's Division.

Eastham, Philip A., enlisted September, 1861; Co. B, 7th Virginia Cavalry; Jones' and Rosser's Brigade, Jackson Division; first lieutenant.

Farish, G. G., enlisted September, 1864; Co. E, 9th Virginia Cavalry, W. H. Lee's Brigade, Fitz Lee's Division.

Farish, Robert T., enlisted in Co. E, 9th Virginia Cavalry; W. H. Lee's Brigade, Fitz Lee's Division; killed September, 1863, in Culpeper county near Cedar Mountain while scouting for General Stuart.

Fant, John S., enlisted April 17, 1861; Co. H, 4th Virginia Cavalry, Wickham's Brigade, Fitz Lee's Division; wounded at Winchester September 19, 1863.

Finks, H. W., enlisted December 1, 1862; Co. L, 10th Virginia Cavalry, Walker's Brigade, Ewell's Division; promoted first sergeant; wounded June 17, 1863, at Winchester; captured May 19, 1864, at Spotsylvania C. H., held at Fort Delaware.

Foster, Warrington D., enlisted August, 1863, Co. A, 39th Battalion Cavalry, Lee's body-guard; captured November 29, 1863 at Mine Run; held twelve months at Point Lookout.

Foster, McKidru F., enlisted April, 1861; Co. E, 6th Virginia Cavalry; '63 transferred to General Lee's body-guard.

Foushee, Frank R., enlisted June 1, 1861; Co. A, 7th Virginia Infantry, Terry's Brigade, Pickett's Division; captured April 7, 1865, at Farmville.

Fox, Henry, enlisted May, 1861; Co. F, 21st Virginia Infantry, Jones' Brigade, Johnston's Division; killed at Petersburg.

Fray, William H., enlisted April, 1861; Co. A., 7th Virginia Infantry, Kemper's Brigade, Pickett's Division; captured April 6, 1865, at Sailor's Creek; held at Point Lookout.

Freeman, George, enlisted 1861; Pelham's Battalion Horse Artillery; participated in all the battles of his command; captured May, 1862; held at Point Lookout.

Freeman, J. G., enlisted April, 1861; Deering's Artillery, Ewell's Brigade, Longstreet's Division; promoted commissary sergeant.

Freeman, William T., enlisted February, 1863, Deering's Artillery, Ewell's Brigade, Longstreet's Division; captured near Richmond; exchanged in a few days; died 1872.

Gaines, B. F., enlisted March 14, 1862, Co. L, 1st Virginia Reserves Artillery; captured July 3, 1863, at Gettysburg; was carried about two miles and dodged the Federals by jumping behind an old shop and escaped.

Gaines, Henry L., enlisted April, 1862; 4th Virginia Cavalry, Wickham's Brigade, Fitz Lee's Division; killed at Williamsburg, near Richmond.

Gaines, Reuben M., enlisted April 17 1861; Co. L, 7th Virginia Infantry, Kemper's Brigade, Pickett's Division; killed at first Manassas July 21, 1861.

Garnett, John K., enlisted August, 1863; Co. C, 39th Virginia Battalion.

Gibson, Daniel W., enlisted January 1862; Crenshaw's Company, Pegram's Battalion Artillery; captured at Five Forks; held at Point Lookout two months.

Gibson, John W., enlisted January, 1862; Crenshaw's Company, Pegram's Battalion Artillery.

Gibson, Thomas C., enlisted March, 1861; Co. E, 13th Virginia Infantry; in Crenshaw's Company, Pegram's Battalion Artillery.

Gordon, Albert S., enlisted April, 1861; Co. E, 13th Virginia Infantry; was afterwards in Jackson's Brigade; discharged August, 1861.

Godfrey, Alexander, enlisted April, 1862; Co. A, 18th Virginia Cavalry, Imboden's Brigade.

Goodwin, Daniel A., enlisted April 17, 1864, after the burning of the Military Institute; Infantry, Breckenridge's Division; wounded at Maryland Heights.

Grimsley, Daniel A., enlisted April 17, 1861; Co. B, 6th Virginia Cavalry, Payne's Brigade, Fitz Lee's Division; promoted major.

Hackley, William, enlisted April, 1861; Co. A, 2d Virginia Infantry, Stonewall Brigade; battles, four; service two years; discharged 1863.

Hale, Daniel W., enlisted June, 1861; Co. C, 15th Virginia Infantry, Pegram's Brigade; Ewell's Division; wounded at Gaines' Mill, Hatcher's Run, and February, 1865, at Fisher's Hill.

Hall, F. S., enlisted June, 1861, first under Captain Nolan in D. H. Hill's Artillery and under Captain Braxton in A. P. Hill's Artillery; promoted assistant surgeon in Pegram's Battalion.

Holliday, W. D., enlisted April, 1862; Co. A, 13th Virginia Infantry, Early's Brigade, Ewell's Division; wounded June 8, 1862, at Cross Keys, in arm; September 1, 1862, at Ox Hill, in thigh; May 12, 1864 at Spotsylvania, lost an arm; discharged December 7, 1864.

Hatcher, Mahlon G., enlisted 1861, Co. C, 17th Virginia Infantry, Corse's Brigade, Pickett's Division; promoted color sergeant; wounded May 5, 1862, at Williamsburg, captured 1862 in Loudoun county, [illegible] escaped. Dead.

Hawkins, [illegible] F., enlisted 1863; Co. B, [illegible] Virginia Infantry, Kemper's Brigade, Pickett's Division; [illegible] conscript officer, service [illegible] 1864.

[illegible] at the time of Stuart's death, near B[illegible]

Hawley, John A., enlisted [illegible] 1862; Fry's Artillery, [illegible] Corps.

Hawley, M. R., enlisted April [illegible] 1862; 6th Virginia Cavalry, Payne's Brigade, Fitz Lee's Division.

Heflin, John L., enlisted February, 1864; Co. E, 13th Virginia Infantry, Kemper's Brigade, Pickett's Division.

Hill, William H., enlisted April, 1861; Co. C, under Colonel Porter, Pickett's Brigade, Longstreet's Division; promoted corporal; killed at Gettysburg July 3, 1863.

Hitt, Festus, enlisted May, 1861; Co. G, 49th Virginia Infantry, Smith's Brigade, Early's Division.

Hitt, Blewford A., enlisted May, 1861; Co. G, 7th Virginia Infantry, Kemper's Brigade, Pickett's Division; died September, 1861, at home in Culpeper county.

Hitt, James W., enlisted March, 1862; Co. A, 7th Virginia Cavalry, Stuart's Brigade, captured August 6, 1863, near Brandy Station, held at Point Lookout.

Hitt, Martin L., enlisted May, 1861; Co. G, 7th Virginia Infantry, Kemper's Brigade, Pickett's Division; discharged January 4, 1865, on account of disability.

Hudgins, Albert G., enlisted April 14, 1861; midshipman on the steamer "Sumter," Confederate States Navy; promoted lieutenant.

Hoffman, F. W., enlisted July 1, 1861; Stribbling's Battery, Pickett's Division; wounded March 26, and captured April 2, 1865, at Petersburg, held at Newport News; discharged July, 1865.

Holliday, John Z., enlisted May, 1861; Co. G, 20th Virginia Infantry, Garnett's Brigade; re-enlisted in Co. A, 3d Virginia Cavalry, Fitz Lee's Brigade, Stuart's Division; captured 1861 at Rich Mountain; paroled.

Holmes, F. Wallace, enlisted April, 1861; Co. F, 18th Virginia Infantry, Stonewall Brigade; wounded July 18, 1861, at Manassas; discharged July 18, 1861.

Hooe, George G., enlisted April 17, 1861; Co. G., 4th Virginia Cavalry, Wickham's Brigade, Fitz Lee's Division; captured several times, always escaped; was on general scout duty all through the war.

Howard, Thomas C., enlisted April, 17, 1861; Co. A, Huger's Battalion Artillery, Jordan's Battery; promoted sergeant.

Hudson, Bruce, enlisted 1864; 4th Virginia Cavalry; killed at the Wilderness.

Hudson, James W., enlisted April 17, 1861; Co. G, 7th Virginia Infantry, Kemper's Brigade, Pickett's Division; wounded July 3, '63, at Gettysburg.

Hudson, Samuel T., enlisted April 17, 1861, Co. G, 7th Virginia Infantry, Kemper's Brigade, Pickett's Division; captured April 3, 1865, at Richmond; held at Point Lookout.

Hudson, Thomas J., enlisted October, 1862; Camp Lee Guards, City Battalion at Richmond; served until January, 1865; re-enlisted, Co. B, 13th Virginia Infantry.

Hoffman, Moses A., enlisted March, 1861; Co. K, 7th Virginia Infantry; [illegible]'s Brigade, Kemper's Division.

[illegible]ne, R. E., captured and held at [illegible] Lookout.

[illegible]ney, Asberry, enlisted October [illegible] courier for General Hill.

[illegible]ries, Robert S., enlisted 1863; [illegible] Virginia Infantry; captured 1865; [illegible] Point Lookout.

[illegible]ler, Ferdinand, enlisted April, [illegible] Virginia Cavalry, Rosser's Brigade.

[illegible]y, Andrew J., enlisted May [illegible] Co. G, 7th Virginia Infantry, Kemper's Brigade, Pickett's Division, wounded July 3, 1863, at Gettysburg.

Kilby, H. C., enlisted August, 1861; [illegible] G, 7th Virginia Infantry, Hill's, [illegible]ylor's, Kemper's Brigade, Long[illegible]'s Division; wounded and cap[illegible] at Frazier's Farm; held at Fort [illegible]ure.

Kilby, James P., enlisted March [illegible] 4th Virginia Cavalry.

Kilby, Joseph M., enlisted 1862; 6th [illegible]inia Cavalry, Kemper's Brigade, [illegible]ett's Division.

Kilby, Thomas M., enlisted April 18, [illegible]; Co. G, 7th Virginia Infantry, Kemper's Brigade, Pickett's Division; [wo]unded slightly at Seven Pines, May [illegible] 1862.

[L]ampkin, J. W., enlisted 1861; Co. [illegible] 38th Battalion Virginia Artillery; [wo]unded July, 1863; paroled; wounded July 6, 1864, at Petersburg.

Lampkin, Thomas O., enlisted 1861; [illegible] Virginia Infantry, Walker's Brigade, Ewell's Division; discharged on [acc]ount of disability.

Leavel, James W., enlisted 1861; Co. [illegible] 7th Virginia Infantry, Kemper's Brigade, Pickett's Division; promoted [ord]erly sergeant; wounded August 30, [illegible] at Manassas.

Leavell, William A., enlisted October [illegible] 1861, Co. E, Mosby's Battalion.

[illegible]er, Ambrose C., enlisted 1863; [illegible] Virginia Infantry, Johnston's Division; killed at Spotsylvania C. H.

[illegible]ge, James W., enlisted April [illegible]; Co. C, 13th Virginia Infantry, [Peg]ram's Brigade, Early's Division.

[illegible]ge, Peyton E., enlisted September [illegible] 1862; Co. C., 13th Virginia Infantry, Pegram's Brigade, Early's Division; captured October, 1864, at [Cul]peper; held at Washington.

[illegible] Richard, enlisted 1861; Co. [illegible] Virginia Cavalry, Fitz Lee's [illegible] Stuart's Division, captured [illegible] Ashland; held at Fort Del[aware] [illegible] May 6, 1864, at Wi[lderness].

[illegible]

[illegible] Division.

[M]ajor, E. F., enlisted May 186[illegible], [Wi]se's Company of Wise's Legion; [pr]omoted adjutant; killed May 31, [18]62, at Seven Pines.

Major, Langdon C., enlisted 1864; [Co.] E, Mosby's command.

Major, Samuel, enlisted March 17, [18]63; Sturtevant's Battery; [illegible] [Jo]nes' 12th Va., Field Artillery, An[derson]'s Corps. Participated in the battles in and around Richmond.

Major, W., Jr., enlisted May, 1863, Sturtevant's Battery. October 14, 1864, wounded by the explosion of the magazine.

Marsh, C. W., enlisted September 1864; Co. F, 2d Virginia Reserves, Walker's Division.

Massey, John, enlisted April 10, 1861; Co. I, 6th Virginia Cavalry, Payne's Brigade, Fitz Lee's Division; died December 18, 1883, in Texas.

Massey, T. C., enlisted April 1, 1862; Co. I, 6th Virginia Cavalry, Payne's Brigade, Fitz Lee's Division; wounded November 15, 1863, at Stevensburg and November 1, 1864, at Winchester.

Maupin, H. A., enlisted 1862; Co. [illegible], 7th Virginia Cavalry, Ashby's Brigade, Rosser's Division.

McConchee, William A., enlisted April, 1861; Co. I, 11th Virginia Infantry, Kemper's Brigade; promoted corporal.

Miller, Henry T., enlisted July, 1861; Co. I, 7th Virginia Cavalry, Ashby's Brigade, Jackson's Division.

Miller, Robert B., enlisted 1864; 1st Virginia Reserves; second lieutenant; captured near Richmond; held at Fort Delaware.

Milton, John W., enlisted 1862, Co. [illegible], Mosby's Cavalry, transferred to Co. C, 13th Virginia Infantry, Pegram's Brigade, Pickett's Division.

Morgan, William B., enlisted April 1861; Co. B, 7th Virginia Infantry, Kemper's Brigade, Pickett's Division.

Nale, G. B. W., enlisted October 12, 1863; Co. D, Cadet Corps, Virginia Military Institute, Breckinridge's Division; first sergeant.

Nolan, John, enlisted April 17, 1861; Co. C, 13th Virginia Infantry, Pegram's Brigade, Early's Division; promoted corporal; captured September [illegible] 1864, at Fisher's Hill; held at Point Lookout; exchanged in one month.

O'Callahan, William, enlisted 1861; Co. K, 49th Virginia Infantry, Smith's Brigade, Early's Division; promoted first sergeant; wounded 1862, at Seven Pines; captured 1862 at Sharpsburg; held at Fort Delaware; service four years; discharged at close of war.

Pattie, D. M., enlisted April 1861; Co. K, 17th Virginia Infantry, Pickett's Brigade, Longstreet's Division; promoted department marshal of Eastern Virginia under confiscation act.

Patton, Hugh M., enlisted April 18, 1861; 7th Virginia Infantry, Kemper's and Cook's Brigade, Pickett's and Heath's Division; promoted first lieutenant; wounded at second Manassas.

Patton, James, enlisted April 18, 1861; Echols Brigade; promoted lieutenant; wounded at Giles C. H.; died March 30, 1862.

Patton, W. T., enlisted April 18, 1861; 7th Virginia Infantry, Kemper's Brigade, Pickett's Division; captain; promoted colonel; wounded at second Manassas; killed at Gettysburg.

Payne, J. W., enlisted April, 1864; Black Horse Cavalry, Co. D, Stuart's Brigade, Fitz Lee's Division; served till close of war.

Payne, Joseph F., enlisted March 9, 1862; Co. H, 4th Virginia Cavalry, Wickham's Brigade, Fitz Lee's Division; wounded and captured March, 1863, at Kelly's Ford; held at Washington, D. C., "Old Capitol building," three months; exchanged and returned to company.

Payne, Robert W., enlisted 1861; Co. A, 7th Virginia Cavalry, Rosser's Brigade; Fitz Lee's Division; wounded 1862, at second Manassas; 1863, at Gettysburg; 1864, at Ream's Station and four other times.

Pendleton, Edmund, enlisted 1862, 1st Virginia Infantry, Kemper's Brigade, Pickett's Division; died 1863.

Penick, N., enlisted May, 1861; Co. A, 38th Virginia Infantry, Smith's Brigade, Johnston's Division; lieutenant; promoted adjutant; served in infantry till autumn 1861; entered artillery service 1862 as captain Co. A, Poague's Battalion Artillery.

Pendleton, John R., enlisted June, 1861; Co. H, 7th Virginia Cavalry, wounded at Hanover Junction and Jones' Brigade, Fitz Lee's Division; Reams' Station; captured at Mount Jackson and in Albemarle county; held at Fort Delaware seven months.

Perry, George P., enlisted August 1861; 7th Virginia Infantry, Kemper's Brigade, Pickett's Division.

Perry, W. G., enlisted April 12, 1862; Co. G, Horse Artillery, Stuart's Brigade, Jackson's Division.

Pierce, J. M., enlisted 1862; Co. D, Gowe's Regiment Arkansas Infantry, Churchill's Brigade, Hindman's Division; wounded 1864 at Mansfield.

Pinkard, A. A., enlisted May 15, 1861; 49th Regiment, Pegram's Brigade, Early's Division; ensign; killed June 26, 1862 at Mechanicsville.

Porter, John J., enlisted September, 1861; Co. F, Mosby's command, promoted to Mosby's staff; captured in Culpeper county, October 1, 1863; held ten days at Culpeper C. H.; discharged at Winchester, April 12, 1865.

Ratrie, Henry H., enlisted March 10, 1862; Co. K, 4th Virginia Cavalry, Jones' Brigade, Fitz Lee's Division.

Rixey, Samuel, enlisted June, 1863; under Captain Taylor in conscript service [illegible] close of war.

[Robe]rtson, William A., enlisted March 1862, Po[illegible] Brigade, Field's [illegible]

Robson, W. T. [illegible]

[illegible] enlisted [illegible] quartermaster department [illegible] Co. C, Mosby's Rangers [illegible]

Scott, J. M., Jr., enlisted April 1861; Co. F, 10th Virginia Cavalry, Hampton's, then Chamberlain's Brigade, Fitz Lee's Division; sergeant of guards; slightly wounded at Gettysburg and Brandy Station; captured October 11, 1863, at Brandy Station; held at Old Capitol and Point Lookout 16 months.

Shackelford, John M., enlisted February, 1863; Co. C, 4th Virginia Cavalry, Wickham's Brigade, Fitz Lee's Division; wounded at Five Forks, April 2, 1865; captured at Richmond, April 4, 1865; held there.

Shaw, Jackson N., enlisted 1864, Captain Franklin's Company, Mosby's command; lost an eye below Upperville, 1864.

Sims, William B., enlisted September 28, 1862; Co. A, 4th Virginia Cavalry, Wickham's Brigade, Fitz Lee's Division.

Slaughter, Thomas T., enlisted April, 1861; Co. B, 6th Virginia Cavalry.

Smith, Early, enlisted August 9, 1861; Co. L, 10th Virginia Infantry, Taliaferro's Brigade, Jackson's Division; captured March, 1864, at Hamilton, Loudoun county; held at Fort Delaware.

Smith, Elza, enlisted May, 1861; assigned to quartermaster department.

Smith, John W., enlisted August 9, 1861; Co. L, 10th Virginia Infantry, Taliaferro's Brigade, Jackson's Division; captured April 1, 1865, at Five Forks, held at Fort Delaware.

Smith, Joseph T., enlisted March, 1863; Co. F, 21st Virginia Infantry, Terry's Brigade, Johnston's Division.

Smith, Philip, enlisted May, 1861; Taylor's Company, 7th Virginia Infantry, Kemper's Brigade, Longstreet's Division; killed at the Seven Days fight.

Smith, Thomas J., enlisted September, 1862; 21st Virginia Infantry, Stuart's Brigade; captured in Culpeper county; held at Point Lookout [illegible]

Somerville, C. B., enlisted November, 1863; Douglass' Pontoon Corps.

Somerville, J. W., enlisted May, 1861; Co. G, 20th Virginia Infantry, Pegram's Brigade, Garnett's Division; discharged July, 1861; re-enlisted 1863, 3rd Alabama Regiment, Rhodes' Brigade; wounded at Rich Mountain and Boonesboro Gap.

Somerville, Langdon, enlisted November, 1863; Douglass' Pontoon Corps; died April, 1864.

Somerville, Walter, enlisted 1861; surgeon at Yorktown; died 1863.

Somerville, R. B., enlisted May, 1861; Porter's Company, 7th Virginia Infantry, Kemper's Brigade, Pickett's Division; killed at Gettysburg.

Sparks, Champ C., enlisted May, 1861; Co. G, 7th Virginia Infantry, Kemper's Brigade, Pickett's Division; promoted corporal; wounded [illegible] 1862, at Williamsburg; wounded and captured July 3, 1863, at Gettysburg; held Williamsburg; wounded and captured July 3, 1862, at Gettysburg; at Fort Delaware and died there October, 1863.

Sparks, Robert W., enlisted April, 1861; Co. A, 7th Virginia Infantry, Kemper's Brigade, Pickett's Division.

Stallard, Randolph R., enlisted 1861; Captain Vanderslier, 49th Virginia Infantry; mortally wounded November, 1864, at Spotsylvania C. H.

Starke, A. E., enlisted August 9, 1861; Co. I, 49th Virginia Infantry, Smith's Brigade, Early's Division; promoted sergeant; 1863 transferred to Co. K, same regiment; October, 1864, wounded and captured at Cedar Creek, held at Point Lookout.

Stewart, Broaddus, enlisted January 1863; cavalry; died 1882 in Missouri.

Stewart, James W., enlisted April 29, 1861; Co. I, 30th Virginia Infantry, Corse's Brigade, Pickett's Division; wounded June 26, 1862, at Chickahominy; died June 29, 1862.

Stewart, Joseph, enlisted May, 1861; infantry, Stuart's Brigade, Pickett's Division.

Stewart, Richard, enlisted May, 1861; cavalry; died 1868.

Stringfellow, B. W., enlisted May, 1861; Co. I, 11th Virginia Infantry, Kemper's Brigade, Pickett's Division; lieutenant; wounded May 31, 1862, at Seven Pines; captured 1862, in Orange county; paroled; captured 1864, at Petersburg; held at Old Capitol, Washington.

Stringfellow, Martin S., enlisted April 16, 1861; Co. A, 13th Virginia Infantry, Early's and Pegram's Brigade, Ewell's and Walker's Divisions; promoted first lieutenant; slightly wounded at Chantily.

Strother, George F., enlisted March, 1863; as assistant commissary.

Strother, Philip W., enlisted April, 1861; Co. F, 13th Virginia Infantry, Early's Brigade, Ewell's Division; lieutenant; wounded May 12, 1864, at Spottsylvania C. H.; discharged same day.

Taliaferro, Alex. G., enlisted May, 1862; 13th, then 25th Virginia Infantry, Johnston's Division; promoted captain, lieutenant colonel, and brigadier general; wounded at second Manassas.

Taliaferro, John K., enlisted February, 1863; Co. H, 4th Virginia Cavalry, Wickham's Brigade, Fitz Lee's Division; wounded at Trevilian Depot; captured April 1, 1865, at Five Forks; held at Point Lookout two months.

Tanner, John W., enlisted March, 1862; Co. E, 7th Virginia Infantry, Kemper's Brigade, Pickett's Division; wounded June 3, 1862; at Frazier's Farm; discharged July, 1862.

Thomas, G. S., enlisted March 13, 1862; Purcell's Battery; Hill's Division.

Towles, G. R., enlisted 1863; 17th Virginia Infantry, Kemper's Brigade, Pickett's Division; killed May 16, 1864 at Drury's Bluff.

Throckmorton, John [illegible], enlisted April, 1861; [illegible]th Virginia Cavalry [illegible]

Tarrant, Lewis C., enlisted [illegible] Co. I, 11th Virginia Infantry, Kemper's Brigade, Pickett's Division; captured 1862, at Williamsburg; held at Fort Delaware; released and discharged 1862.

Turner, T. H., enlisted 1863; Pelham's Battalion Horse Artillery; participated in the principal battles of the command.

Vaughan, Franklin D., enlisted 1863, Co. E, Mosby's Rangers.

Vaughan, Henry J., enlisted 1861; teamster, served on hospital duty, and engineers' corps, Colonel Talcott, Captain Johnson.

Vaughan, Peter, enlisted July, 1861; quartermaster department, carpenter and scout.

Wager, James P., enlisted April, 1861; Co. E, 13th Virginia Infantry, Kemper's Brigade, Pickett's Division; discharged 1862.

Waite, C., enlisted April 3, 1861; Co. B, 9th Virginia Cavalry, Fitz Lee's Division; captain; promoted major; served on General Lee's staff from May 1, 1862, till close of the war.

Walker, Thomas G., enlisted March, 1862; Crenshaw's Company, Pegram's Battalion Artillery, A. P. Hill's Division; wounded July 3, 1863 at Gettysburg; captured April, 1863, at Louisa C. H.; held at Washington one month; captured April 1865, at Five Forks; held at Point Lookout three months.

Wallace, A. Henderson, enlisted October, 1864; Co. C, 30th Virginia Infantry, Corse's Brigade, Pickett's Division.

Wayland, John W., enlisted 1861; Co. A, 7th Virginia Infantry, Kemper's Brigade, Pickett's Division; served two years in quartermaster department.

Wharton, Stanton, enlisted April, 1861; Co. E, 13th Virginia Infantry, Pegram's Brigade, Early's Division; wounded at second Manassas; captured at Petersburg in 1865; held at Point Lookout four months.

Wheatley, James G., enlisted April, 1861; 4th Virginia Cavalry, Fitz Lee's Division.

Whitlock, Martin, enlisted 1864; Co. I, 6th Virginia Infantry, Wickham's Brigade, Fitz Lee's Division; wounded 1864, at Manassas.

Winston, Arthur W., enlisted May, 1861; 7th Virginia Infantry, Kemper's Brigade, Pickett's Division.

Winston, L. D., enlisted April, 1861; Culpeper Minute Men, Purcell's Battery, Hill's Division.

Wise, John B., enlisted 1862; wounded 1863, at Leesburg; died 1873, at Shreveport, Louisiana, of yellow fever.

Wise, Louis A., enlisted 1861; Richmond Howitzer Company Artillery.

Wood, P., enlisted 1863; Co. D, 13th Virginia Infantry.

Wood, Robert W., enlisted June 6, 1861; Co. D, 23rd Virginia Infantry, Taliaferro's Brigade, Jackson's Division; lost all toes by frost; discharged February 9, 1862.

Yancey, Edwin D., enlisted 1861; artillery; promoted lieutenant.

Yowell, John, enlisted September 1, 1863; Pegram's Battalion Artillery.

Yowell, William L., enlisted September, 1863; Co. C, 4th Virginia Cavalry, Wickham's Brigade, Fitz Lee's Division.

LIBRARY AND ARCHIVAL COLLECTIONS

Doris A. Hamburg

Library and archival collections encompass a wide range of materials—from documents, maps, books, and manuscripts, to posters, advertisements, broadsides, ephemera, and stamps. The common denominator of the materials discussed in this chapter is the paper support, although some also include parchment, leather, and cloth. Art on paper and photographs involve overlapping considerations and are addressed in other chapters. Preservation is influenced by the original materials and methods of fabrication, as well as the environment in which the items are kept. Many steps can be taken to ensure the preservation of library and archival materials. Housing, handling, and care procedures have significant impact on long-term preservation. Informed periodic review of an object's condition and housing will help to assess and address the conservation needs of the collection in a systematic approach. The following comments should serve as a springboard for discussion and action, to be supplemented by personal observation and further reading. (See the bibliography at the end of this book.)

Poor-quality adhesives can cause discoloration and embrittlement of paper, as is the case with the bookplate shown here, which was adhered with rubber cement.

Opposite:
This newspaper has become brittle over time due to the low quality of the pulp from which it was made and poor storage conditions, including prolonged exposure to light. Repeated folding caused tears in the paper. The subsequent ill-advised use of pressure-sensitive tapes for repair led to further damage.

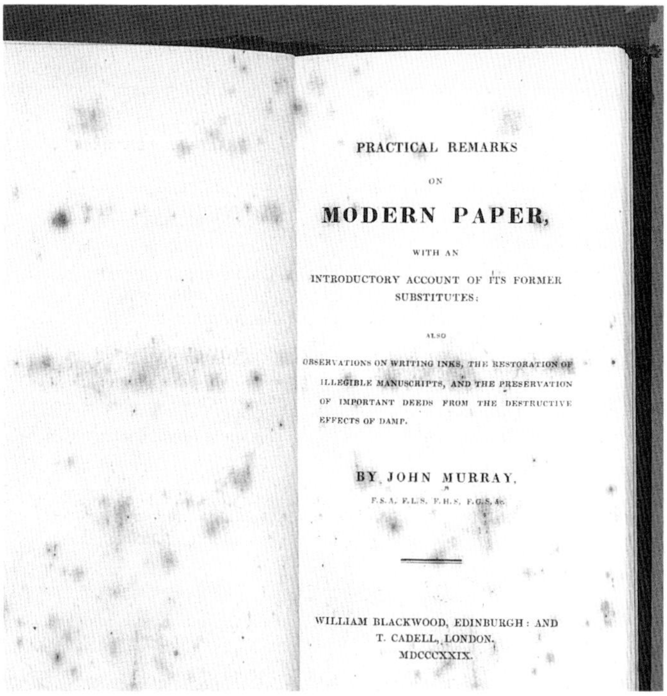

PRACTICAL REMARKS

ON

MODERN PAPER,

WITH AN

INTRODUCTORY ACCOUNT OF ITS FORMER SUBSTITUTES;

ALSO

OBSERVATIONS ON WRITING INKS, THE RESTORATION OF ILLEGIBLE MANUSCRIPTS, AND THE PRESERVATION OF IMPORTANT DEEDS FROM THE DESTRUCTIVE EFFECTS OF DAMP.

BY JOHN MURRAY,

F.S.A., F.L.S., F.H.S., F.G.S., &c.

WILLIAM BLACKWOOD, EDINBURGH: AND T. CADELL, LONDON.

MDCCCXXXIX.

The reddish brown stains on the book pages are known as foxing *spots, which develop most commonly upon exposure to humid conditions.*

The Nature of Library and Archival Materials

The manufacturing method and materials significantly influence the long-term stability of library and archival items. Early in the history of paper and books, the quality of the materials used tended to be very high, and, if kept in a good environment, the paper would be well preserved over time. In the nineteenth century the demand for paper, and the growth in printing, led to the development of new, lower quality manufacturing techniques and the use of materials that were highly acidic. Research has shown that the presence of acidity creates an inherently unstable condition in paper, causing it to deteriorate over time. The self-destruction rate is hastened further if the paper is stored in areas of high humidity, high temperature, and/or exposed to light. Deacidification of the paper can neutralize the acid and deposit an alkaline compound to buffer against future acid attack. Deacidification may be desirable in cases where the paper support, inks, and other mediums will not be affected adversely. Deacidification is not appropriate for leather or parchment. A number of deacidification processes have been developed and are chosen for use according to the nature of the materials. This procedure should only be done by a professional conservator. In any case, protective housing with alkaline (acid-free, buffered) paper or card and a good, stable environment can help mitigate further deterioration.

Today there is an effort to encourage the use of alkaline paper in printing. Paper that meets American National Standards Institute standard Z39.48 1984 displays the infinity symbol on the verso of the title page. Once a paper mill has converted to an alkaline processing system, the costs for alkaline and acid paper are competitive.

Reddish-brown spots that appear in a random pattern in older paper may be *foxing* spots. Generally, they develop under humid conditions and are thought to be caused by trace metals in the paper and/or mold. There is little that can be done to reverse the visual effect of foxing without risking further damage to the paper support.

Inks and paints can be a source of *inherent-vice* deterioration. For example, a common type of writing ink, called iron gall ink, used until the beginning of the twentieth century, was formulated with many different recipes; however, all contain some amount of acid. The acid, particularly with exposure to humid conditions, can attack the paper, causing breaks and holes. Other concerns related to mediums involve inks that are not well bound to the paper support. Such inks may flake off or be friable. Those mediums, such as gouache and poster paint, that are thickly applied, are vulnerable to cracking, and one must take care to avoid flexing the paper support. Early maps were sometimes hand colored with a green pigment often made from copper (such as verdigris). In humid conditions copper-based pigments can turn brown and become deleterious to the paper support. Care must be taken with fragile pages. A conservator should be consulted for treatment.

Binding styles vary and affect the durability of and the way in which a book functions. The increased demand for leather in the eighteenth century resulted in modified processing techniques that produced an inferior-quality leather. Over time some of these leathers have developed *red rot*, becoming powdery or embrittled, leading to detachment of the covers from the book. The increasing quantity of mass-commercial binding has led to the production of weaker bindings that are particularly vulnerable to damage from improper handling.

Environment

The papers that make up archival and library materials range widely in quality. All, however, are susceptible to damage if displayed or stored in an environment that is damp, very dry, or hot. Storage in an attic or basement is always to be avoided, unless there are controls and insulation for providing the proper relative humidity and temperature. The recommended conditions are 40 to 55 percent relative humidity and 72 degrees Fahrenheit or lower. (Recent research suggests that the lower end of this RH range is preferable.) In addition, it is most important to avoid changes in these conditions. Cycling one day from 40 to 50 percent RH and back again the next day causes the paper to expand and contract as it absorbs and loses moisture from the atmosphere. If changes are to occur they should be gradual and as few in number as possible. High humidity and high temperature encourage chemical reactions in paper cellulose that lead to embrittlement and discoloration. Appropriate storage containers can help provide a more stable microenvironment as they modulate the environmental changes before they reach the artifacts.

Paper objects are affected by the light-intensity level combined with the length of exposure. We can expect that any paper item will change if left in the light over time. Light causes changes in the paper structure itself as well as the mediums, leading to bleaching, fading, darkening, and/or embrittlement. Because this kind of damage cannot be reversed, we must provide appropriate conditions for displaying library and archival collections. Since ultraviolet radiation is the most damaging component of light and provides no benefit to our viewing, it should be filtered out. It is important to recognize that the visible light that remains *also* causes the detrimental changes cited above and therefore light levels should be kept low—5 to 10 footcandles maximum.

Some paper types and mediums are particularly susceptible to light damage. Newsprint and other papers of similarly poor quality, such as might be used for ephemera, telegrams, paperbacks, handbills, and posters, contain *lignin*, a woody substance in trees that deteriorates very quickly in the light, causing the paper to become brown and very brittle. One only need leave a newspaper in a window for a short time to see the dramatic change that occurs. Colored manuscript inks, felt-tip-pen ink, iron gall inks, colored papers and book cloths, watercolors, and certain dyes also tend to be highly susceptible to changes, particularly fading, from light exposure. The length of exposure should be strictly limited and the light level kept at the lowest ranges indicated above. Display periods preferably should not exceed three months per year. Archival and library collection materials with intrinsic importance should never be considered for permanent or long-term exhibition. Facsimiles made by photography, photocopying, or printing may make practical substitutes for longer displays.

Gas contaminants such as sulfur dioxide, nitrogen oxide, and ozone and airborne particulates can harm library and archival materials over time. Sources include car and truck exhaust fumes, aerosols, and heating systems. Filtration of outside or circulating air may be beneficial; however, good, protective housing is also very important in providing the object with a barrier to surrounding pollutants as well as buffering the object against environmental changes.

Paper and books are prime food sources for insects and vermin, whose presence is detected by evidence of dust piles or droppings in the collection area, abrasion of the paper surface, or holes in the paper. If an infestation is particularly active, the insects or rodents may be visible. Warm, damp conditions, as well as household dirt, will encourage infestation by all these pests. Traps are available to help monitor for pests. An early call to a conservator will be the best course of action to

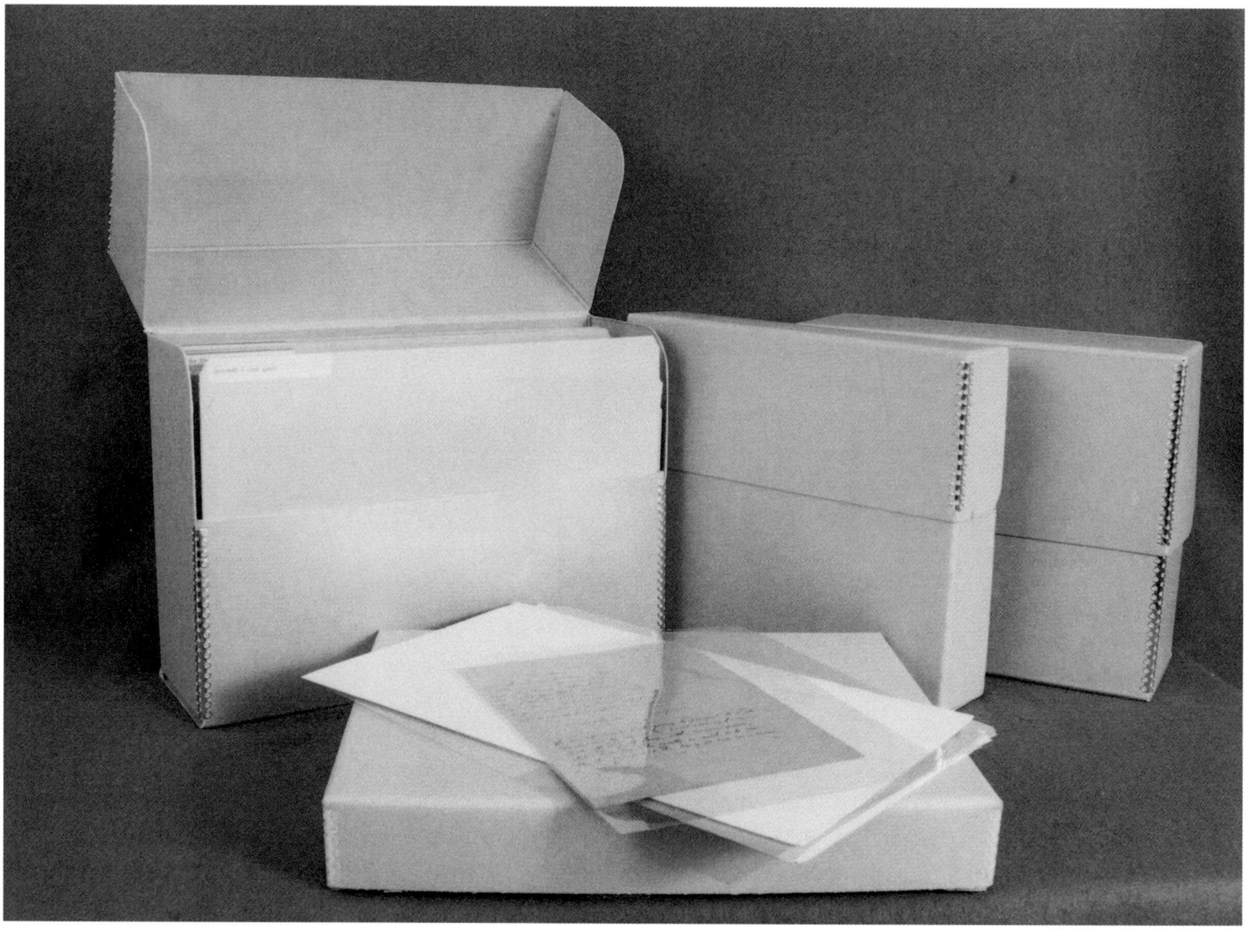

Acid-free and/or alkaline-buffered manuscript file and flat storage boxes are available in various sizes. When combined with folders of similar size, many types of library and archival materials may be stored safely.

find an appropriate and expedient solution for dealing with pest problems in archival and library collections.

High humidity (above 65 to 70 percent RH), dust, and stagnant air also provide a conducive environment for the growth of mold. There are many, many types of mold that, if left to grow, will weaken the paper and its sizing and with time lead to holes, discoloration (sometimes brilliantly colored!), or even adhesion of one paper to another. Regular inspection will help to catch problems before they become major. A musty smell, and also, of course, the appearance of fuzzy spores, can help alert you to the possible presence of mold. If mold develops, it is best to remove the affected items to a dry area to reduce the moisture level. On a sunny day, take the item outside and lightly brush the mold with a soft camel-hair brush to remove the spores. Avoid brushing the spores onto other vulnerable materials or toward yourself. Dabbing with a kneaded eraser can be helpful if testing shows that the medium and support will not be disturbed as a result, but never rub with an eraser. Some items are sufficiently delicate due to their medium or the condition of the paper, that it is safest to take them to a conservator to avoid further damage. Fumigation may be considered in some cases; however, due to toxicity issues, there are relatively few choices of chemicals available. If the size of the problem suggests the need for fumigation, it will be necessary to call a conservation professional. In any case, good air circulation and reduction of the relative humidity are key to avoiding mold problems.

Storage: Protective Housings and Enclosures

The immediate housing conditions for archival and library materials can have a direct impact on the preservation of the collection. Flat documents, maps, posters, books, and manuscripts require a variety of storage conditions depending on size, mediums, condition, quantity, type and frequency of use, and availability of funds. Since acidity can migrate from one paper to another, it is important to choose high-quality protective materials for storage. Therefore, alkaline-buffered papers or boards (also called acid-free, buffered) are best for providing chemical protection in storing paper objects. Although good-quality acid-free papers (pH around 7), which do not have an alkaline buffer, will provide nondeleterious housing, they will not provide equal protection against attack from acids. Avoid those paper storage materials that contain lignin or pigments or dyes that are water soluble. Paper storage materials should be made from rag, cotton linters, or chemically purified wood pulp (lignin removed) to which a calcium or magnesium buffer compound has been added, yielding a pH of 6.5 to 8.5.

Certain film materials, such as uncoated polyester film (DuPont Mylar Type D or ICI Melinex 516), uncoated polypropylene, and uncoated polyethylene, can be used to make stable housing enclosures as well. Avoid plastics that contain chlorinated compounds (such as polyvinyl chloride, called PVC), external plasticizers (as in vinyl-covered binders), and ongoing solvent activity (as might occur from an antistatic coating). Polyester and other plastic films should not be used in direct contact with friable mediums, such as cracking inks, pastels, heavy pencil, or flaking paint. Film materials tend to be transparent and as such they can facilitate retrieval of an item. In addition, relative to its thickness, polyester can provide considerable physical support in handling. Unfortunately, films do not offer the same chemical safeguards for an acidic item as does an alkaline-buffered paper. Therefore when storing acidic materials in film housings, it is desirable to include a buffered paper or card on at least one side of the item.

Unfortunately, current advertising standards are not clear-cut, and it is important to ask about the components of the materials being selected rather than rely on the statement that something is "archival." Most of the high-quality materials must be purchased from suppliers of archival products. The possible permutations for safe housing formats are innumerable; those discussed below serve as models in providing the appropriate solutions for the particular materials under consideration.

Manuscripts, Documents, Ephemera, Stamps

Smaller documents, manuscripts, and ephemera of letter or legal size are most effectively housed in acid-free, buffered folders, which are placed in an acid-free, buffered manuscript file box to protect against dust and light and reduce environmental fluctuations. The quantity per folder will depend on their shapes, thicknesses, and fragility, and should allow an easy fit. The dimensions of the folders should exceed the size of the manuscripts by at least a quarter to a half inch on each side. The folders should fill the box without stuffing, and, if the box is underfilled, an acid-free card support of similar size should be placed behind the folders to keep them upright. Folders and manuscript boxes should be clearly labeled for easy retrieval. Avoid the use of paper clips and staples as they rust, crimp, and crease the paper.

It is important to isolate highly acidic materials such as newspaper clippings or telegrams from other papers to avoid acid migration, which causes discoloration and embrittlement of the adjacent materials. Highly acidic items may be separated by putting them in individual alkaline-buffered card or polyester film folders. If it is appropriate to consider reproductions in another format as a method of preserving the information, photocopy the news clippings or similar material onto alkaline-buffered paper. A curatorial assessment is required to determine whether or not the original format has intrinsic value and should be retained.

In general one should minimize the amount of handling any item receives. If a particular item is going to be handled a lot, it would be worthwhile to consider making a surrogate (photograph, photocopy, microfilm) for first-level use, reserving the original for special-need occasions. Polyester-film folders (sealed on one or more sides) are also useful for holding items that are fragile or to be handled regularly. When four sides are sealed, the process is called *encapsulation*. The polyester holds the item in place with static and provides support. If the document has not been deacidified, a piece of buffered paper slightly larger than the item should be placed behind the document in the polyester folder.

Stamps and postal covers can be placed in uncoated polyester film with prefabricated pockets, or in acid-free, buffered paper sleeves. Due to the adhesive on the back of stamps, it is important to avoid humid conditions and the possibility of sticking. The adhesive on the back of a stamp should not be disturbed by hinging as this will affect the stamp's value.

Large Flat Paper Objects

The overall goal in housing is to provide support for the paper so that it will not be likely to crease and bend. It is preferable to create a larger size housing for an unfolded item rather than fold it to fit into a housing. As larger items are considered, the storage issues become more complicated. In general it is most advantageous to keep items of like size together in order to provide uniform support for the object and most efficient use of space. Acid-free, buffered-card stock folders can be used to hold large documents, handbills, broadsides, posters, and maps. The objects and folders can then be placed in similarly sized, acid-free, buffered card boxes with lids. The objects and folders should be arranged so they do not shift in the boxes. The weight of materials being stored needs to be supported adequately by the box, and in turn the shelf should fully support the box on the shelf. If there is only a handful of oversize items, a stiff, acid-free portfolio may be adequate. Another alternative is to store large objects in folders in flat file cases made from stainless steel covered with a fused-powder coating or baked-on enamel. These cabinets become indispensable for very large items. The use of alkaline-buffered card and/or polyester folders inside the flat file case may be necessary in helping to aid safe retrieval of the items from the drawer. A nearby staging area should always be maintained and kept clear for temporary placement of items.

If an object exceeds the size of the largest flat-file case, it may be necessary to roll the oversize artifact onto the outside of a card tube (either made of acid-free card or lined with polyester and acid-free, buffered paper). The tube diameter should be at least three inches, and possibly more, depending on the stiffness of the item. Use a buffered tissue as interleaving when rolling the item onto the tube. If the object is very stiff, it may not be possible to roll. In some situations, it may be possible to arrange a hanging storage system for large oversize items such as posters. This may involve hinging the object within a polyester encapsulation and securely hanging it from a rod and track system. A hanging system facilitates access to the collection, since relatively little handling is needed to view the objects.

Mounting an oversize item onto some type of board or lining it onto linen is not recommended as a routine course of action, due to changes that occur in the original character of the object and concern for the long-term effect of these processes. If lining is necessary for a fragile item, Japanese paper and wheat-starch paste applied by a professional conservator is the recommended procedure.

Books and Pamphlets

Books are best stored on smooth, clean shelves, preferably away from the light, in a well-ventilated area. It is best to shelve books according to their sizes so that they receive appropriate support from the adjacent books. If not supported fully, the taller ones tend to splay out and become deformed. This is particularly acute for books with limp covers and parchment bindings. If a book is too tall for the shelf or too heavy to stand upright—such as many scrapbooks or oversize volumes—it should be laid flat on its side on a shelf that is wide enough to accommodate its width. If a shelf is not wide enough, place a stiff card below the book to make sure it has the necessary support. No more than two or three oversize books should be stored on top of each other due to the difficulty in retrieving any

A sturdy bookend and an arrangement of the books that takes into account their relative sizes will provide good support. Note the dust jacket of the fourth book from the right, which shows wear from pulling at the headband.

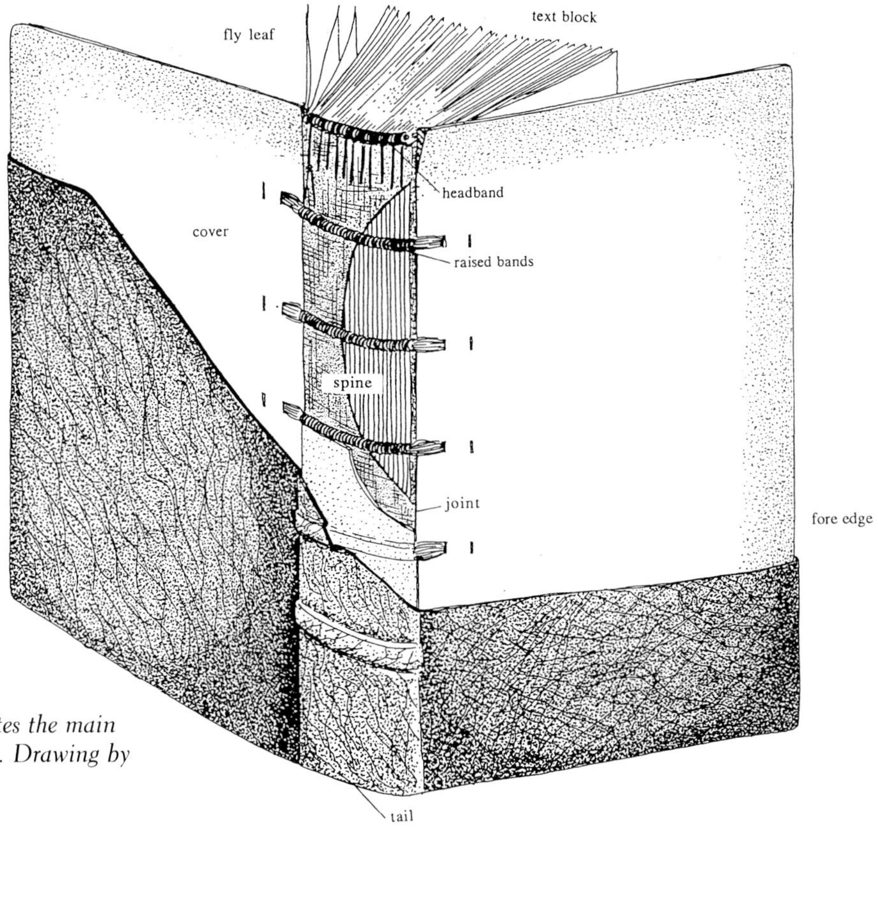

This diagram illustrates the main components of a book. Drawing by Margaret R. Brown

one of the items. For folio volumes, the addition of extra shelves will be helpful. Occasionally, it may be appropriate to turn a slightly oversize or very thick book on its spine (not on its fore edge) to fit within the height of the shelf and keep it with related books. Make sure the covers have adequate support so they will not splay out to the sides.

Cabinets with glass doors can help reduce the dust exposure, although adequate ventilation must be considered. Once dust becomes embedded in the paper, it is difficult to remove. The best-designed bookends have sufficient weight to stand upright independently on the shelf, do not abrade a book's tail or cover, and have sufficient surface area to provide overall support at the cover.

The best protection for a book is a custom-made box to protect it from light and dust, provide support in handling and transport, and mitigate changes in the environment. There are several styles, but a custom double-tray book box (also known as a *clam-shell box*) will accomplish these goals most effectively. The box should fit the book precisely; otherwise, the book can become damaged in transport. A clam-shell box can be quite elaborate, or, with recent advances in technology, quite simple. Slipcases accomplish some of the stated goals; however, they leave the spine exposed to the light (fading is often seen), and it can be difficult to remove the book from the slipcase. A four-flap portfolio box, called a *phase box*, made from acid-free, buffered card, accomplishes the goals for the types of protection and can be low cost, though plainer in appearance.

Original dust jackets should be preserved, as they add to the value of the book. A polyester wrapper will be helpful in keeping the book and/or dust jacket in good condition. While a book is being used, it may be appropriate to store the dust jacket separately until the book is returned to storage.

Storage of a pamphlet collection can be approached in the same way as a manuscript collection by placing the pamphlets in folders and boxing. If it is important to store individual pamphlets interspersed in a book collection on shelves, they should be placed in acid-free, buffered-card wrappers in envelopes or in stiff-card pamphlet portfolios. Avoid adhering the pamphlet to a stiff cover as usually the pamphlet structure will not hold up with use.

Guidelines for Display

Display of books and archival materials once again requires proper physical support and environmental conditions. Poor exhibit practice can lead to considerable damage. When exhibiting an open book, a cradle or book block of adequate size is needed underneath so that the weight of the covers and gravity do not pull on the joint and binding. The degree of opening depends on binding flexibility and desired opening location. Polyethylene bands can be used to gently keep the text from springing. A book conservator can advise on providing the safest conditions for especially fragile material.

Displays should be temporary, not exceeding a few months, so that light does not cause fading or discoloration to the open pages. Changes in relative humidity and temperature environment should be avoided to minimize problems from expansion and contraction of the paper and binding adhesive. Long-term exhibition can lead to permanent deformation of the binding and difficulty in safe closing.

Flat paper objects can be displayed by hinging with Japanese paper and wheat-starch paste onto acid-free, buffered mat board. Custom photo corners made from polyester film or paper can be used if the documents are small or stiff enough so there is no danger that the object will fall out of the corners when placed vertically. Such photo corners avoid the need to undo hinges after display if the object is not normally matted for storage.

The display of very large archival materials such as posters requires creative solutions. Either encapsulation in polyester or hinging at the top, followed by separation from the glazing with a spacer, is appropriate for flat items of medium size or smaller. Pressure mounts, which are made by placing the poster in a polyester film sleeve and then between glass or acrylic glazing and a backboard in a frame, may be used for short-term, temporary exhibits. This is not desirable for longer

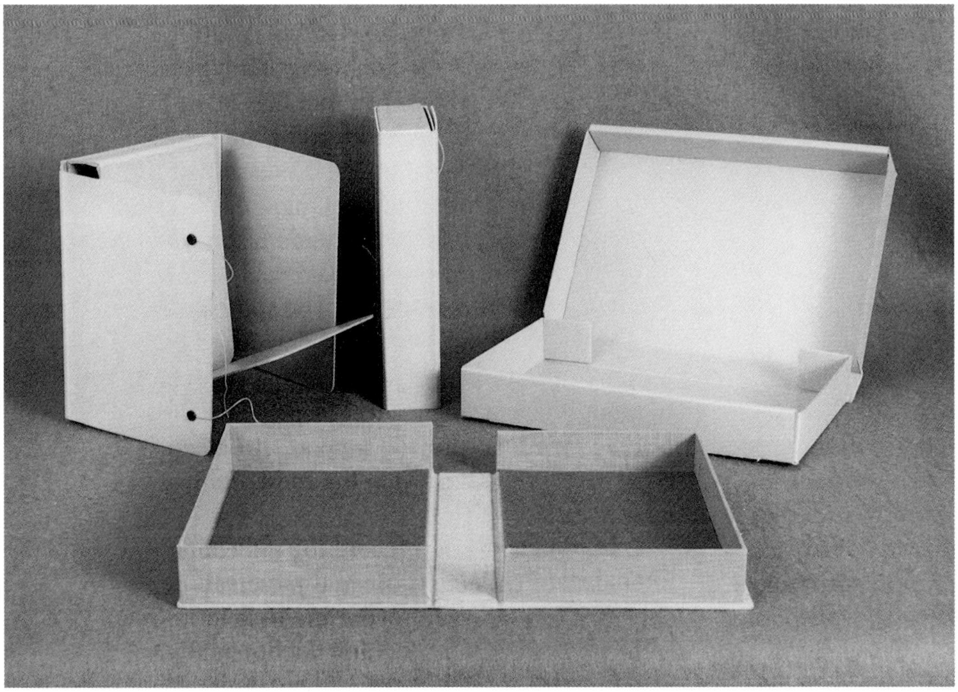

Books are best protected by storage in custom-fitted boxes such as those shown here (left to right): *phased box (open and closed); custom-made, traditional clamshell box; custom-fitted, die-cut clamshell box.*

Each of these book cradles can safely support books, without causing stress to the bindings, while they are on display (left to right): *custom-fitted acrylic cradle; card support under open cover, with polyester or polyethylene strapping to hold fly leaf; custom-fitted card cradle. Adjustable, reusable cradles also are available commercially.*

term display as the poster will become cockled (wavy) as it responds to changes in relative humidity and temperature yet is restrained by the mount. Dry mounting is to be avoided due to concerns about the long-term reversibility and stability of the dry mounting and the backing materials. Also the character of a paper object is altered as it becomes thick and stiff.

Preservation Guidelines

In caring for a collection, it is important to try to think ahead to prevent accidents and to avoid situations that have the potential to cause damage. Be sure hands are clean and dry before handling collection materials. The use of gloves (clean, white cotton or latex) helps prevent fingerprints but reduces dexterity in handling. After use, collection materials should be inspected for any changes in order to catch problems before they become major.

Food or drink should not be in the collection area. If water is needed for some reason, it should be placed at a lower level than the collection items so that a spill would create minimal damage. Smoking should not be allowed due to the residue that collects on the materials and the very real potential for fire. Only pencils should be allowed in the vicinity of collection materials, since a stray pen mark is very difficult to remove and requires a professional conservator. Avoid leaning on or writing on collection materials. If it is necessary to record identifying information on a collection item, use a number-2 pencil in an unobtrusive area. Pressure-sensitive notepapers should not be used, since they can leave behind residues that are difficult to remove. Avoid marking a location in a book with a three-dimensional object such as a pencil; instead, use a bookmark made from a medium-weight, acid-free, buffered paper.

If large, flat objects need to be moved from one area to another, a stiff card portfolio with handles, A-frame dolley, or cart will be required. Avoid curling folders for underarm carrying, as the item inside can become crimped or creased.

When removing a book from the shelf, hold the spine or sides of the book rather than the head cap, which is much weaker. Another method is to reach to the back of the shelf and push the book forward from the fore edge. Do not overfill bookshelves so that the books are tightly packed; provide adequate support so that they stand comfortably upright. When reading the book, rest it on a table with support on each side so that the binding is not strained in opening.

Photocopying should be undertaken with care; not all books can be photocopied safely due to tight bindings or brittle text pages. The spine or back of the book should not be pressed downward onto the glass as the force of this pressure can easily crack the binding. Place a single sheet in polyester film before copying to provide support. An electrostatic copy machine will provide the most archival-quality copy.

Maintenance of a record log indicating frequency of collection use and preservation concerns can be useful over time in determining collection needs. Cataloguing documentation may be annotated to indicate size orientation and location. It is worthwhile periodically to review the collection for condition evaluation. An informed evaluation of condition, preferably by a conservator familiar with the type of collection material, will help assign conservation priorities. Conservation factors to consider include appropriateness of housing, medium problems (flaking, abrasion, loss, fading), support problems (tears, losses, embrittlement, inherent vice), treatment urgency, cleanliness of storage area, procedures for use by readers, and environmental conditions. A condition survey needs to be evaluated in conjunction with curatorial priorities, such as value, frequency of use, and relative importance to the collection. A written long-range plan will be useful in establishing steps for preservation action.

When Damage Occurs

Despite one's best efforts to prevent it, damage—such as dirt, tears, embrittlement, or flaking pigments—can occur, and stabilization will be needed. If pieces become detached, they should be retained in an envelope clearly indicating the item from which they came. The envelope should be kept with the item or a notation should be made on the folder. For tattered papers, polyester film can provide more support than a paper or card folder and avoids the need to handle the item directly. A buffered sheet of paper is desirable behind the document if it has not been deacidified. A conservator should advise on treatment options.

Stray pencil marks or overall surface dirt on paper generally can be removed with a soft vinyl eraser or eraser crumbs grated from a vinyl eraser. Other erasers can be too rough and may abrade the paper. As with any treatment, a small unobtrusive area should be tested before proceeding. When surface cleaning, avoid ink or other mediums. Whenever in doubt, do not proceed further. Book collections will require cleaning from time to time if there is a dust buildup. Use cheesecloth or a soft cloth to dust the covers. If necessary, lightly vacuum the edges of the text block with hose end that has been covered with cheesecloth. A very soft brush can be helpful in lifting the dirt; be sure to avoid rubbing against the text block.

The tendency is to want to repair damage as it is noted on paper and books. The most obvious solutions for tears, such as any of the pressure-sensitive tapes, should never be used for archival materials. The tapes provide a short-term answer but over the long term will create worse problems, such as irreversible disfigurement, embrittlement of the paper, and alteration of inks requiring more difficult and costlier solutions. Some tapes are advertised as "archival"; however, there is no universal definition of the word and, considering the long-term effects, pressure-sensitive tapes should be avoided. At present, pure wheat-starch paste or methyl cellulose and Japanese paper provide the best answers for mending tears. Use of these materials, however, is best done by someone trained in their proper application.

If parts of a book, such as covers or spine, are detached, wrap the book in acid-free paper so that all the parts are kept together and supported. A four-flap portfolio or phase box will give excellent protection until the book can be treated. If it is not possible to provide a box, tie white cotton twill tape around the covers and text block, tying a bow at the fore edge.

Use of leather dressings and oiling is *not* a routine procedure; a book conservator should be consulted prior to any use of these materials.

For leather-bound books suffering from red-rot deterioration such that the leather powders off when lightly rubbed, wrap the book in acid-free, buffered paper or put a polyester film or acid-free card jacket cover around the binding to prevent everything from getting dirty until it can be treated by a book conservator. If treatment for problems such as acidity, embrittlement, flaking pigments, discoloration, distorted boards, red rot, broken bindings, presence of tapes and poor-quality adhesives, or water damage is warranted, contact a paper or book conservator who has experience in working with these issues and materials.

A disaster-preparedness plan put in place prior to the event of flood, fire, hurricane, tornado, or water-heater or pipe leaks could make the difference in saving a collection. Immediately accessible information on experts and suppliers to call as well as organized procedures for action will allow a ready and beneficial response. Also, quick and appropriate self-help may make the difference in saving materials. Wet flat paper and books should be interleaved with absorbent paper, such as thin blotters or towels, or stood upright to fan dry them. Take care to avoid stressing a binding with too much interleaving or insufficient support. If the problem is a large one, wrap the water-logged paper and book materials individually so they may be frozen until further action is possible. If wet coated paper is allowed to dry without interleaving or freezing, the pages will stick together permanently.

As in most things, caring for collections involves common sense, weighing options, and making informed choices. Proper environment, housing, display, and handling can lengthen significantly the life of library and archival materials. The recommendations discussed above are guidelines to be considered in view of the special characteristics of such collections. To gain additional and new ideas that may be appropriate, look at other collections, explore written sources, and always ask many questions when consulting an expert.

John Nahl
316 Lackawanna Ave.
Scranton, Pa.

PHOTOGRAPHS

Debbie Hess Norris

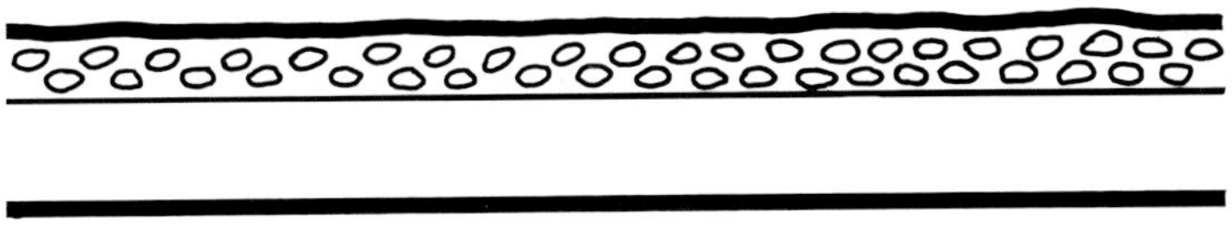

Cross section of a typical photograph illustrating its three basic components. Diagram by Patrick J. O'Brien

A typical collection of family photographs is likely to contain a wide variety of photographic processes that share certain common properties. Most photographic materials are laminate structures composed of a *final image material, binder layer,* and *primary support*. The final image material is that substance which absorbs and scatters light to produce a photographic image. A wide variety of final image materials have been utilized throughout the history of photography, including metallic silver, platinum metal, pigments, and dyes; many are subject to deterioration in the form of fading and yellowing. The binder is the transparent layer in a photograph in which the final image material is suspended and protected. Binders play an important role in determining the optical properties and overall stability of photographic images. Binder materials most commonly used include albumen, which is the white of hens' eggs; collodion, a form of cellulose nitrate used in the nineteenth century; and gelatin, a highly purified, commercially prepared protein produced from animal hides and bones. Finally, the primary support, which may be paper, metal, plastic, or glass, provides the photograph's binder layer with structural support.

All of these different types of photographs will exhibit distinctive characteristics relating to their chemical composition and deterioration mechanisms, which in turn will affect preservation concerns. First and foremost, the custodian of these irreplaceable images must be able to identify the various photographic processes and their deterioration problems. Although completely accurate identification of all photographic processes represented in such collections may not be possible, basic information such as the years during which they were popular, methods of manufacture, and principal deterioration mechanisms may be useful.

Opposite:
Photographic prints can be protected from handling damage by storage in good-quality plastic sleeves and archival boxes.

These tintypes illustrate various deterioration problems. Note the rust formation at the outer edges of the portrait at the upper right and the loss of image (revealing the japanned iron support) at the lower left.

Daguerreotypes, Ambrotypes, and Tintypes: Identification and Deterioration

The earliest photographic process to gain popularity in America was the *daguerreotype*, in active use from the period 1840 to 1860. A daguerreotype consists of a silver-plated sheet of copper with the whites or highlights of the image being a combination of silver, mercury, and gold and the darks pure silver metal. The daguerreotype surface is therefore mirrorlike and reflective. To enhance their effect, daguerreotypes were often hand-colored with pigments.

The daguerreotype's silver surface is easily affected by airborne moisture and pollutants and may appear darkly tarnished or corroded. The deterioration usually is most prominent at the outer edges of the plate. Under no circumstances should attempts be made to remove such disfiguring corrosion. Most cleaning procedures will irreversibly alter the daguerreotype's chemical and physical properties, causing greater damage.

The *ambrotype* was popular in America from 1850 to 1870. Like the daguerreotype, the ambrotype is a direct-positive process, which means that negatives were not involved in their production. Rather, a piece of glass was hand-coated with collodion, a thick, syrupy binder that holds the light-sensitive salts in suspension. The glass plate was made light sensitive by immersion in a solution of silver nitrate; then it was exposed to light in a camera and immediately developed,

These ambrotypes illustrate loss of the collodion binder layers and breakage of the glass supports.

washed, fixed to remove the remaining light-sensitive silver salts, and varnished. At this stage, the highlights in the ambrotype glass plate consisted of white, highly reflective silver image particles, with shadow areas of clear, collodion-coated glass. To complete the photograph, the photographer often painted the back of the glass support with black lacquer.

Ambrotype images will exhibit numerous deterioration characteristics, including discoloration or yellowing of the varnish and collodion layers, flaking of the collodion binder and/or the black lacquer, and breakage of the fragile glass support. The final varnish layer appears to protect the ambrotype's silver image from oxidation, and for this reason these images do not often tarnish or fade.

In the *tintype* process, patented in 1856 and in use throughout the remainder of the nineteenth century, collodion was coated onto a sheet of black-lacquered iron to produce a direct-positive image in a method similar to the ambrotype process. The tintype image is often dull gray in color, with creamy white highlights. Exposure to moisture may cause the tintype's iron support to rust severely, causing further damage to the image.

Once completed, daguerreotypes, ambrotypes, and some tintypes were sealed to a metallic (usually lacquered brass) mat and cover glass, thus preventing dust and other pollutants from marring their fragile surfaces. (Tintypes frequently were pasted into paper cards with window openings surrounded by a decorative embossed border.) These protective packages were then fitted into standard-size decorative miniature cases. Owing to excessive handling and poor storage, these miniature cases are often in many pieces. Further, the glazing materials used to protect these photographic images often were chemically unstable, and their corrosion or decomposition products are often visible on the interior surfaces of the glass. Because it is an especially serious problem, this type of deterioration should be brought to the attention of a trained photographic conservator for evaluation.

Photographic Printing Processes: Identification and Deterioration

Metallic Silver, Platinum, and Cyanotype Processes

The *salted-paper* process, one of the earliest photographic printing processes, was introduced in 1841 and used throughout the following decade. Like all *printing-out* processes, in which the light-sensitive paper is placed in contact with a negative and set out in the sun until the image visually "prints out," this process produced warm-toned images. Prints from this process exhibit a *matte* (nonglossy) surface and may be heavily retouched.

Introduced in 1850, the *albumen* print was the most common photographic process available during the period from 1855 to 1885. To make albumen prints, a thin, smooth, high-quality paper was floated on a solution of homogenized egg white (albumen), which contained a small amount of sodium chloride. The albumenized paper was then placed in a silver nitrate solution to make it light sensitive. The paper was placed in direct contact with a negative and exposed to daylight until the image visually printed out. Following printing, these photographs were toned with gold chloride, fixed in a sodium hyposulfite bath to remove the remaining light-reactive salts, and thoroughly washed.

Because the paper stock on which they were printed was very thin, most commercial albumen prints were mounted onto a secondary support of decorative cardboard. These mounts varied in size and shape, although the *carte-de-visite* (2½ by 4¼ inches) and *cabinet-card* (4¼ by 6½ inches) formats were particularly popular during the nineteenth century.

Albumen prints in excellent condition usually look purplish brown or black. However, the finely divided form of printed-out silver in these photographs is very susceptible to oxidation. As a result, approximately 85 percent of extant albumen prints exhibit moderate to severe image fading, discoloration, and a significant loss of highlight detail. Subtle facial features and details in clothing, such as lace, for example, may be lost entirely. Many of these photographs are also heavily stained in their white or highlight areas due to the degradation of the albumen protein.

Albumen prints may be identified accurately by their characteristic deterioration, primarily fading and yellowing, as well as their surface, which appears cracked or crazed, caused by the albumen binder expanding and contracting differently from the thin paper support.

Collodion-chloride printing-out paper, manufactured in glossy and matte textures and used primarily for studio portraiture, was one successor to the popular albumen photographic process. These papers, available from 1890 to 1920, were coated with light-sensitive salts dispersed in collodion at the factory. This light-sensitive paper was placed in contact with a negative and exposed to sunlight or strong electric light. The resultant image was then washed, toned with gold and/or platinum salts, and fixed.

The tonality of the collodion-chloride print varies depending on the toners utilized. Generally, a glossy collodion-chloride print is warm (gold toned) in color, whereas a matte-surfaced paper is olive-black (gold and platinum toned). In all cases the collodion binder may become embrittled, and these prints therefore may appear abraded. Gold- and platinum-toned papers tend to be in excellent condition because they protect their silver image from oxidation.

Silver-gelatin photographic printing paper was introduced in the 1880s and predominated the market through the 1960s, at which time it was replaced by color photographic processes. Silver-

These cased daguerreotypes exhibit active glass deterioration (left) *and advanced corrosion of the silver-plated copper support* (right).

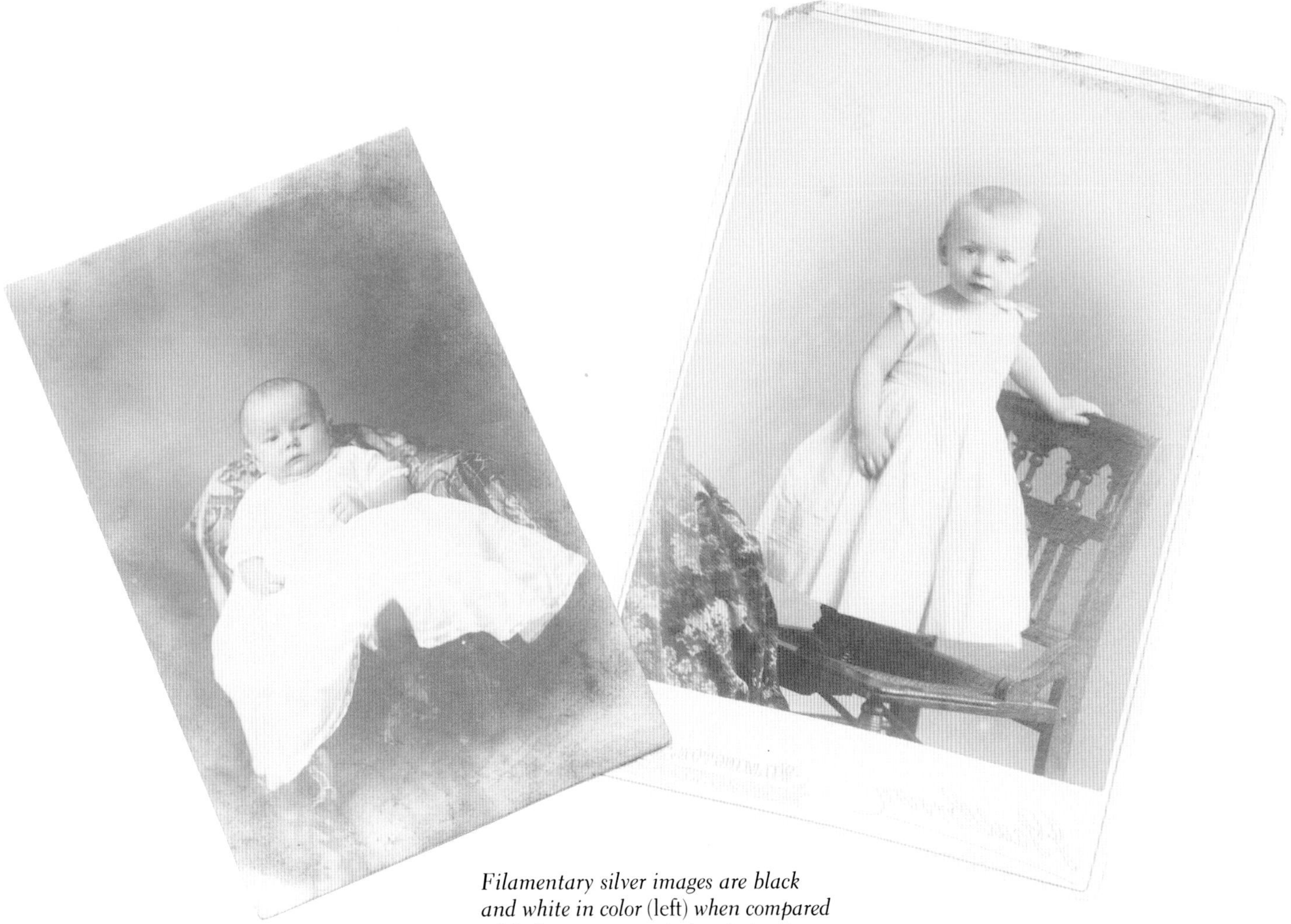

Filamentary silver images are black and white in color (left) *when compared with the warm-toned photolytic silver images characterized by the albumen process* (right). *Note the presence of silver mirroring at the outer edges of the silver gelatin photograph on the left.*

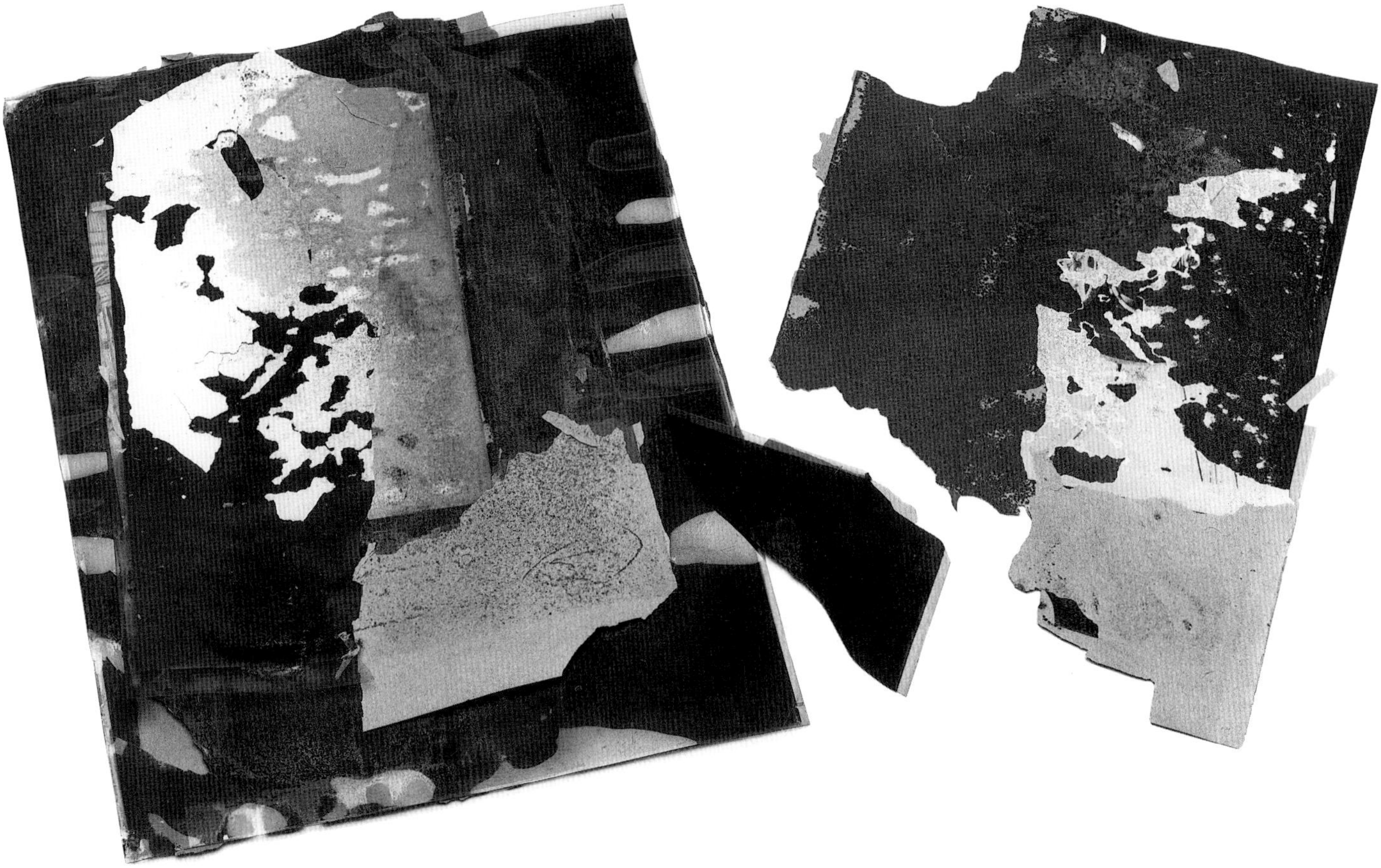

In advanced stages of cellulose-nitrate film deterioration, embrittled negatives are fused together.

gelatin printing-out papers were popular at the turn of the century, and prints made with them are usually warm in tonality. As in the albumen process, these prints were produced by placing the light-sensitive paper in contact with a negative and exposing it to sunlight. Silver-gelatin *developing-out* papers, however, were not printed out in the sunlight; rather, they were exposed directly to light in an enlarger. Following exposure, the image was chemically developed in a reducing agent, fixed, and washed. Silver-gelatin black-and-white prints may be matte, glossy, or highly textured.

All silver-gelatin processes are susceptible to irreversible image deterioration in the form of fading and yellowing, much of which may be attributed to improper processing (inadequate fixing and/or washing) during manufacture. Aged silver-gelatin photographs also may exhibit a highly reflective iridescence in their dark image areas, a phenomenon commonly referred to as *silver mirroring*. Although mirroring may occur in other processes, it is most common in the silver-gelatin developing-out process.

Platinum prints and *cyanotypes* (blue prints) are examples of two of the more common nonsilver processes that may be found in a family collection, and both were in popular use at the turn of the century. Platinum prints exhibit a matte surface texture and are often cool gray in tonality. In contrast to silver prints, these images do not discolor or fade. Cyanotypes are easily recognized by their characterisic royal blue image color.

In many cases, coatings were applied to all of these historical photographic materials to alter their surface or protect them from atmospheric pollutants. These surface coatings also served as a ground for coloring by hand, which consisted of watercolors, oils, pastels, and/or aniline dyes.

Color Processes

It is very likely that color photographs will be a major component of one's family heritage. These materials differ from many of the previously discussed processes because they contain organic dyes rather than metallic silver as the final image-forming substance. The permanence characteristics of these materials are therefore distinctively different. Owing to the instability of most organic dyes, these images may fade, often at an uneven rate, creating a shift in image color.

Some of the least stable contemporary color materials are produced by *chromogenic* processes, which employ color couplers to produce dyes in their emulsion layers during processing. In dark storage, unreacted color couplers may induce staining, which produces an overall yellow discoloration, readily visible in the highlight areas. Chromogenic materials include all of the papers used for printing color negatives, some papers used for printing from positive color transparencies, and all color-negative films.

Special Hazards to Photographic Materials

The very nature of the photographic process poses a hazard to the preservation of photographs. Chemical instability due to improper processing during manufacture, specifically insufficient washing and/or the use of exhausted fixing baths, is an important factor in the deterioration of photographs. Improper processing can produce a severely yellowed and stained photographic image. The damaging effects of residual processing chemicals are intensified by exposure to high temperature and relative humidity conditions. All copy prints and negatives must be processed to published standards specified by the American National Standards Institute and housed in a stable environment to ensure their long-term preservation.[1]

Chemical instability may contribute greatly to the eventual deterioration of some photographic materials, including cellulose-nitrate and cellulose-acetate film base and contemporary color materials. The chemical deterioration of cellulose-nitrate film, for example, has been well documented. This film ignites easily and burns rapidly, giving off toxic gases. In the presence of atmospheric moisture, these gases combine with water to produce corrosive nitric acid. Nitric acid attacks the negative's individual components, causing the film's gelatin binder to become soft and tacky, the silver image to fade, and the cellulose-nitrate base to crack and embrittle. If contained in a family collection, these negatives should be examined closely for advanced stages of deterioration and duplicated (or at least reprinted if a print in good condition does not exist) when necessary. Cellulose-nitrate film must never be housed in a hot attic. Contact a conservator for specific advice on the safe disposal of severely deteriorated film.

The damage observed in early "safety" (cellulose acetate–based) films includes severe shrinkage of the film base and subsequent separation of the films' various layers, a process accelerated by exposure to adverse environmental conditions.

Contemporary color photographs can deteriorate radically over a short period of time because their dye layers fade (often at different rates, resulting in a significant color shift) in both the light and the dark. The permanence of these dyes varies with process and is also related to conditions of storage and use.

Prevention of Deterioration

With such a diversity of materials and substances, it is no wonder that photographs are subject to damage and deterioration. Deterioration may be referred to as any chemical or physical change in the condition or appearance of the original material. More often than not such changes are the result of exposure to adverse environmental and storage conditions, mishandling, improper processing during manufacture, and/or the chemical instability of the individual components, which causes these materials to deteriorate over time.

The Importance of Proper Environmental Conditions

Exposure to adverse environmental conditions is the primary cause of deterioration in all historic and contemporary photographic materials. Relative humidity levels above 60 percent will greatly accelerate harmful and often irreversible chemical reactions and interactions. In fact, relative humidity is the single most important factor in preserving most photographic materials. Image fading in albumen photographs, for example, is primarily a function of exposure to moisture. As discussed earlier, its manifestations are loss of highlight detail, an overall fading and yellowing of the image, and a shift in image color from a purplish brown to a warmer, yellowish brown. Other irreversible forms of deterioration activated by exposure to high relative humidity include the formation of mold, softening of binder layers, fading of dyes, distortion of plastic film bases, corrosion of metal and glass primary supports, and silver mirroring of photographic prints and negatives, as well as deterioration of poor-quality mats and mounts.

Under conditions of very low or fluctuating humidity, binder layers may crack or peel and become severely embrittled. Frequent fluctuations in temperature and humidity are most damaging because the different layers of photographs expand and contract at different rates in response to changes in the environmental conditions. Such fluctuations result in instability and physical separation of the layers as well as curling of the paper supports.

Exposure to high temperatures will accelerate many of the severe deterioration problems discussed earlier. Therefore, photographic collections should be housed at a temperature of 68 degrees Fahrenheit with a constant relative humidity of 30 to 40 percent. Ideally, conditions should be kept within these ranges with a minimum of cycling, 24 hours a day, 365 days per year. Such conditions generally can be achieved most easily within an enclosed space, but not, as is often the case, in the attic of a residence; a closet in an air-conditioned room, for example, may be an excellent storage location.

Temperature, not relative humidity, is the controlling factor in the stability of contemporary color photographs; therefore, storage at low temperatures (cold storage) is particularly advised for these materials.[2] Many institutions with large cultural collections, such as the Smithsonian Institution and the Art Institute of Chicago, utilize carefully controlled cold-storage vaults to house their color photographic materials.

Atmospheric pollutants affect the stability and permanence of photographic materials. Sulfur dioxide, for example, will combine with oxygen and moisture in the air to form sulfuric acid, which, in very small amounts, will cause silver images to fade and discolor. Likewise, exposure to gaseous by-products given off by fresh paint fumes, plywood, deteriorated cardboard, and many cleaning supplies may accelerate image deterioration in historic and contemporary photographic materials. As will be discussed later, this is the reason why photographs should be stored in nonacidic containers.

Exposure to visible light is potentially damaging to photographic materials. Following exposure to light, paper supports may become brittle and binder layers, particularly those of albumen, become yellowed. Many components of miniature-cased photographic materials, such as their dyed fabric interiors and hand-colored surfaces, are susceptible to severe fading. Extended display, especially under bright light, will destroy color prints.[3]

Do not hang framed photographs on exterior walls in direct sunlight. If at all possible, replace direct sunlight with incandescent lighting, and cover windows with blinds or drapes. Ultraviolet-filtering Plexiglas is recommended for use in framing.

Color transparencies also are adversely affected by prolonged exposure to light. Therefore, projection of these materials should be kept to a minimum, especially if they are Kodachrome films. Valuable slides, particularly those that have faded or shifted in color, should be duplicated and the duplicates used for projection.[4]

Handling

Great care is required when handling original photographs, as these materials, if handled improperly, are often subject to disastrous damage, including tears, cracks, losses, abrasions, fingerprints, and stains.

Resist quick rummaging through stacks of mounted and unmounted photographs. One should avoid touching these fragile materials because salts present in human perspiration may damage their delicate surfaces. Handle unsleeved negatives and prints, when possible, with cotton gloves, which are readily available from both conservation- and photographic-supply companies. Photographic prints that are adhered to acidic and brittle mounts should be well supported with both hands, or preferably with an auxiliary sheet of four-ply ragboard from beneath, to avoid potential damage.

Storage Materials

Proper storage materials are essential to the long-term preservation of all photographic materials. Photographs must be housed in protective enclosures to shield them from atmospheric particulates such as gritty dirt and dust, which can abrade images, retain moisture, and deposit contaminants. Enclosures provide photographs with increased physical support and may act as an effective barrier between the photograph and environmental changes.

Suitable photographic-enclosure materials may be made of chemically stable plastic or paper materials, which are free of sulfur, acids, and peroxides. Avoid highly reactive and problematic storage materials such as acidic paper envelopes and sleeves, polyvinyl chloride (PVC) plastic, rubber bands, paper clips, and poor-quality adhesives such as pressure-sensitive tapes and rubber cement. Contact with these materials may greatly accelerate the rate of silver image deterioration (in the form of fading and mirroring) and contribute to the formation of irreversible staining in the photographs' binder layers and primary supports.

Acid-free, lignin-free paper-storage enclosures are available in many forms in both buffered (pH 8.5) and unbuffered stock, including central- and side-seamed envelopes, heavyweight and lightweight folders in a variety of standard sizes, and seamless enclosures.[5] Buffered storage enclosures currently are not recommended for contemporary color materials, albumen prints, and other nineteenth-century printing processes, including cyanotypes, although their potential use continues to be investigated. Buffered materials are recommended, however, for deteriorated film-base negatives, brittle prints, and photographic prints that have been mounted onto poor-quality secondary enclosures. Paper enclosures are opaque, thus preventing unnecessary light exposure; porous; easy to label in pencil; and relatively inexpensive.

Suitable plastic-enclosure materials are uncoated polyester film (DuPont Mylar Type D or ICI Melinex 516), uncoated cellulose triacetate, polyethylene, and polypropylene. These plastics are exceptionally strong, durable, and chemically stable. Plastic enclosures have the obvious advantage of allowing an image to be viewed without removing it from the enclosure, thus minimizing damage from handling. When using plastic enclosures, special concern must be given to humidity control, as photographic emulsions may tend to stick to the slick surface of plastic at high relative humidity levels. If humidity levels absolutely cannot be maintained below 80 percent relative humidity on a consistent basis, then plastic materials should not be used. Furthermore, plastic enclosures must not be used for glass-plate, nitrate, or acetate-based negatives.

When not in use, historical photograph albums should be housed flat in acid-free boxes to protect the photographic images from the intrusion of air and moisture.

Photographic prints of significant historic value should be matted with acid-free rag or museum board to provide protection during storage and display. Depending on the type, condition, and format of the print, good-quality (100 percent rag fiber) paper photo corners or lightweight paper hinges may be used to safely secure the print in its window mat. This must be done by an experienced framer or under the direction of a trained conservator.

Store color transparencies in acid-free or metal (with a baked-on enamel finish) boxes or polypropylene slide pages. Commonly available polyvinyl-chloride slide pages, easily identified by their strong plastic odor, should never be used because of their extreme chemical reactivity.[6]

Slip early miniature-cased photographs carefully into acid-free paper envelopes and house flat in good-quality boxes. House loose tintypes in polyester sleeves or, if flaking is present, in paper enclosures.

Store all matted and sleeved prints and negatives in acid-free boxes of durable construction, such as those sold by most conservation supply companies. If possible, keep negatives separate from print materials.

Storage of family photographs in albums is often desirable, and many commercially available albums utilize archival-quality materials. Avoid photographic albums constructed with highly colored pages, as these materials are often acidic and very damaging. Also, never use commercially available magnetic or "no stick" albums for the storage of contemporary or historic photographic prints in black-and-white or color. The plastic, adhesives, and paper boards used in their construction will deteriorate quite quickly over time.

Calling a Conservator

Deteriorated photographic print materials may require conservation treatment. In devising an appropriate preservation plan, the photographic conservator will consider the chemical composition and physical condition of the deteriorated photograph, as well as its historic and aesthetic integrity and the short- and long-term risks and merits of a particular treatment procedure.

Those photographic prints exhibiting active mold growth, flaking binder layers, the presence of pressure-sensitive and rubber cement adhesives, and severely embrittled or deteriorated secondary and primary supports may be considered highest priority for treatment by a trained photographic conservator. Safe and reliable treatments for the intensification of faded photographic images do not exist at present. In some cases, severely faded and discolored images can be photographically copied for improved image resolution.

NOTES

1. The various processing procedures to produce films and papers that are essentially free of residual processing chemicals have been well documented. Consult American National Standard Institute PH4.8-1985 *Residual Thiosulfate and Other Chemicals in Films, Plates, and Papers—Determination and Measurement* for specific guidelines.
2. A frost-free refrigerator may be used for the low-temperature storage (40° Fahrenheit or below) of color materials. In doing so, very specific guidelines must be strictly followed. Consult Henry Wilhelm, "Storing Color Materials: Frost Free Refrigerators Offer a Low Cost Solution," *Industrial Photography* 27, no. 10 (October 1978), 32-35 for additional information.
3. For this reason, it may be recommended that copy prints of important images be made, with the copy being displayed and the original housed in dark storage. Fujicolor Super FA, Cibachrome, or Fujichrome Type 34 papers are recommended. In fact, for additional protection, two copies should be made, one for permanent dark storage. See "Going! Going!! Gone!!!" *Popular Photography* 97, no. 6, for information pertaining to the relative stabilities in light and dark storage of these and other photographic materials.
4. For duplication of color transparencies Fujichrome Duplicating Film is recommended. See "Going! Going!! Gone!!!" *Popular Photography* 97, no. 6.
5. There are many companies that currently manufacture or sell these archival materials. See the resource lists at the end of this book.
6. An easy method to indicate the presence of polyvinyl chloride requires the use of two-foot lengths of #8 or #10 copper wire and a propane torch (with protective goggles). Strip the vinyl cover off a portion of the copper wire and burn off the residual vinyl (from the wire cover) in this area. When the flame is orange, touch the red-hot copper tip to the unidentified plastic sleeve and then place the copper wire back in the flame. If it burns green, then vinyl chloride is present and the enclosure should not be used.

FURNITURE

Brian Considine

One of the most interesting aspects of furniture conservation is the great complexity of materials encountered. In dealing with furniture, we regularly see objects made from combinations of several woods and wood veneers, brass, silver, steel, chrome, pewter, tin, bone, ivory, horn, tortoiseshell, mother-of-pearl, leather, various textiles, gesso with metal foils or paint, lacquer, and of course a wide array of plastics and other modern materials. The word *combinations* is very important because most pieces of furniture are made up not only of several different organic materials but also of inorganic materials. *Organics*, materials made from animal or vegetable materials that once were alive, are very sensitive to forces of nature such as light, changes in temperature and relative humidity, biological attack, and pollution. *Inorganics*, such as metals, are far less sensitive, although, with the exception of gold, they are susceptible to corrosion. Pieces of furniture are, then, composite architectural objects in which each part is reacting to the environment and seeking its own equilibrium.

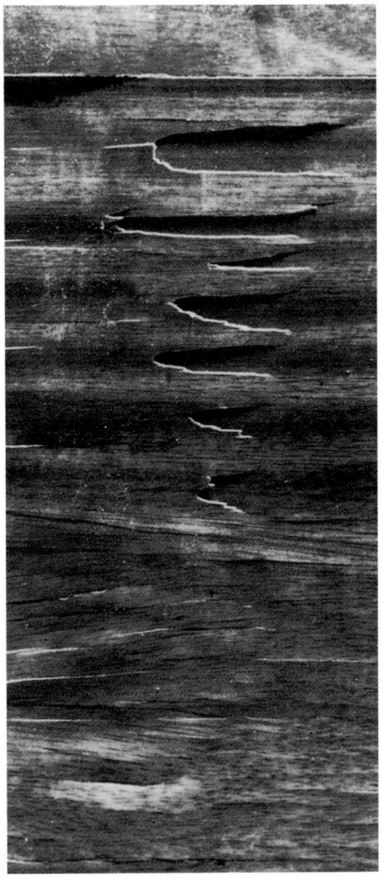

Detail showing damage to veneer resulting from movement in the substrate. Built-in stress between the two layers exists when the grains lie at right angles to each other.

Unfortunately, the various component parts that make up a piece of furniture sometimes have very different needs. It is important for the collector to understand the needs of the individual parts in order to create an environment that meets the requirements of all the parts. This chapter will concentrate on traditional furniture, not out of a bias but because it is, on the whole, more sensitive than contemporary furniture. Recommendations for traditional furniture also are valid for contemporary pieces.

The goal of all conservation is to preserve, as much as possible, an object in its original condition. Because furniture is functional art, most pieces bear traces of wear, and the conservator looks upon these traces as a part of the object's historical significance. Nicks, dents, worn drawer runners, and even blemished finishes and worn textiles are to be preserved as part of the artifact's history. Further, any treatment of an object should change that

Opposite:
The raised leaf of this table clearly shows the damage to the top caused by direct exposure to sunlight. Not only will sunlight bleach the color, it also will break down the finish.

object as little as possible. While many modern art-conservation materials are appropriate for use on furniture, wax and other traditional finishing products should be used wherever possible. It is important to remember that only preventive conservation, that is, providing a sympathetic environment and avoiding sources of deterioration, can prolong the life of a piece of furniture.

The Importance of Accurate Records

The first step in caring for a collection of furniture is to establish a well-organized system of record keeping. For each object there should be a file where all relevant documents are kept. These records should include what is called a *condition report;* that is, a detailed description of the piece, including dimensions and any notations about its condition. Any losses, splits, or other damages should be described and measured. Detailed photographs should also be included. The file also should include a description of the special conditions that the object might require, as well as notes on any recommended conservation treatment, fumigation, or special handling instructions. Each piece of furniture should be numbered so that any mention in inventories, insurance policies, or conservation records will be precise. This can be done in an obscure spot by brushing on a small square of Soluvar varnish as a barrier layer and then painting a registration number over it with acrylic paint. Notes on any comments concerning the object—such as appraisals, authentications, or correspondence regarding its purchase or loan—should be put in its file. These records will prove invaluable over the years for monitoring the condition of an object.

Creating the Proper Environment

Preventive conservation focuses on the prevention of damage to the objects from light, problems with relative humidity, pests, and accidents. Ultimately this is the only way to extend the life of a piece of furniture because damage caused by these sources is never reversible. The importance of providing the proper environment for a collection cannot be overemphasized. This requires monitoring the levels of light, temperature, and relative humidity. Remember too that all heat, air conditioning, and monitoring equipment needs to be maintained regularly.

Light

Light is perhaps furniture's most insidious attacker because the deterioration it causes is gradual rather than dramatic. Light radiation attacks furniture in several ways: it breaks down the finish; fades and destroys the structure of applied textiles, leather, and synthetic coverings; causes embrittlement of wood and glue through the convection of heat and the subsequent loss of moisture content; and changes the color of the wood itself. The color of wood is determined by the proportion of *cellulose* (white), *lignin* (brown), and other wood *extractives* that are present. With exposure to light, light-colored woods such as the distinctive yellow and pink tulip wood, will tend to yellow or darken. Conversely, darker woods like amaranth or walnut will fade. Any colorants—stains or dyes used on the wood—also will fade with prolonged exposure to light.[1]

Deterioration caused by light has been discussed in greater detail in the chapter on Creating and Maintaining the Right Environment; this chapter will address some of the principles that relate to the preservation of furniture. While some materials are particularly susceptible to fading by specific wavelengths of light, in general the shorter the wavelength the greater the harm to the object. Since ultraviolet light has the shortest wavelength, it is of critical importance to eliminate an object's exposure to it. However, it is not enough to eliminate only ultraviolet light because visible light can also cause fading. Further, infrared light, which has the longest wavelength and transfers heat, causes the embrittling of objects and glue. Therefore, we must bear in mind that it is an object's total exposure to light that counts. This means that prolonged exposure at a low light level can cause the same damage as brief exposure to a high light level. This is true even if you are

The edge of this seat cushion shows fading of the upholstery fabric, which originally was black, caused by exposure to sunlight.

comparing prolonged exposure to visible radiation with brief exposure to ultraviolet radiation. Total exposure can be calculated in footcandle hours per year. Preventive conservation dictates keeping the yearly exposure to an acceptable level.[2]

Before you can regulate your collection's exposure to light you have to monitor it with equipment that will tell you not only the total illuminance but also the percentage of that illuminance that is made up of ultraviolet light. Visible light is measured with a luximeter, which consists of a selenium photo cell connected to a meter. The widely accepted guidelines call for optimum levels of 15 footcandles for most organics and 5 footcandles for textiles and colored furniture. An ultraviolet monitor will indicate whether an ultraviolet filter is needed or when one needs to be replaced.[3] The principles of monitoring ultraviolet light are very important, but even if a collector is not able to install elaborate monitoring and filtering equipment, there are very simple measures that should certainly be followed. Sunlight must never be allowed to fall directly on an object. At certain times of year, an object can get the recommended yearly exposure in a number of hours. Pulling simple scrim shades can be very effective, but even more important, darkening a room that is not in use can amount to an effective preventive measure. One can also filter light in a number of ways.

Relative Humidity

Incompatible or widely fluctuating levels of relative humidity pose a particularly serious threat to pieces of furniture because every piece is made of various

Gesso preparations found on painted or gilded furniture will chip and flake when air pockets develop between the gesso and the wood substrate. This is caused by the wood shrinking more than the gesso layer. Detail of giltwood torchère, one of a pair. Collection of the J. Paul Getty Museum, Malibu, Calif.

organic and inorganic materials, and each component is moving in its own way to maintain its own equilibrium with the environment. This movement can cause serious problems. When the relative humidity rises, all organic materials will absorb water from the environment, swelling in the process. They also will give off moisture, or shrink, in the face of falling relative humidity. This taking on and giving off of humidity causes objects to warp, twist, or split, and very often these deformations are permanent. Veneered furniture is particularly susceptible to dislocation between parts due to fluctuations in relative humidity. Low relative humidity can embrittle some glues, while high relative humidity can soften others. Excessive (above 65 percent) relative humidity will also allow mold to grow.

Maintaining a proper environment for a furniture collection is a matter of compromise: wood furniture does well between 50 and 60 percent RH while the metal components on furniture are better preserved at very low levels. The best environment for furniture then, is a compromise of 68 degrees Fahrenheit, plus or minus 2 degrees, and 55 percent RH, plus or minus 5 percent. The specific level of heat or relative humidity, however, is less critical than avoiding radical fluctuations. Wood can accommodate changes if they occur gradually, at a rate of no more than a 10-percent change per month; repeated cycles of broad swings, such as heating a house just for a weekend, will have serious consequences.

Humidity can cause further problems for a collection of furniture: above 65 percent RH, objects will be subject to biological attack. Mold spores are always present in the air and require only the right conditions to grow. It is therefore very important to keep the relative humidity below 65 percent. Mold and fungi also grow more rapidly in the dark and with still air, so if conditions of high humidity are encountered, turning on a light and increasing the circulation of air will impede the growth of mold spores.

Pests

Another serious threat to furniture made of organic materials is pest infestation. The well-known term *woodworm* is commonly used for a variety of vermin such as Anobidae, furniture beetle, deathwatch beetle, Bostrychidae, and Lyctidae. In addition to these, the wood or upholstered components of furniture are prey to silverfish, clothes moths, termites, carpet beetles, cigarette beetles, and more.[4] Detection is a problem because the eggs are laid in crevices, and the grubs then feed by boring into the wood, where they remain for one to five years before they make exit holes by which they can be seen.

Since woodworm infestation can spread throughout an entire collection, close initial inspection of a new acquisition and constant vigilance are very important. Before bringing an object into a collection, the object should be examined overall with a bright light. Fresh wood powder, called *frass*, coming out of exit holes is a good indication that there is active infestation. If this is spotted on a new object, or even one that has been in the collection, the first thing to do is to isolate the object in a large polyethylene bag. Place a sheet of black paper under the area in question. Leave it in the bag like this for a few days. If when you reinspect it there is fresh frass on black paper, it is a strong indication that there is an active infestation. (Or with masking tape attach a piece of polyethylene over the suspected area and later look through the plastic for new frass.) If you find such evidence, you should contact a professional conservator for advice, as fumigation treatments all carry risks and none of the options prevents reinfestation. If you believe an object to be infested, you should check all the surrounding objects in the manner described. It is sometimes possible to disinfect an object by putting it in a closed bag with a No Pest strip, taking care to keep the No Pest strip out of contact with the object. After twenty-four hours, check to be sure there is no damage to the finish from the No Pest strip, then seal the bag for two weeks. The treatment should be repeated after several months to prevent reinfestation by a new generation of larvae. There are additional insecticide products available, but because of the risk of damage to the finish, they should be used only by a conservator. Depriving vermin of a hospitable atmosphere is the best defense for a collection. This entails keeping the objects as well as their environments clean and dust free.

Installation and Storage

The prevention of accidents and response to them is another important aspect of furniture conservation. This involves considering the sources of trouble when installing or storing an object. Keep furniture away from sources of direct heat such as steam pipes, radiators, or hot-air ducts. Note possible sources of flooding and avoid storing furniture beneath overhead piping. Never leave an object in storage directly on the floor, and be sure the material on which it rests is not water absorbent. When installing a piece of furniture, it is very important that its weight is supported evenly by all of its feet. Wedges or shims can be used to achieve this if necessary. Also, old case pieces should not be heavily weighted. Keep drawer contents light, open them infrequently, and wax the runners to reduce friction.

In areas of possible seismic activity, the stability of an object should be carefully studied and pieces with a high center of gravity attached firmly to the wall or stabilized in another way. Also consider traffic patterns so that vulnerable objects are not put at undue risk. Emergency supplies can make a great difference if an accident does occur. Always have on hand rags to blot any spills on furniture and plastic sheeting to cover objects in the event of a water leak. Drying should be slowed to prevent a disequilibrium between the interior of an object and its surface. Mold growth is also a serious threat in these situations, so a professional conservator should always be consulted in the event of such an accident.

Storage conditions should provide added security to objects rather than a different set of risks. Keep light to a minimum, with outside windows heavily filtered and shades drawn. As in areas where

Detail showing frass coming out of exit holes in a chair rail. Notice that some holes are dark whereas others are filled with fresh frass, possibly indicating an active infestation.

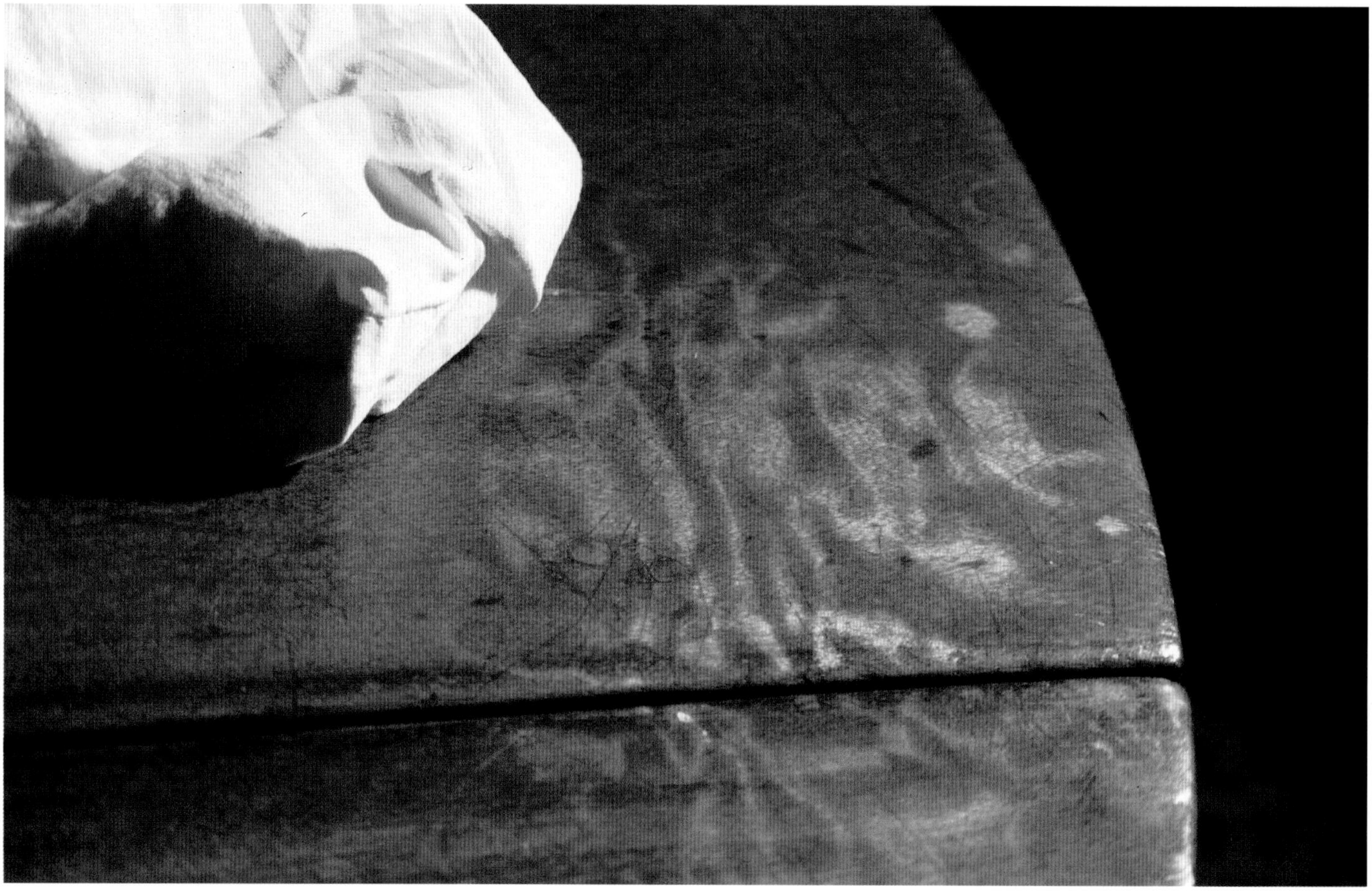

A cloth dampened with a cleaning preparation, which was left on a table, has dissolved the finish and discolored the table.

furniture is used or displayed, monitor the temperature and relative humidity in storage areas and examine objects periodically for pest infestation. Temperature and air circulation should be within normal guidelines, and storage areas should be kept scrupulously clean by frequent vacuuming to discourage pest infestation.

Storage should be systematic and well organized. Never stack objects; rather, secure them to rigid shelving made of inert materials, such as enameled steel, which has itself been secured to the wall. Always cover furniture with fabric that can breathe to prevent trapping moisture, and keep dust to a minimum, for it can provide food for vermin, leave an acidic film, and trap moisture, all of which can attack the finish. Store small objects in inert containers. Avoid materials that give off residual gas, and never bring food, drinks, or flammable solvents to a storage area.

Cleaning and Routine Maintenance

Cleaning around furniture should be taken seriously, for it can either protect the collection or subject it to unnecessary wear. It is important to draw up detailed instructions and review them frequently with whoever is doing the cleaning. Great care must be taken not to snag any lifting veneer, loose pieces of carving, or flaking paint or gesso. Clean these delicate areas with compressed air or a sable brush with an air bulb at the bottom of the stem. With one exception (see next page), water-based cleaning solution should never be used on any surface. Clean, lint-free rags that are washed frequently are best for dusting, although a soft drafting brush can be used if great care is taken. No aerosol polishes or dust attractors should ever be

This detail shows an area where water gilding has been wiped off inadvertently during an attempt to clean it. Detail of giltwood torchère, one of a pair. Collection of the J. Paul Getty Museum, Malibu, Calif.

used as they can harm the finish. Vacuum-cleaner heads should be padded.

Furniture's complexity presents many varied surfaces to clean. Glass, for example, can be cleaned using any kind of alcohol on cotton swabs with a small amount of calcium carbonate added for difficult spots. Calcium carbonate can also be used with water to polish silver mounts. Marble tops can be cleaned with mild soap and water with a tablespoon of calcium carbonate added, then waxed. Painted surfaces must be cleaned with extreme caution, and only if there is no flaking or loose paint and if there is a varnish layer. Under these conditions, a painted surface can be wiped very lightly with mineral spirits. Gilding is applied in either a water-based or oil-based medium, and it is frequently quite difficult to distinguish between the two. Because these two mediums are cleaned in very different ways, gilding should be kept dust free but cleaned only by a conservator.

Routine care of wooden furniture is surprisingly straightforward, for, contrary to popular belief, wood does not need to be fed. Since grime is harmful as well as unsightly, it is most important to keep the finish of a piece of furniture clean. If necessary, this can be done by using a very mild (1:50) solution of Murphy's oil soap in distilled water. Use a soft cloth and wring it out so that it is damp, not wet, and gently wipe the finish. Rinse with a cloth dampened with distilled water, and dry. This is a delicate operation and should be done with extreme care. A test should always be carried out on an obscure part of the furniture to be sure there will not be *blanching*, or a penetration of the moisture into the finish, causing it to whiten.

Rewaxing the finish can restore its shine and offer a degree of protection. The wax should be used sparingly and only once a year. Beeswax is very good and can be made into a paste by grating it into a jar, covering it with an equal amount of mineral spirits, closing the jar, and letting it stand until the wax has dissolved. This or other waxes can be toned to blend with the existing finish by adding dry pigments. Cosmolloid (plastic) waxes made from petroleum refining, such as Renaissance wax, are also good and can be combined with beeswax and carnauba (palm) wax to achieve a durable wax finish that is easy to apply without streaks. Butchers, Staples, and Goddards are other brand-name blended waxes with good working properties. To apply wax, use a small amount of mineral spirits to moisten a clean, lint-free rag. Apply the wax sparingly in a circular motion, then finish by wiping with the grain. Let stand several hours and buff with another soft, lint-free rag.

Never clean brass handles, knobs, or mounts in situ because the alkaline cleaning solutions will attack the surrounding furniture finish. Number the mounts and lay them out in order on a cardboard in the same way that they are on the object. Apply a weak solution (1:100) of ammonia with a cotton swab and rinse generously with distilled water, then dry thoroughly. Mounts should not be cleaned more than once a year because any residual water can encourage corrosion. If the mounts are used frequently and tarnish quickly, protective coatings are available but should be applied by a conservator. Before cleaning, give careful consideration to the aesthetic value of patinated copper alloy mounts. Dull brasses can be very beautiful, especially when they are waxed.

Upholstered pieces should be maintained by thorough vacuuming, including the underside. Take care not to create wear marks on the outermost or show fabrics, or to have part of a period textile dislodged by the process. Never touch the textiles, either by ungloved hands or the machinery being used to maintain the object. Vacuum period textiles with a low-suction vacuum that has a fine-wire screen over the nozzle. Soft brushes are on occasion appropriate for mechanical removal of soil but should be used with extreme caution. Also, never sit upon period upholsteries.[5]

Always keep a Mylar-backed cork pad (not felt, which absorbs water too easily) underneath plants or flowers. Any water or alcohol spilled on the surface must be blotted and wiped dry immediately. Never place plants or flowers on gessoed furniture.

If small bits of gesso, veneer, or stringing become separated during cleaning, label the pieces and put them in a ziplock bag, noting the date, object, and precise location from which they came. A central file for all such objects will facilitate their eventual reattachment by a conservator. If dents or scrapes occur, they can be toned in with watercolor or filled with pigmented wax. If blanching or whitening of the finish or a mild burn occurs, it can be rubbed with cigarette ashes, rottenstone, or very, very fine pumice in a light oil (never linseed oil as it contains drying oils, which make its effects irreversible).

Furniture should be double crated so that any shock will be absorbed by the outer crate. Bumpers made of Ethafoam and Volare are used to hold the piece in place. The bumpers are positioned at the piece's strongest points and are wrapped with sulfur-free fabric where they come in contact with mounts. The crate should be lined with waterproof paper and gasketed. Coffer on stand. Collection of the J. Paul Getty Museum, Malibu, Calif.

Packing and Shipping

Many different types of problems can arise from packing and handling furniture. When moving a piece of furniture, all of its separate parts should be removed. Withdraw drawers from chests; remove marble or glass tops from their bases and always carry and store them vertically. Secure loose but attached parts, such as doors, by putting a blanket over the piece and attaching it with a string or large elastic band. Furniture should always be moved by at least two people, who should first inspect the piece and be shown its vulnerable points. Handlers should never wear rings or watches or hang keys from a belt. While it is best to handle finished furniture with bare hands, always wear gloves to handle metal or upholstered furniture. Lift objects by their lowest supporting member, always below their center of gravity; never tilt, drag, or push. Never allow mirrors to rest on their carved bottom

Water allowed to stand on a finish will produce black stains.

rails; rather, hang or screw them to cleats. When a piece of furniture is transported in a car or van, all of its surfaces should be padded. It should be laid on its back to lower its center of gravity and either tied in place or generously padded. Never place separate parts within the body of a piece but pad them separately. Thermal shock is a danger in cold climates, so any vehicle should be preheated.

Crating and shipping museum-quality furniture requires great expertise and should be entrusted only to specialists. First, it must be determined that the condition of the object in question is suitable for shipment—that it is structurally sound and free of loose parts, flaking gesso, etc., and that the environment to which it is going does not differ significantly from the environment from which it is coming. If the environments differ, professional advice should be sought on making a microclimate and gradually acclimatizing the object to its new environment. This can be done by building a frame to fit over the object with two-by-fours and covering it with polypropylene sheeting. A humidifier or a dehumidifier is then placed in the tent with the piece of furniture with a hygrometer to give a readout of the relative humidity, which can then be adjusted very gradually. Crates themselves actually work as environmental chambers. To avoid a rapid readjustment in temperature or relative humidity, always allow crates to sit at their destination for twenty-four hours before being opened.

Professional Treatment

Professional attention is important to the conservation of a collection of furniture. Assessing the gravity of a problem or knowing when to have an object treated can be difficult. The best way to know is to commission a professional survey of the collection. This should include not only a condition report on each object and an analysis of environmental problems, but also recommendations on preventive conservation issues as well as treatments.

Never undertake restoration projects, such as refinishing and reupholstery, without consulting a conservator; conservation ethics and practices differ from the approach of a restorer, whose goal is usually to renew the appearance of an object. For example, old, worn finishes, even when not original, should be preserved, and degraded finishes often can be reformed by a conservator rather than stripped. An exception is an inappropriate finish that was recently applied. In any case, finish work always should be handled by a professional. An adroit amateur can consolidate lifting veneer by injecting or brushing dilute liquid hide glue, covering with Mylar and a soft pad, and applying very light pressure with a clamp. Beyond this type of stopgap measure, however, eventual professional treatment risks being complicated by intermediate intervention. Foundations and show covers of original upholstery, which enhance an object's historical significance and serve as models to other treatments, need to be scrupulously preserved.

In seeking a conservator, a referral from the American Institute for Conservation of Historic and Artistic Works (AIC) may be helpful, as can a conservator or curator at a local museum. All conservation must be reversible and should be carried out in accordance with the Code of Ethics and Standards of the AIC as described in their directory.

NOTES

1. N. S. Brommelle, J. A. Darrah, and A. J. Moncrieff, Papers on the Conservation and Technology of Wood, I.C.O.M. Committee on Conservation, Madrid, October 1972.
2. Garry Thompson, *The Museum Environment*, 2nd ed. (London: Butterworths, 1986), 30. The maximum recommended levels of annual illumination are 65,000 footcandle hours for objects subjected to 20 footcandles and 20,000 footcandle hours for objects subjected to 5 footcandles.
3. Thompson, 21. UV readings above 75μ with meter are unacceptable.
4. Robert F. McGiffin, Jr., *Furniture Care and Conservation* (Nashville: The American Association for State and Local History, 1983), 152.
5. Elizabeth Lahikainen, correspondence dated June 4, 1990.

ACKNOWLEDGMENTS

The author would like to thank Linda Strauss, Rita Gomez, Gordon Hanlon, Elizabeth Lahikainen, and Rosamond Westmoreland for their contributions to this chapter.

1798

TEXTILES

Sara J. Wolf

Methods used in the past to attach textiles in frames, such as adhesives and nails, can cause irreparable staining of the fabric, as seen in this sampler from 1849.

Textiles are associated with nearly every aspect of our lives. We are wrapped in them when we are born; they provide us warmth for sleep; they are crafted carefully into garments that are worn for the important rites of passage of our lives, such as christenings and weddings; they record the first stitches of a child's alphabet; they adorn our walls; they cushion our feet.

The term *textile* covers a wide range of objects, from heavy tapestries to delicate pieces of lace, and from decorative quilts to utilitarian clothing and rugs. Textiles also make up portions of other objects, such as fans, dolls, and upholstered furniture.

While some textiles—notably tapestries and Oriental carpets—have been highly valued by collectors, most are preserved for their sentimental or historical value. Recently, however, textiles have become more collectible as decorative works of art. Today it is as likely that you will see a textile piece framed and exhibited on the wall as a print or painting. Proper display,. therefore, is one of the most important considerations for the long-term preservation of textile objects.

The textiles that you collect and preserve generally will fall into two categories: those that you will want to display, and those that you will want to use in a limited way, but still try to preserve for the future. The latter category often includes items such as wedding gowns, quilts, and household linens that require special handling and care. In using these textiles, there must be the tacit understanding that while you are doing your best to hand these items from one generation to the next, they will eventually become too fragile to use or may be damaged beyond repair. Damage cannot be

Opposite:
A mat of archival cardboard can be used as a spacer to separate a textile from the glazing material, as was done for this sampler. Collection the author

reversed, even in the hands of a conservator. A tear may be mended, and stains may be removed in cleaning, but each use of a textile causes wear that weakens the structure, the yarns, and the fibers themselves.

The Properties of Textile Fibers

Most historic and ethnographic textiles are made of natural fibers, including wool, silk, cotton, and linen. This chapter will discuss textiles constructed from these natural fibers. Modern textiles that contain synthetic fibers such as rayon and acetates have unique preservation problems, which should be referred to a conservator for advice.

In order to care properly for your textile collections, it is important to know something about the properties of these natural fibers and those factors that cause their deterioration. Of the four major textile fibers, two are of animal origin (silk and wool), and two are of plant origin (cotton and linen).

Animal fibers are composed of proteins, which are deteriorated by strong alkalis. In high humidity, these fibers can absorb about 20 percent of their weight in water, and when wet, they lose strength. Plant fibers are easily deteriorated by acids. Flax (the fiber from which linen is made) is particularly sensitive to high relative humidity. It absorbs moisture very readily, changing dimension and losing strength.

The physical and chemical characteristics of these fibers lead the conservator to make certain decisions about the kinds of materials that should be used in mounting and storing textiles. These characteristics also affect decisions about treatment. As an example, the scaly structure of wool allows the fibers to attach to each other and, when manipulated in water, to form felt. Cleaning of wool, then, can be a very delicate operation that must be carried out without any agitation.

The Primary Enemies of Textiles

One of the greatest threats to textiles is light. The worst damage is caused by ultraviolet radiation from natural daylight and from fluorescent lamps. However, while UV causes damage most rapidly, the entire light spectrum causes textile dyes to fade and the fibers to become brittle. Keeping window shades pulled down or shutters closed during the sunniest parts of the day and using UV-filtering glazing materials when framing textiles provides some protection. The best protection for the long term, however, is to keep your textiles away from sources of natural light and to rotate your collection on view. Ideally, rotation should be done seasonally.

High temperatures can exacerbate the embrittlement of fibers, and heat accelerates the rate of chemical reactions. High relative humidity in combination with warm temperatures promotes a favorable environment for insects and mold or mildew (see the chapter on Creating and Maintaining the Right Environment for guidelines). When caught early enough, fungal growth can be removed before staining takes place; however, irreparable damage can occur if it is left unchecked. If mold or mildew is detected, the textile should be moved to a more stable environment, and a conservator should be contacted immediately for treatment options.

Air pollution also is an enemy of textiles. Sulfur-dioxide fumes from automobile exhaust and industry affect some dyes. In addition, airborne dust and dirt can settle on the surface of textiles and work their way into fibers as they expand and contract in response to relative humidity changes. Dirt particles are very gritty and work like small knives to cut into the fibers.

Textiles made of protein fibers (silk, wool) are particularly susceptible to infestation by clothes moths and carpet beetles. Cotton and linen textiles are not generally consumed by insects, but starch finishes are attractive to silverfish. The presence of silverfish in your collections may also indicate that the relative humidity is too high.

The best protection against insect pests is good housekeeping. When you are bringing a new piece into your collection, it should be vacuumed (see section on maintenance below) and then isolated from other objects until you are sure that it is free of insect eggs, larvae, and adults. An object can be isolated by wrapping it in a piece of clear

Some components of dyes and mordants can be responsible for the deterioration of a textile fabric. This type of deterioration is often referred to as inherent vice *because it cannot be reversed or treated. The Textile Museum, Washington, D.C., Acc. no. 91.445*

polyethylene sheeting and carefully sealing the package with twist-ties or packing tape. If no evidence of insect activity (larvae, adult insects, frass) is seen after two or three weeks, it should be safe to prepare the textile for display or store it with the rest of your collection. If pests are seen, contact a textile conservator immediately for advice. Do not apply pesticides or other chemicals to the textiles as this might cause irreparable damage.

Certain textiles also can be affected by properties that conservators refer to as *inherent vice*, problems caused, for example, by the manufacturing process or the construction of the object. These characteristics lead to deterioration even if you provide a good environment and proper care. For instance, iron was used in the past as a *mordant* (fixative) to produce black and brown dyes. In cases where these mordants have been used on cotton, the fibers frequently have rotted away, producing a hole in the textile. Certain dyes—particularly some of the early chemical dyes produced during the late eighteenth and early nineteenth centuries—are so fugitive that they can bleed into surrounding colors when they become even slightly damp, which makes cleaning of these materials especially difficult. Also during the nineteenth century, when silk was an extremely popular clothing fabric, metallic salts were included in the manufacturing process to add weight and crispness to the fabric. In time, however, this "weighted" silk becomes extremely brittle and begins to crack and powder. This process is, unfortunately, irreversible and is accelerated by light. Examples of weighted silk fabrics are found, not only in costume, but also in many of the Victorian "crazy quilts." Weighted silks are difficult to stabilize and must be treated carefully in order to preserve them at all.

Textiles can be damaged from adjacent materials or objects. Some of the worst deterioration occurs when improper materials are used for display and storage. Textiles placed against wooden framing members or in a wooden drawer will suffer from acidic degradation. Cotton and linen in particular darken and become brittle when placed in contact with wood. In the past, textiles were frequently nailed over wooden supports in frames. In addition to the damage caused by the

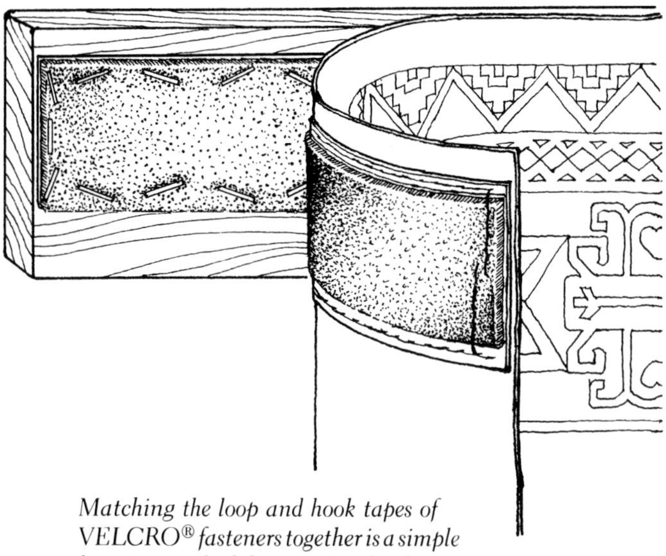

Matching the loop and hook tapes of VELCRO® fasteners together is a simple hanging method for some kinds of textiles, such as Navajo rugs and Oriental carpets. Drawing by Jian Wu

wood, the iron nails frequently rusted, staining and often rotting the textile surrounding the nails.

Both for storage and display, it is extremely important to use archival materials in contact with textile objects. Some of the terminology used in identifying different types of archival products are as follows:

Archival quality is a generic term indicating that the product is appropriate for use in contact with your collection objects.

Acid free is also a general term indicating that the product is free of acids, or has a pH of approximately 7.0. This term is often used incorrectly to describe materials that contain an alkaline buffer.

Alkaline-buffered products contain an alkaline compound (such as calcium carbonate) designed to neutralize any acids that are present or retard the evolution of acids in the future. Alkaline-buffered products should be used with textiles made of plant fibers (cotton, linen) to protect them from acid deterioration.

Unbuffered or **nonbuffered** products have no alkaline reserve. Generally, they are a neutral pH (7.0) or acid-free material. Unbuffered products should be used with textiles made of animal fibers (silk, wool), since proteins are known to be sensitive to bases or alkalis.

Proper Hanging and Display

Mounting Textiles for Display

There are a number of acceptable ways to mount a textile. The choice is ultimately based on the condition of the piece. The following descriptions are presented to facilitate your discussions with a conservator in determining the most appropriate type of mount for your individual textiles.

A textile in sturdy condition can be hung from a VELCRO®[1] fastener strip. Objects that might be hung in this way include quilts, tapestries, Navajo rugs, and Oriental carpets. The female (fuzzy) tape is machine-stitched to a cotton webbing strip cut to the size of the textile's hanging edge. The webbing strip is then hand-sewn to the textile. The male (hook) tape is then tacked or stapled to a varnished wooden strip fastened to the wall, and the two tapes are then pressed together. This system has the advantage of being easily adjusted and is strong enough to hold the weight of larger textiles. As a caution, when taking the object down, slide your hand between the two tapes and gently pull the layers apart. The fastener strips are so strong that pulling on the upper edge of the textile will most certainly cause the textile to tear before the tapes separate.

As a variation on the VELCRO® system, the textile can be fitted with a lining similar to that used for draperies, which will act as a dust cover. In this instance, the lining is sewn to the textile first, and the webbing strip is hand-sewn through both the lining and the textile.

Larger textiles that are not sturdy enough to be hung from one end can be mounted on a fixed, square or rectangular wooden frame, called a *strainer,* over which a mounting fabric has been stretched. The textile is carefully sewn to the stretched fabric in a manner that will provide overall support to the piece. Sewing just at the edges, for example, would be insufficient, as the center would remain unsupported, and the upper edge of the textile would have to bear most of the hanging weight. The sewing tension must be perfectly executed; if the sewing is too loose, the textile is poorly supported, and if too tight, the textile will have the appearance of having been quilted. Textiles that could be mounted on a strainer include paisley shawls and large batiks. Because virtually any size strainer can be constructed, this method is appropriate for both large and small textiles as well as fragments. A caution: the textile object should always be sewn to a support fabric. Never stretch the textile itself over the edges of the strainer.

A variation of the strainer mount includes a panel of archival cardboard in the center of the strainer, behind the mounting fabric, to provide a solid support. This has advantages over the traditional strainer alone because it prevents the stretched backing fabric from sagging. Again, stitching has to be carefully placed to provide overall support to the textile. Depending on its size, a strainer with or without a solid support can be glazed and framed.

As an alternative to the strainer with a solid support, smaller textiles can be mounted on a fabric-covered archival cardboard or mat board. This technique is generally appropriate only for textiles that will be framed, as the mat board or cardboard easily absorb moisture and can warp if not restrained by a frame.

The materials chosen for a mount are as important as the evaluation of the best kind of mount to support the textile. Use as few wooden materials as possible. While some mounts may contain wooden parts, the wood should always be coated with shellac or a moisture-borne polyurethane to seal in wood acids. Even when sealed, the wood must never come in contact with the textile.

Archival mat boards and cardboards should always be used for solid supports and inserts in strainers. Mounting fabrics should always be prewashed to remove excess dyes as well as finishes and sizings. The best choice for mounting fabrics are 100 percent cotton or cotton/polyester blends. Silks and silk velvets are usable but may not be the best choice because of their vulnerability to insect infestation and because they deteriorate so rapidly. Linen is not an appropriate fabric for a mount because it absorbs moisture from the atmosphere so readily, causing sagging and distortion, which reduces the ability of the fabric to provide proper support for the textile object. Wool is also inappropriate as a mounting fabric because it stretches and sags easily and because of its susceptibility to insect infestation.

Framing Textiles

One of the questions asked most frequently about framing is, "Should my textile be framed behind glass?" There is more than one answer to this question and opinions differ; however, the following considerations will assist in making the appropriate choice.

Location Will the textile receive indirect lighting from natural daylight? If so, it is wise to use a glazing material like Plexiglas that contains a UV filter (such as UF-3 Plexiglas) to reduce the damage from at least that portion of the light spectrum.

Size The standard size of a piece of Plexiglas is four by eight feet. It is difficult to obtain a glazing material beyond this size to protect your textile.

Environmental Control If dust and dirt are a problem, glazing is recommended. Without protection, a textile is subject to more frequent cleaning, and the more treatments the piece is subjected to, the shorter the life span of the object. If there are smokers in your household, it is imperative that textiles be protected. In addition, framing materials can help to modify the effects of fluctuating relative humidity, because the backing fabrics and archival cardboards used in a mount will absorb and release moisture in response to environmental changes.

Drape Handmade textiles are frequently somewhat irregular in shape and may tend to ripple as they hang on the wall. This three-dimensional character is lost with framing and glazing, unless a very deep, "shadow-box" type of frame is used. In these cases, the decorative look you are trying to achieve with the textile may determine whether or not to use a frame.

In choosing a glazing material, it is usually preferable to use Plexiglas rather than glass. First, Plexiglas is more flexible and breaks less easily. Irreparable damage can occur where glass has broken and torn through a textile. Second,

Plexiglas is significantly lighter in weight than glass, which makes it much easier to handle and hang larger framed items. One drawback of Plexiglas is that it has electrostatic properties that can pull loose fibers of a textile onto the inside surface of the Plexiglas. It may be better, therefore, to frame a very brittle piece, such as an archaeological textile, behind glass.

It is very important that glass should never come in direct contact with your textile. In high humidity, mold can grow in areas where the glazing material is in contact with the textile. Also, salts contained in the textile can transfer to the glass, absorb additional moisture, and cause increased degradation of the textile.

There are two techniques to separate the glazing material from your textile. First, a window-mat cut from archival cardboard (like those used in mounting prints and drawings) may be placed over the edges of the textile to provide an attractive finish and hold the glazing material away from the surface of the textile. The second technique is the use of a spacer in the frame. Your framer can construct a frame so that thin strips of Plexiglas are attached along the framing edge directly behind the glazing material. When the frame is assembled, these Plexiglas strips will hold the glazing material away from the mounted textile.

While it is generally not recommended that Plexiglas be placed in direct contact with a textile, there is one exception. A "pressure" mount is sometimes used to frame very fragile textiles for display. With this kind of mount, the textile is placed on a well-padded support. The frame exerts pressure on the Plexiglas placed on the face of the textile, thus holding the textile in place on the padded mount. This type of mount is designed only for short-term display. Contact a conservator to evaluate whether or not this type of mount would be appropriate for a specific textile.

A great deal of damage has been done to textiles by gluing them down to an acidic cardboard as part of the framing process. Samplers, in particular, have often been framed in this way using animal glues, which become very brittle and stain the textile, and with white glues and wood glues. It is extremely difficult to remove these adhesives and nearly impossible to remove the stains they leave behind. There are instances, however, when adhesives are the only choice to stabilize a textile. While not entirely reversible, adhesives designed for conservation use can be the last resort to save badly degraded textiles.

Unconstructed costumes, like ponchos and tunics, or garments that do not have set-in sleeves, like kimonos, can be mounted on the wall on a padded rod. Either a Plexiglas or varnished wooden dowel can be used. The rod should be padded with polyester quilt batting to round out the shoulder areas, and covered with a piece of washed, unbleached muslin.

Displaying Textiles that Cannot Be Mounted

If a quilt or coverlet is too large or fragile to be hung, an alternative method of display is to place the textile on a bed in a guest room for display. This area should be a low-traffic area and, as with other items in your collection, the textiles should be rotated seasonally. Be sure to protect these pieces from sunlight; it is very common to see fading along one side of a quilt that has been placed on a bed

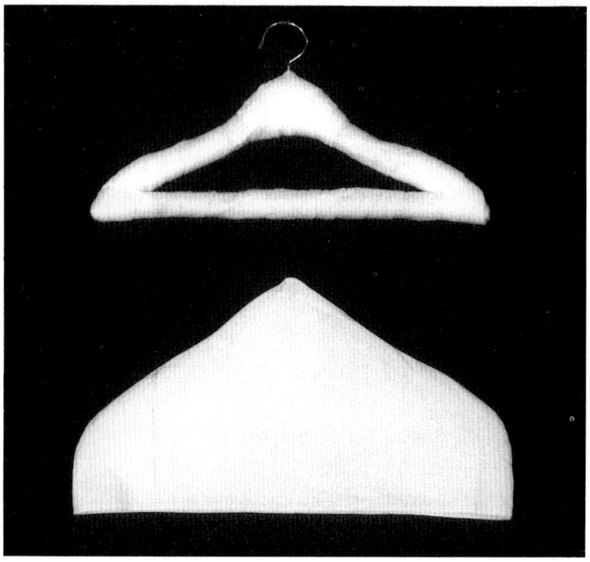

In order to hang a structured garment for storage, a padded hanger can be constructed by wrapping a wooden hanger with polyester quilt batting and a simple muslin cover.

next to a window. This is also an alternative method of display for other large textiles such as shawls.

Proper Shelving and Storage Conditions

The best location in your house for storing textiles is a cool, dark, dry room. If a closet is to be used, make sure there is sufficient air circulation to discourage fungal growth and pest infestation. Rust-free metal shelving is appropriate hardware for storing textiles that have been boxed or rolled with an outer protective layer of muslin. Avoid using wooden shelves or drawers. If wood is your only choice, seal the wood with shellac or water-borne polyurethane varnish. Line drawer bottoms and sides with archival cardboard (preferably alkaline buffered), and place archival cardboard on shelves to further isolate the textiles from the wood.

The decision to hang a costume or to store it flat in an archival box must be made on the basis of the condition of the textile. The following guidelines use a wedding gown as an example but apply to all costumes.

It is critical that every textile object be stored in a clean state. A food spill may not be visible immediately as a stain, but discoloration may become evident over time. Also, the visible and invisible food stains in textiles can provide fertile ground for insect or fungal attack. In addition, perspiration, which is acidic and may be invisible at first, forms alkaline ammonium compounds as it slowly ages. These compounds would cause deterioration of a silk fabric, making it brittle and more easily split or torn. Based on information such as the construction of the garment and the fiber content of fabrics and trims, a textile conservator can offer an opinion as to whether hand washing or dry cleaning would be more appropriate for a new wedding gown. The issues of cleaning an antique gown are more complex.

Once it has been cleaned, a lightweight gown—without heavy trims, beading, or a train—can be hung. Choose a hanger that is the correct shape for the slant of the shoulders and strong enough to properly support the weight of the dress.

Basting cotton twill tape suspenders into the waistband of a dress will lessen the stress of weight on the shoulders of a garment hung for storage. Drawing by Jian Wu

The shank of the hanger should be long enough to prevent creasing of stand-up collars. Wrap the hanger in layers of polyester quilt batting to pad the shoulder area and widen the area of support. The batting should be covered with a washed, undyed muslin cover that can be removed easily for cleaning.

Even when a hanger is padded for the shoulders of the garment, the weight of the skirt can cause stress at the waistline as well as the shoulder area over the long term. To reduce stress on these areas, a cotton twill tape can be basted into the seam allowance of the waistline. Additional twill strips attached to the waistline support can be slipped over the hanger, like suspenders, to reduce the downward pull.

Finally, a garment hung for storage should be protected by a dust cover that completely envelops the object. Again, a washed, undyed cotton muslin fabric is ideal for this application; plastic "cleaners" bags, which are printed with inks that can rub off, and vinyl garment bags, which are chemically unstable, are not appropriate for storage.

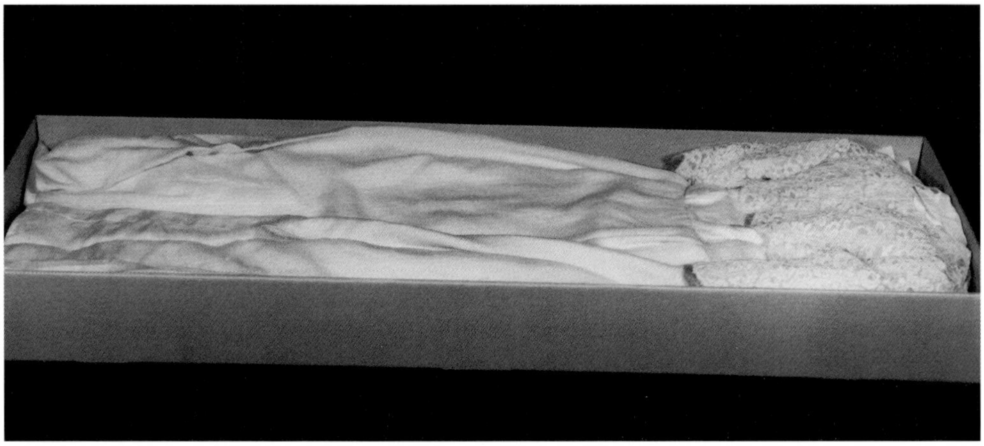

Wedding and christening dresses boxed for storage should be carefully padded with archival tissue to reduce creasing.

Heavily beaded dresses, and those cut on the bias, should be boxed for storage. An archival costume box is generally about eighteen inches in width and sixty inches in length. While the box will accommodate the length of most garments, it probably will be necessary to fold garments along the length to fit them into the box. Archival tissue should be crumpled into the bodice of the dress, inside the sleeves, and into each fold to curve rather than crease the fabric. It is important to avoid making creases, as these areas of stress are prone to splitting as the fabrics age.

There are two simple techniques for storing flat textiles. Small items, such as lace, can be layered between sheets of archival tissue and placed in an archival storage box. Larger items, such as a paisley shawl, can be rolled around an archival rolling tube.

Textiles are best rolled along the warp, which can be identified by fringed or unfinished edges. Place the textile face up on your clean, padded work space. Roll a piece of archival tissue one turn around the archival tube (until the end of the tissue is caught in the roll), and center the textile on the tissue. Roll the textile snugly, interleaving with more tissue as you roll. Finish the roll with a layer of tissue, then place a layer of washed muslin over the entire roll to shield the textile from light and dust. Tuck the muslin into the ends of the tube and secure the middle of the roll with two or three cotton twill-tape ties. Pile textiles, such as velvets and rugs, should be rolled in the direction of rather than against the pile. A textile that has been lined is difficult to roll smoothly. Always roll with the lining facing up to force the lining rather than the textile to absorb any wrinkles.

Routine Care and Maintenance

A fabric weakened by age can easily be torn if handled improperly. When moving a textile from one location to another, it is a good idea to gently fold it (if it is pliable) and place it on a support, such as a piece of archival cardboard. Always plan where you are going to move the object and prepare your work space ahead of time.

Whenever you are working with your textile collection, be sure to remove any jewelry that could catch on loose threads. Wash your hands thoroughly—your skin contains oils, as well as acids, salts, and soils that can easily be transferred to the textile. Work on a clean, well-padded surface. Placing a mattress pad on your dining-room table and covering that with a clean, white sheet makes an ideal work surface.

Never eat, drink, or smoke around your collection objects. Regardless of how careful you are, accidents do happen. A splash of coffee could cause an irremovable stain or cause a dye to bleed. Crumbs could attract insect pests, and the aerosols and particulates in smoke leave a residue on the surface of textiles that is difficult to remove.

Textile objects on display and in storage should be inspected on a regular schedule to check for changes of condition, and especially to see whether they are free of insects. Regular vacuuming is particularly useful in helping to prevent insect infestations of silk and wool objects.

A low-power, hand-held vacuum is the best tool for vacuuming a textile. Textiles with a nap (velvets, pile rugs) should always be vacuumed in the direction of the nap. Lightweight and/or fragile textiles should be vacuumed through a fiberglass

Vacuuming a textile through a screen is an important part of a regular maintenance program for a textile collection. The Textile Museum, Washington, D.C., Acc. no. 6.138

Oversize flat textiles can be rolled for storage on an archival rolling tube. The Textile Museum, Washington, D.C., Acc. no. 6.138

window screen. Carefully place the nozzle of the hose down over the screen, lifting the nozzle and moving it to the next area without "scrubbing" it back and forth.

The schedule of vacuuming will depend on how the textile is used. For example, an Oriental pile carpet used on the floor should be vacuumed routinely, as you would with any floor covering. In addition, the carpet should be turned over and vacuumed from the back at least once each month to remove dirt and grit that has accumulated at the base of the knots. The underside of the carpet also is a likely place for carpet beetles and moths to colonize, so regular maintenance of both sides of the carpet is important. The back side of a Navajo rug hung on the wall is an equally likely location for a pest infestation; therefore, semiannual inspections and annual vacuuming of wall-hung textiles also are essential.

When to Hire a Conservator

Unlike many other kinds of objects that we collect, textiles are frequently used, cleaned, mended, and reused until they bear little resemblance to their former splendor. And, because we are used to undertaking these tasks as part of our daily routine, it may make sense to us to undertake the cleaning and reframing of a sampler executed by great-grandmother. After reading this chapter, you can see that the treatment of a textile is rarely as simple as it first appears.

You can preserve your textile collection by carefully maintaining your objects, rotating the collection on view, and using archival materials for storage. A conservator will recommend treatments based not only on his or her experience with similar objects but also upon careful examination of the piece.

Textiles and costumes are important, not only for their beauty, but also for their meaning in our lives. Despite their fragility, they can be made to last for generations with thoughtful, proper care.

NOTE

1. VELCRO® is a registered trademark for fasteners made by Velcro Companies.

DECORATIVE ARTS

Meg Craft

The decorative arts include almost every material imaginable: ceramics, glass, metal, wood, textiles, leather, ivory, bone, tortoiseshell, horn, pearls, mother-of-pearl, eggshells, plastics, wax, coral, and stone, including rock crystal and gemstones. Artists frequently combine several materials into a single creation of great beauty and opulence. Whether functional or for display only, decorative works are intended to be attractive and often to exhibit high standards of craftsmanship. Aesthetically, the decorative arts must be presented in good condition and repair to fulfill their original intent. The combination of materials makes preservation of the objects difficult due to the possibility of conflicting requirements of individual material. The needs of the most vulnerable material must be given first consideration and a compromise reached to preserve the entire object.

Before (opposite) *and after* (above) *treatment of a broken export porcelain plate with overglaze enamel landscape and gilded border. China, early nineteenth century. Private Collection*

Many of the materials found in decorative-art collections, such as wood, textiles, and stone, are covered in other chapters. Therefore, this chapter will focus on the care and preservation of ceramics and glass, with a brief review of the special needs of several of the other materials.

Ceramics and glass, with some notable exceptions, are fairly stable relative to the environmental elements of temperature, light, relative humidity, and insects. With proper handling, storage, and display, ceramics and glass are among the easiest materials to preserve. The majority of damage to stable ceramic or glass objects is caused by improper handling or storage and display. Therefore, preventive maintenance is critical to insure preservation of one's collection.

Ceramics and Glass

For purposes of conservation, ceramics can be divided into three groups: unfired clay, earthenware or terra-cotta, and stoneware and porcelain. The groups are roughly defined by their degrees of *porosity*, or presence of voids in the clay body, and firing temperatures. The porosity and degree of *vitrification*, or glassiness, achieved in the clay body during firing determine the types of damage that will occur in an accident, what flaws or weaknesses are likely to be present, and, to the conservator, what materials and methods may be appropriate to repair damages to the object.

Unfired clay, such as mud and clay adobe, is water soluble and unstable. It requires special environmental controls and handling that differ from those for fired clay. Underfired clay (fired well below 1000 degrees Centigrade or 1832 degrees Fahrenheit) or archaeological artifacts, such as Tanagra figurines, may behave like unfired clay.

Earthenware is fired at temperatures ranging from 1000 to 1200 degrees Centigrade or 1832 to 2192 degrees Fahrenheit. The temperatures reached render the object water insoluble but do not allow formation of an extensive glassy or vitreous network within the ceramic body. The body remains porous, and water can penetrate. The porous body permits the object to undergo some shock, such as in cooking, without breakage. To make the vessel water impenetrable, glaze must be applied. Glaze forms a vitreous or glassy coating that "fits" over the surface of the earthenware body in a primarily physical, not chemical, bond. In a cross section of an earthenware piece, the glaze would appear as a separate and distinct layer sitting on top of the ceramic body.

Since the glaze is not chemically bound to the clay body, a variety of agents are able to disturb the bond, causing conservation problems. A crackle pattern, often an intentional decorative element, is actually a weakness in the glaze "fit." An impact or scratches from cutlery can cause glaze losses. Losses are especially aggravated if there is a thick, powdery layer of *slip*, or a wash of clay between the glaze and body, as in Pennsylvania-German slipware plates. If the glaze fit is disturbed, the surrounding glaze becomes vulnerable and easily detached.

When a glazed earthenware object breaks, even if the fragments fit cleanly together, it is likely that small chips of glaze will be lost along the breaks. If there is a crackle pattern in the glaze, fragments in the shape of the pattern are likely to detach.

Porosity in earthenware allows moisture to penetrate the ceramic body through unglazed areas, damages, or crackle in the glaze. Stains and repair materials will seep into the body and are prevalent in utilitarian earthenware forms, such as punch pots, teacups, coffee pots, and platters.

Porcelain and stoneware are fired at the highest temperatures for nonindustrial ceramics, in the range of 1200 to 1400 degrees Centigrade or 2192 to 2552 Fahrenheit. There are two types of china; *soft-paste*, or low-fired, china and *hard-paste*, or high-fired, true porcelain.[1] Porcelain clay mixtures, which all contain fine white kaolin clay, feldspar, and quartz, fire to form a very hard, brittle, and relatively nonporous body. Soft-paste china contains other additives to yield a white body but at a lower temperature. When bone ash is added, for example, the ware is called bone china. Soft paste was used in England and Europe in the nineteenth century to imitate Chinese porcelain. Spode, Chelsea, and Bow factories produced soft-paste wares. Because of the lower firing temperatures, soft-paste china may behave more like earthenware for conservation purposes.

Porcelain objects may be fired at high temperatures prior to glazing to promote vitrification.[2] Left without glaze, the resultant ware is called bisque. Looking at a cross section of porcelain, the boundary between the body and the glaze may not be visibly discernible or just barely so. Loss or flaking of high-fired glazes or underglaze decoration does not readily occur as it does on earthenware. For example, few glaze losses are noted on underglaze blue-and-white nineteenth-century Chinese export porcelain. The pattern of decoration is level with the surface, not raised. The high temperatures, however, destroy many glaze colors. Overglaze decoration and gilding, applied in later firings at lower temperatures, are susceptible to loss. Since the overglaze or enamel colors are applied on top of the previously fired surface, the overglaze is raised above the surface and not as well adhered. Gilding, applied for the last and lowest temperature firing, is most fragile and is easily abraded by excessive handling.

Related to ceramics and glass, enamels such as *cloisonné*, *plique-à-jour*, and *champlevé* are made by applying ground-glass powder, or *frit*, to a metal substrate, often copper. While there are several techniques of retaining the frit, basically, firing fuses the frit, which is then ground to level when cool. The enamel often is not attached securely to the metal substrate, which can corrode, causing the enamel to detach or crack. Differing rates of movement caused by temperature variations encourage the enamel and the substrate to separate. Enamels must always be treated by a conservator. They should never be wetted, heated, or cleaned commercially using an ultrasonic bath.

Two majolica plates, with the glaze on the right-hand plate showing damage by heat from an old repair. Left: *Gubbio. Molded dish with seraph, c. 1530–50.* Right: *Gubbio. Molded dish with female martyr saint, c. 1530–40. The Corcoran Gallery of Art, Washington, D.C. William A. Clark Collection*

Environment

While glass and ceramics are fairly stable in a wide range of environmental conditions, extremes or sudden changes in temperature can cause breakage, cracks, or loss of glaze. A common example of damage from sudden changes in temperature occurs from warming porcelain dinner plates. Not only may the porcelain or china develop an extreme crackle pattern in the glaze, but it may break or crack. The worst risk of breakage happens when china is placed in a preheated oven or a hot plate is plunged into cold water. Heating can also occur due to careless placement of incandescent spotlights or photographic lights, especially when working with dark-colored glass, which readily absorbs heat. No valued ceramic or glass artifact should be heated or cooled rapidly.

A more unusual cause of temperature-related damage is refiring associated with dangerous methods of repair or alteration. Signs of refiring, which is seldom successful, are pits or holes in the

Adhesive from tape has pulled the surface off this Chinese ceramic piece. Courtesy of The Center for Conservation and Technical Studies, Harvard Art Museums

glaze and body from the explosion of air pockets and mineral inclusions. *Crawling* or dripping of the glaze also can occur. Blackening or burning may occur locally or overall. Glaze colors can be altered, especially overglaze colors or gilding, which are applied last and at the lowest temperatures.

Damage from freezing may occur in porous earthenwares, which retain moisture. If sufficient moisture is present during freezing, the expanded size of the ice crystals inside the body will cause *spalling*, or general weakness in the ceramic, and repeated freezing cycles can cause the destruction of the artifact. Such deterioration can be seen on soft, porous, unglazed terra-cotta tiles or exterior bricks in historic structures. Freezing can also disturb the physical bond between the ceramic body and the applied glaze.

Stable, intact ceramics and glass are not sensitive to a broad range of relative humidity—from 10 to 65 percent. A concern at relative humidities greater than 60 to 65 percent may be mold growth supported by dust, food, or organic residues from use or repair. Mold can stain ceramics, but fortunately most mold growth is superficial and removable by routine maintenance procedures. Stains left by mold growth are difficult to remove if they have penetrated the body and are under the glaze.

Fired ceramics and glass are damaged at moderate to high light levels only by the associated temperature changes. However, in composite objects, paint or secondary materials may be sensitive to light, and in these cases, the needs of the most sensitive element must take precedence.

Handling and Moving

Ceramics and glass in decorative-art collections must be considered in a different perspective from expendable items intended for daily use. Once an object is part of a collection, its preservation becomes the highest priority. Use poses a risk, both of loss from an accident and of deterioration from wear and handling; hence, utilitarian functions should be eliminated or minimized.

The guidelines for proper handling of ceramics and glass are based on common sense. Proper care does not require sophisticated knowledge of ceramic- or glass-material science to understand the consequences of improper handling. Ceramic and glass surfaces tend to be smooth and slippery. Therefore, they should be handled with clean, bare hands or with latex gloves. Remove jewelry to prevent chips or scratches.

Self-adhesive stickers or tape should not be applied to ceramic surfaces. The adhesives become discolored and very tacky and cause staining as they deteriorate. Some adhesives shrink and become brittle with age. If the strength of the adhesive is significant, weakly adhered glaze or fragile body elements can be pulled off. Gilding on ceramics or glass is readily removed by tape adhesive. The temptation to apply temporary loan numbers, identification information, or sales tickets or to secure broken fragments with tape or stickers, even on a temporary basis, should be resisted. Information can be applied using methods suggested for professional museum registrars.

Fingerprints normally do not cause the permanent damage, staining, or corrosion that occurs on metal artifacts. Exceptions are some lusterware metallic glazes, where handling or contact with specific foods results in surface staining or discoloration. For example, unstable glasses may readily be marked by fingerprints that can disfigure permanently (see p. 106).

When handling ceramic or glass objects, one should completely and uniformly support the weight of the piece, utilizing the center of gravity. Never use handles, spouts, or any extremities to support the main body of an object, such as a teapot. Sections of repair and restoration, which may not be reliable, also should never be used for lifting. Remove loose or detachable parts, lids, stoppers, or stands and wrap separately before handling or transportation. Carry objects in padded baskets, boxes, or carts. If multiple objects are being moved in a single container, insert padding between each item to prevent contact or shifting during movement. Cloth diapers, plastic foam, or crinkled tissue make suitable wrapping material for short moves. Use only conservation-quality materials for long-term packing, and avoid stacking.

Prior to movement of ceramic and glass artifacts, take precautions to prevent accidents. Have an adequate number of people available to aid in the movement of large items or many pieces. Clear the chosen path of obstacles such as throw rugs or door mats. Prop doors open or have a second person available to help negotiate doors, elevators, or stairs, and prepare a clear, clean destination surface before beginning movement. Handle the object(s) over a clean, padded surface rather than over the floor. Appropriate surface padding includes clean cotton mattress pads, short-pile carpet, or closed-cell, stable polyethylene foam.

Storage

Storage facilities should be located in a secure area, away from traffic patterns, where the environment is stable. Storage locations to avoid include closets adjacent to fireplaces or where extremes in temperature occur, such as unheated attics, basements, or barns. Interior spaces are preferable to those with exterior walls.

Make the storeroom, closet, or shelving unit as dust-free as possible, and use dust covers over open shelving units. Patch or caulk cracks in plaster. Finish and seal all construction, gypsum board, concrete block, or plaster. Seal wood with shellac, acrylic latex paint, or water-borne polyurethane varnish. Air out new construction for a minimum of two weeks before use to allow polluting gases to escape.

Ceramics and glass can be safely stored on shelving composed of either enameled steel or sealed solid-wood shelving. Stable, intact ceramics and glass are not particularly sensitive to gaseous vapors or contaminants given off by oil-containing paints, varnishes, or shelving and building materials. Use caution, however, if secondary materials such as silver, copper, or pewter rims, stoppers, or stands are present. Consideration for the most sensitive materials must receive highest priority.

Individual shelves with a lip prevent an object from rolling off during an accident or earthquake. A wide elastic or cloth strip can be retrofitted across the front of almost any shelf; its size depends on the stored artifacts.

Shelves require padding to reduce abrasion and chipping. Closed-cell polyethylene foam, white polyester felt, and heavyweight, acid-free paper can be utilized. In selecting the covering material, several factors must be considered. The stability or center of gravity of the items to be housed may dictate how soft or thick the padding should be. Tall, stemmed goblets will not stand steadily on soft or thick foam, so a thinner acid-free paper or polyester felt might be a better choice. Stacked plates, heavy platters, or serving pieces benefit from resting on thicker, denser products, such as polyethylene foam. Often the underside, rough feet, or rims, such as on some Chinese export ware or unglazed bases, can catch on polyester felt, causing damage. More practical factors of ease and ability to clean the shelf covering, replacement cost, and amount of wear also should be considered.

There are several materials to avoid. Wool felt attracts and harbors insects such as moths and silverfish, which may harm other collection materials. Polyurethane foam is not conservation quality and deteriorates over a short period of time, leaving deterioration products that are sticky and acidic.

Leave enough space around each item to allow handling without threatening adjacent objects. Crowding frequently results in breakage or chipping.

Artifacts should not be stacked unless absolutely necessary. Plates and saucers, which frequently must be stacked, need separators between each item to prevent abrasion and chipping, as the foot rim of a plate or saucer is capable of scratching the glazed surface below. Gilding is particularly susceptible to abrasion. Commercially made separators of cotton flannel, polyester felt, or muslin can be purchased. Rounds of acid-free paper or DuPont Mylar Type D also can be cut to fit the size. The separator should cover the entire upper surface of the plate or artifact.

Stacks of plates should never exceed four to six pieces. Place the larger or heavier items on the bottom and smaller, lighter weight pieces on top. Place repaired pieces on top of the stack *only.*

Display

Ceramics and glass can be displayed in the open or in cases or cabinets. Enclosures reduce dust accumulation and the risk of accidents. Stands or hangers to support plates or tiles must not put pressure on the object or cause abrasion around the edges. Keep edges, corners, and prongs of stands smooth and polished, not sharp, abrasive, or ragged. Cover rough edges with moleskin or felt. Spring-loaded wire hangers are not recommended, particularly if any cracks or repairs are present. Sticky wax can be used to secure artifacts that are slightly unsteady or are subject to minor vibrations.

Lighting should be designed to avoid heating the object, especially glass objects. Locate incandescent spotlights outside of the cases. Internal lighting should only be fluorescent. Ventilation must be provided in either case to prevent heat buildup.

Valuable or irreplaceable objects should never be used for food or flower displays. Insert liners inside to protect the less-valuable object, or consider using silk flowers and artificial food instead of the real things. Use is undertaken with acceptance of the risk of damage or loss.

Maintenance and Conservation

Routine maintenance of glass and ceramics, a regular aspect of collection care that can usually be done by a nonconservator, includes dusting, infrequent wiping or washing, inspection, and proper storage and display.

The least aggressive cleaning should be attempted first. Always dust objects first to remove loose dirt. Leaving loose dirt on the surface during washing creates "mud," which is more difficult to remove. If this does occur, wipe with a clean, soft cloth, such as a cotton diaper that has been dampened with plain, room-temperature water, which should be sufficient to remove light grime.

Dust ceramics and glass with a soft, clean paintbrush or a clean cloth, such as a diaper or Dust Bunny,® which is an electrostatically charged, synthetic cloth. No cleaning sprays, oils, or liquids should be applied or rubbed into the surface. If the surface is rough or highly textured, use only a brush or an air jet. Lint, especially from cotton wool, will become entangled, dangerous, and tedious to remove. If the surface is unstable or damaged, the object should not be dusted and should be housed in a closed environment until professional evaluation can be arranged.

Even with regular maintenance, objects stored or displayed in the open occasionally will require more extensive cleaning than dusting, depending upon the particulates and pollution in the environment. Collections housed in urban centers or where cigarette smoking is permitted will require more frequent cleaning. Display in a case or cabinet reduces accumulations of grime. Most stable, intact ceramics and glass can safely be wiped off or washed in room-temperature water. Exceptions include objects that are repaired or overpainted; unstable objects, such as ceramics contaminated with salts or crizzling glass; unglazed earthenware; and objects with paint, unfired, underfired, or friable glaze or clay bodies. Never wash or submerge objects with materials that are not properly identified. Plaster and gesso can be mistaken for low-fire ceramics, and serious surface erosion will occur upon wetting them. For safety's sake, test all procedures on an inconspicuous area before cleaning the entire surface.

Stubborn or oily soil may require submerging in water. Add several drops of nonsudsing, household-grade ammonia to a sink of room-temperature water. Line the sink with a thick towel and wash only one object at a time to prevent chipping. Objects should not be allowed to soak. Replace the wash water as it becomes soiled, and rinse the objects in clean water immediately. Some conservators recommend adding a small amount of alcohol to encourage water removal. Blot objects with cotton diapers or towels to remove pools and droplets of water and leave to air dry.

Breakage or damage from improper care or an accident cannot be reversed. Damage to a ceramic, or especially a glass object, substantially reduces its monetary value. This loss is permanent even if subsequent conservation treatment minimizes the visibility of the damage. Treatment renders the object more displayable but should never be undertaken solely to restore any decrease in monetary value.[3] Valid considerations for repair are artistic value, historical significance or association, and sentimental value.

In case of an accident, save all fragments, slivers, and chips, no matter how small or insignificant; the fragments should be wrapped individually in tissue but housed together. Information from the accident, including date of accident, number of fragments in the box, finder, and any other pertinent information, should be written on the exterior of the storage container. Normally, as long as the fragments are properly collected and stored, repairs can be done at any future time.

Speed in repair is not necessary; more important is that eventual treatment of valued objects should be undertaken only by professional conservators. Repairs demanding a professional's skills include reattaching broken fragments, any inpainting of losses, removal of water-soluble salts, stain removal, or consolidation of flaking glaze or paint surfaces. The conservator's knowledge of the characteristics of both ceramics and glass and available adhesives and repair materials allows the selection of the safest and most effective treatment procedure. Improper choice of repair materials or methods may cause permanent damage such as staining or loss of decoration or body along or adjacent to breaks. Cosmetically, repairs done with the wrong material may discolor rapidly, appear aesthetically unattractive, or not hold up well over time. Structurally, improper repairs may fail and cause additional breaks or cracks.

Repairs are made primarily to permit display, and many conservation-quality materials are not designed to withstand the rigors of use. As a result, a large portion of a conservator's work is upgrading or redoing old repairs. Conservation materials are continually being improved and superseded by higher quality products and more sophisticated treatment procedures. Ethics and aesthetics of repairs also change over time; thus, conservation treatments must be reversible to the extent that retreatment in the future is possible.

In the past, the choice of materials for repair was extremely limited. Primarily, only natural materials such as shellac, hide glue, dammar, and mastic resins and oils were available. Prior to the

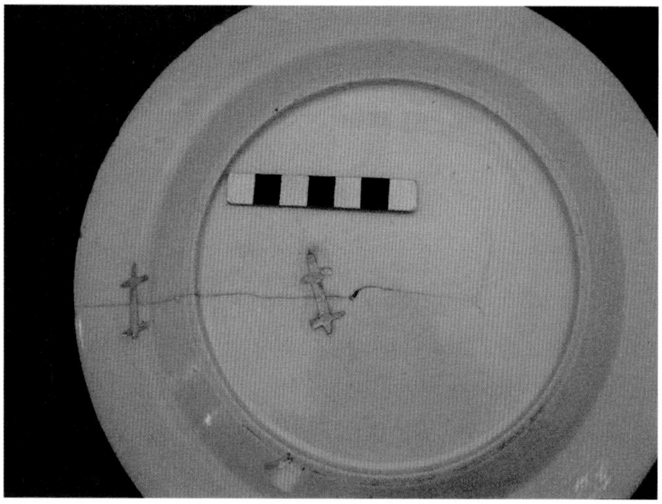

This porcelain was repaired with unsightly iron staple-like rivets sprung into drilled holes.

advent of modern adhesives, rivets or metal staples were used to secure fragments on functional pieces. Rivets are seldom used today due to the permanent damage caused by drilling holes into the ceramic for insertion of the rivet and by the corrosion over time of the rivets themselves.

In the repair of earthenware objects, the porosity of the body helps the conservator determine the proper adhesive to use. The adhesive, which should not penetrate a porous body, must stay on the surface, dry quickly, and remain easily soluble to allow removal. An improperly chosen adhesive that soaks into the body may cause permanent staining by filling the voids to create an optical darkening or by discoloring with age. The degree of permanence depends on the reversibility and/or ease in solubility. Several classes of conservation-quality adhesives, such as acrylics and polyvinyl-acetate resins, can effectively repair many earthenware decorative-art pieces, with the exception of very heavy objects or joins that support a large amount of weight. The repair materials are difficult to handle, and the work should be done by a professional conservator.

The breaks that occur in earthenware are usually rough and jagged in texture and provide a large surface area, making the selection of a relatively weak adhesive possible. In contrast, breaks in porcelain have a smooth, glassy, sometimes conchoidal fracture. The slick porcelain surfaces form weak bonds with the high-quality adhesive resins used in earthenware repair, most of which set by solvent evaporation. Since porcelain is nonporous, solvents are slow to evaporate and the full strength of the bond slow to develop. In order to bond sufficiently to the porcelain, stronger, less readily reversible adhesives, such as epoxies, frequently are chosen. While aging qualities of epoxies have improved over the years, the ideal adhesive for porcelain has not yet been developed.

Due to the methods of manufacture, glass and high-fired ceramics may retain stress within the object. Breakage releases the stress and results in cracks and breaks that are misaligned. This misalignment caused by the release of internal stress is called *springing*. Although the same materials generally are used to repair glass and porcelain, glass repairs are more difficult to disguise due to the difficulty in matching visual characteristics of transparent glass and repair adhesives.

Special Problems

Decorative-art ceramics—especially porous, low-fired wares, such as earthenwares—can be contaminated with water-soluble salts. Sources of salt are frequently related to historic use; for example, solutions of brine or vinegar used for food preservation. Nitrate and chloride salts occur from the use of cachepots, serving pieces, or vases for flower displays or as planters. Chlorides are often left from attempts to bleach ceramics with chlorinated laundry products or, in archaeological artifacts, from burial. Chlorides that are absorbed into the body can be removed by prolonged soaking in water, but it is extremely difficult to remove all of the residues. Even the presence of small quantities of water-soluble salts can wreak havoc on the structural integrity of the body and the attachment of the glaze to the body.

The water-soluble salts exist in liquid form at high relative humidities and change to a solid, crystalline form at low relative humidities. The

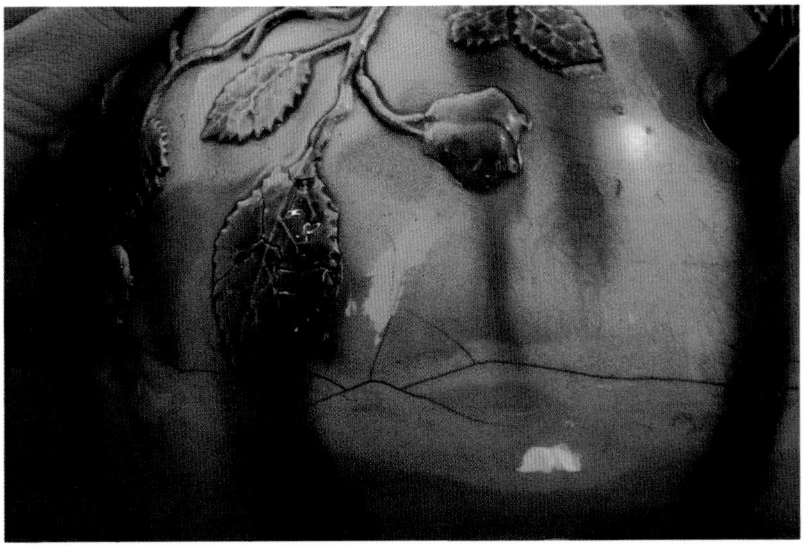

Before and after stain removal from a piece of glazed earthenware. England, early nineteenth century

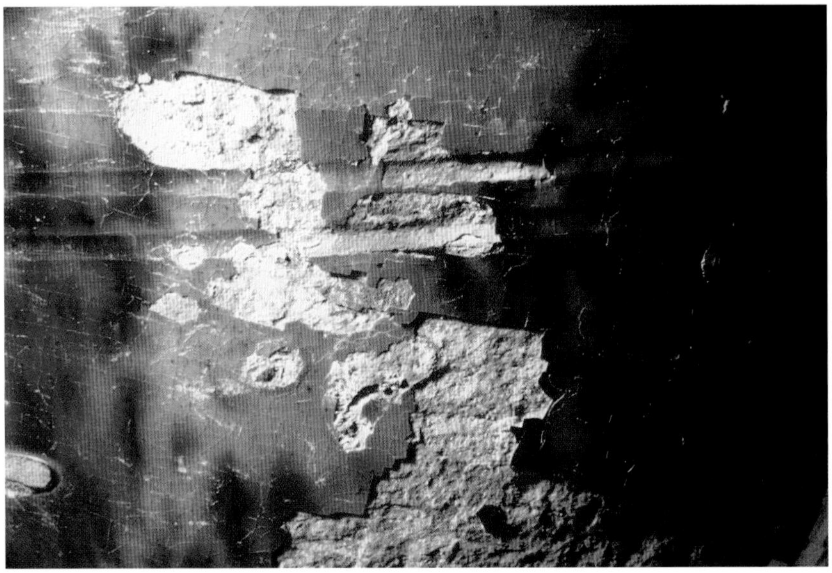

The white efflorescence and spalling body on this detail of a glazed earthenware storage jar was caused by water-soluble salt contamination. American, early nineteenth century

conversion relative humidity is specific to the particular salt. The solid, crystal form is physically larger than the liquid form. The changing physical size and force involved in crystallization causes the ceramic body to crumble and break down. Spalling and exfoliation of the body occur, and the glaze may also be pushed off. Contaminated artifacts require immediate professional treatment and stringent, stable climate control.

Stains commonly occur on ceramics from use with foods, coffee, tea, ale or punch, gravy, and grease. If the glaze on a porous object is crackled or damaged, these contaminants can seep under the glaze and into the body. Stains may also be caused by repair materials that have entered the body. Common offenders are shellac and epoxy, especially on porous bodies.

Stain removal is not assured even with professional conservation assistance. Removal can take two forms. One is actual removal using principles of gravity and evaporation along with cleaning agents, such as nonionic detergents and dilute alkaline solutions with water or organic solvents, either as baths or poultices. These agents may adversely affect inclusions in the body such as iron. Further, movement or solubility of the stain may not be possible, or controlling the direction in which the stain moves may be troublesome and unpredictable. The second method is to bleach or alter the color of the offensive stain with a nonchlorinated bleach, such as hydrogen peroxide. The staining material remains in the body but the color is altered to be less obvious and disfiguring. Occasionally, bleached stains may recur and the color may revert.

Unstable glass occurs due to improper proportions of ingredients in the original recipe. The results of this deficiency or inherent vice are referred to as *weeping* and *crizzling* glass. In weeping glass, the surface of the glass may be damp and highly alkaline. In crizzling glass, the structure of the glass breaks down, causing a small network of fine cracks to appear. Unstable glass is frequently found in cover glasses in cased photographs or on portrait miniatures and in Venetian, English Ravenscroft, Asian, and modern-art glass. Unstable glass can only be preserved by controlling the environment with the guidance of a conservator.

Other Materials

The ceramics and glass discussed so far are inorganic materials and relatively stable. The materials discussed below are primarily organic in origin and extremely sensitive to the environmental factors of light, temperature, relative humidity, pests, and pollutants. Their presence in a decorative-art object demands that the entire object be handled to preserve these fragile and vulnerable materials.

Ivory is technically the tusk of an elephant, but the category can be broadened to include whale, hippopotamus, boar, or other animal teeth. All consist of *dentin*, which grows in a layered structure. Specific identification is done based on the difference in the dentin structure and composition. The composition is both organic and inorganic in nature, making ivory extremely sensitive and reactive. Ivory moves in response to changes in relative humidity. Low relative humidity causes desiccation, shrinkage, and cracking, while high relative humidity will cause warping and swelling. Ivory bleaches when exposed to light and darkens in contact with the skin or oils. Heat fluctuations induce expansion and contraction. Elevated temperatures can result in a series of color changes. The ideal conditions for storage and display of ivory are 45 to 55 percent RH and 65 to 72 degrees Fahrenheit. Conditions should remain constant. Light levels should be kept to a minimum, approximately 5 footcandles. Most solvents and water affect ivory adversely. Professional conservation assistance should be sought to clean or repair ivory.

Bone is used in decorative-art objects, sometimes interchangeably with ivory. The lack of a layered structure and the presence of small pores (which appear black or dark) for passage of nutrients, are characteristics that visually differentiate bone from ivory. Bone is equally sensitive to environmental factors.

Tortoiseshell, horn, and **baleen** are proteinaceous materials that are sensitive to temperature and relative humidity. Environmental ranges comparable to those for ivory and bone are suggested, and light levels should fall below 5 footcandles. Tortoiseshell, baleen, and horn are attractive food sources for many insects, especially dermestids or beetles. The objects often have shallow, roundish holes from insect attack, which in fact can be used to help separate tortoiseshell and horn from plastic substitutes.

Cellulose nitrate, an early plastic under the trademark Celluloid, was used in the late nineteenth and early twentieth centuries to imitate ivory, bone, and tortoiseshell for objects such as comb-and-brush dresser sets, hair combs, desk accessories, buttons, and sewing or manicure kits. Good imitations may be visually difficult to identify, but their chemical characteristics are distinctly different from that of organic materials. Cellulose nitrate is highly soluble in acetone and melts when touched with a hot needle. Bone, ivory, and tortoiseshell are not soluble, and they char but do not melt when touched with high heat. Cellulose nitrate is highly unstable, and its deterioration products are acidic, corrosive, and very flammable. Celluloid artifacts should be stored in isolation to prevent affecting nearby artifacts. Deterioration cannot be reversed or halted, only delayed with proper storage and handling. No treatment is known.

Mother-of-pearl, the iridescent inner layer of a mollusk shell, is often encountered as inlay in decorative-art objects, such as lacquer screens, papier-mâché trays, and paper fans. Pearls are also commonly used. These shell products are composed primarily of calcium carbonate with organic components that are readily attacked by mineral and organic acids. Housing and display materials must be of the highest quality to prevent introduction of formic or acetic acid vapors and other pollutants. Extremes in humidity, especially low relative humidity, are detrimental. The exterior skin or layer of the pearl may become dessicated and peel off. The deteriorated pearl loses its nacreous appearance and looks dull and powdery. Careful handling and moderate environmental conditions can drastically slow the deterioration. Eggshells are similar in composition but are thinner and even more fragile.

Wax is used to create miniature portrait busts, seals, models, and appliqués on wooden polychrome sculpture. The greatest danger to wax is heat. The wax mixtures have low melting points to allow easy manipulation by the artist; hence wax remains soft and is easily marked by contact or handling. No storage materials should come in contact with decorated wax surfaces. Impressions of the storage material or a burnished effect from abrasion may result. Natural-wax mixtures often have additives such as honey or molasses that may encourage mold growth in high (greater than 65 percent) relative humidity. As the wax ages, these plasticizers may migrate or deteriorate, making the wax more brittle and subject to cracking. Wax is also highly soluble in many mild organic solvents found in cleaning products. Wax objects should always be displayed in cases, glazed frames, or other protective covers, and conservation assistance should always be sought for its treatment or display.

NOTES

1. Glass contains many of the same elements found in transparent ceramic glazes but in different proportions in order to be workable and to support itself structurally. For conservation purposes, glass can be repaired using the same adhesives as for porcelain. Repair of stained glass is a specialized field of conservation and should be handled by a professional.

2. Glazed porcelain (or other glazed ceramic ware) may be fired in one process or in two steps, depending on the type of ware being discussed. Neither is more common in antiques.

For a single firing at high temperatures, the air-dried ware is covered with glaze (which often contains clay) before firing. Everything happens in one process in a single firing.

In a multistep firing, the raw, dried porcelain is fired to a high temperature; the resultant ware is called *bisque* or biscuit. Later, the bisque is glazed and refired at lower temperatures, if desired. Lower temperatures allow a broader color palette. The blue in Chinese export porcelain is usually fired at high temperatures, but other colors, such as in the *famille rose, noire,* and *verte* palettes, are destroyed at those high temperatures. Many Western wares are made in multiple firings (delft, majolica). Two firings allow both nonporosity and a wide color palette but are less economical.

3. A well-restored piece may be more easily sold because it can be displayed but the value will be significantly below that of an undamaged item. The only area where breakage is sort of expected or accepted is in antiquity sales (Greek vases, Chinese tomb figures, archaeological material). Broken decorative-art pieces can be almost worthless unless unique or very rare.

METAL OBJECTS

Terry Drayman-Weisser

Since ancient times people have fashioned metal into objects to satisfy their daily needs and to delight the eye. The unique qualities of metal—its luster, color, durability, strength, and ability to be formed by casting or with tools, as well as its intrinsic value—have inspired artists and craftsmen throughout history to create a wide array of artifacts. These artifacts, ranging from coins to sculpture, are admired and collected today. This chapter will guide you the collector in the general care, display, storage, and packing of metal objects. It includes sections on the special needs of objects made of gold, silver, lead, pewter, copper, bronze, and brass as well as special considerations for the care of coins, Japanese metalwork, and outdoor bronze sculpture. It will alert you to danger signals to watch for and let you know when to call in a professional to diagnose or treat your metal objects.

General Care and Preservation

Environmental Conditions

It is useful first to understand why metal objects must be cared for if they are to be preserved. Although metals are generally durable, they are inherently unstable and have a natural tendency to change over time. This is due in large part to the fact that most metals as we know them are not found in nature but begin as ores, stable compounds that resemble rocks and lack the qualities we associate with metals. These ores are gathered or mined and, through various processes, usually involving high temperatures, are converted to metal, which is then shaped into an object by the artist or craftsman. Unfortunately for the collector, the metal immediately begins to convert back to a naturally more stable ore state. We call this process *corrosion* or *oxidation*, one of the most striking examples of which is the rusting of our automobiles. Sometimes, if corrosion is thin, even, and attractive in color, it is called *patina*, which is simply corrosion that is considered desirable. You

Shown opposite are four examples of patinas on bronzes, which can range widely in color and texture. The two on the left have formed naturally during burial. The two on the right were artificially produced for artistic effect. Courtesy The Walters Art Gallery, Baltimore

should not confuse this natural patina with an artificial patina made with chemicals or lacquers intentionally applied to the surface of a metal object by the artist to imitate natural aging or to create special effects, which will be discussed in more detail later.

The collector plays a very important role in prolonging the life span of a metal object, since the rate at which the corrosion of a metal takes place is directly related to its immediate environment. This environment may be your home, a display case, a storeroom, drawer, or wherever you keep your metal objects. In order to preserve a metal object, there are three major factors in the environment that you should be aware of: relative humidity, temperature, and pollution.

Moisture is required for corrosion to take place. Therefore, proper relative humidity for metal objects is as low as possible without going to extreme measures. Forty to 45 percent is considered safe, with 50 percent as the acceptable maximum. If an object has already shown evidence of problems, such as watery or powdery areas—indications of serious corrosion—it should be kept at or below 35 percent RH until a professional conservator can examine it.

Although establishing specific temperature levels for metals is not critical, temperature does affect relative humidity and the rate of corrosion. As the temperature rises, the relative humidity decreases, and vice versa. Therefore, raising the temperature can be used as a tool to control relative humidity. This should be done with caution if the metal is actively corroding since the higher the temperature, the faster the rate of corrosion. Once a consistent temperature has been established in a display or storage area, it should not be allowed to fluctuate widely over short periods of time. A drop in temperature in an enclosed space can cause condensation to occur on metal surfaces. Also, metal can expand and contract with changes in temperature, leading to stresses that may cause existing cracks in the metal to widen.

Most people are aware of the dangers of pollution in the outdoor environment. However, they are surprised to learn that our indoor environment, under certain circumstances, can be just as harmful or even worse for metal objects. Unwittingly we surround ourselves and our collections with natural and man-made products—such as woods, glues, plastics, and dyed fabrics—that emit harmful gases, as well as corrosive acids and alkalis. Many museums are becoming painfully aware of this problem as they build display cases and storage facilities that corrode rather than protect their collections of metal objects.

How, you may be asking, does one know if a material will harm a metal object? Professional conservators can often advise against or for general categories of materials, and the recommendations that follow in this chapter will provide guidance. However, even conservators must perform tests on products since not all ingredients may be known. A simple test—which you can perform—for potential damage from organic acid emissions is to place a small piece of lead, obtained from a hardware store, in the area of concern. If at any time the lead develops whitish patches or spots, the materials in the environment should be examined to find the source of the organic acid contamination.

The best way to prevent serious damage to your metal objects is to examine them on a regular basis and note any changes. If you suspect something is amiss, remove your objects from their current environment and call in a professional for a consultation.

Handling

Aside from corrosion, other common threats to metal objects stem from human carelessness or accidents. Dropping a metal object, allowing it to rub against hard or abrasive materials, even wearing rings while handling it may deform or scratch the surface. Wear clean gloves whenever handling a metal object. Touching with bare hands can deposit potentially damaging salts and oils and permanently etch fingerprints into a polished surface. The fingerprints may not be visible at the time of handling but may show up years later and seriously disfigure and devalue the object. Tape should never by applied to a metal surface since it often creates a mark and leaves a potentially corrosive adhesive residue.

The outward appearance of a metal object may be deceiving when trying to judge its condition and strength. A sturdy-looking object may in fact be brittle due to internal corrosion and easily damaged if not handled carefully. Some metals are inherently brittle. For example, certain bronze mirrors were made in antiquity with higher than usual amounts of tin in the alloy, giving the mirrors a hard surface that would take a high polish and therefore reflect an image well. However, a negative side effect is that these mirrors will shatter if hit or dropped.

Metal objects often undergo internal changes and become brittle with age. In fact, some metal-dating techniques are based on the evidence of these natural changes in the metal structure. Improper restoration or conservation treatment of a metal can cause or increase brittleness. In addition, certain stresses and chemicals can cause cracking. Therefore, treatments of metal objects should be carried out by a conservator who has relevant practical experience and an understanding of metallurgy.

Be aware of loose parts when handling metal objects. Certain types of solder may corrode, creating a weak join, and mechanical joins sometimes work loose and come apart. Parts that become detached should be wrapped in acid-free tissue and placed inside the object or otherwise kept with the object until repairs can be made. Metal objects should never be lifted by projecting parts, even handles, as these parts may be insecure and cause the object to fall. Preferably, objects should be lifted with both hands, with one underneath for support, and carried in a padded basket or cart so that they are protected from scratching, rolling, and falling. Cushioning is best done with acid-free tissue and polyethylene foam sheeting. Cotton wool should never be used as cushioning against the surface of a metal because it can snag on a brittle metal object and cause breakage. In addition, if the texture of the metal or patina is rough, the cotton fibers can become trapped in the surface and disfigure it. Removal of the fibers is tedious, time consuming, and sometimes impossible.

Display

The forms and surfaces of metals can make them the most exciting and beautiful objects to display, inspiring collectors to experiment with dramatic lighting and special mounting techniques. In creating a display environment for metal objects, observe humidity and temperature requirements and avoid materials that will pollute that environment. Enclosing the object in a display case will help keep it free of dust and allow you to establish special environmental controls for objects with specific needs.

Fabric can cushion and aesthetically enhance the display of metal objects. However, there are hidden dangers even here. For example, wool should not be used for long-term display since it contains sulfur, which will eventually attack the metal. Unfortunately, even if a fabric itself is not harmful, the dye, sizing, soil-release agent, fire retardant, or other finishing products may cause damage. It is best to use cotton, linen, or synthetic fabrics after thorough washing and rinsing to remove potentially harmful finishing products.

Special antitarnish papers and cloths can be used in display cases to absorb harmful gases before the pollutants can attack the metal. Corrosion inhibitors that give off vapors should not be used since they have been known to alter the color of the metal in some instances. Because metals conduct heat readily, do not enclose brittle or cracked objects in cases with spotlights that emit high levels of heat. The cycling of high and low temperatures from turning the lights on and off may be enough to cause condensation and dimensional changes in the metal, leading to corrosion and further cracking.

Mounts for metal objects should be sturdy enough to distribute and bear the weight of the object and should touch the object only where it is structurally sound. The mount should not abrade or scratch the metal surface. There should be no sharp edges or burrs at points of contact with the object, and the mount should be padded with a synthetic fiber felt or a thick layer of an acrylic resin, which may be purchased at a good art-supply store. Cover the mounting pins with acrylic resin or a stable plastic tubing such as polyethylene or teflon. Plasticene or oil-based modeling clays often contain sulfur and should never be used in mounts for metal objects. Do not wrap rubber bands around metal since black lines may result, which are often impossible to remove completely. Mounts should be designed to be attached and removed easily without stressing the object. If earthquakes are a possibility in your area, display cases and mounts should be designed with this in mind. Consult a professional conservator for advice since each object may have different needs. In order to prevent accidents, follow the handling recommendations mentioned above when installing the objects in their mounts.

Storage

Good storage is based on common sense and good housekeeping. The storage area should have the same environmental conditions as the display area. Avoid overcrowding as this tends to lead to scratching and accidental breakage. Store an object that is top-heavy or precarious on its side, if this can be done safely; place an object that may roll in a nest of acid-free tissue. Keep the area as clean as possible. If open shelves are used for storage, place acid-free tissue over objects to keep the dust to a minimum. If the objects are wrapped in tissue, label the outside of the tissue for easy identification in order to avoid unnecessary handling.

The storage area should not be near a source of water. If dampness is a problem, install a dehumidifier. The manufacturer or company representative can advise you on models that will meet your specific needs based on the volume of air in the storage area. The dehumidifer should have an automatic cut-off feature for when it is full, and, unless a drain is readily available, arrangements should be made to empty the dehumidifer on a regular basis. Certain salts, such as silica gel, also can be used to control humidity in an enclosed space (see the chapter on Creating and Maintaining the Right Environment).

Metal objects should not be wrapped in plastic except in special circumstances. Some plastics, such as polyvinyl chloride (PVC), give off harmful gases, which form acids in the presence of light and moisture. Over time PVC, as well as other plastics, may deposit sticky substances on metal surfaces. An additional problem with wrapping a metal object in plastic is that moisture can be trapped within and can cause a high relative-humidity environment, leading to corrosion of the metal. Special assistance should be sought from a professional conservator in selecting plastics to be used with metals. Even stable plastic should be ventilated or a drying agent such as silica gel should be placed within the plastic package.

Storage shelves ideally should be made of metal and padded with thin polyethylene sheet foam to protect the objects; however, layers of acid-free tissue or even a washed, synthetic-fiber pad will do. If the metal shelving is painted, the finish should be baked on and no paint or solvent odor should be noticeable. Glass shelves may not be able to bear the weight of metal objects and can cause serious damage if they break. A concern with wood shelves is that they may undergo significant dimensional changes and warping. Therefore, only seasoned wood should be used, if at all, and it should be left in the storage area to acclimate to the conditions there. Wood shelves have collapsed, seriously damaging collections, because the shelves shrank and were no longer held by the shelf supports.

If wood must be used to construct shelves or cabinets, it should be selected carefully. Some woods, including oak, Douglas fir, birch, and beech, among others, produce organic acids. Urea formaldehyde glues used in making many composite wood products, such as particle board, chipboard, and interior-type plywood can give off formaldehyde gas. Not only is this gas harmful to you, but it forms formic acid, which can attack vulnerable metals. If it is necessary to use a composite wood material for storage or display, it is recommended that formaldehyde-free products or marine-grade plywood, some types of exterior-grade plywood, or other products made with less corrosive phenol formaldehyde glues be used. When in doubt, ask the supplier or the manufacturer if the product contains urea formaldehyde glue. If it does, do not use it. Since formaldehyde poses a health hazard, it is likely that more formaldehyde-free materials will be available in the future.

Seal all exposed surfaces of wood products. Self-adhering inert plastic sheeting incorporating a metallic aluminum layer is ideal for this purpose but can be expensive. Otherwise, coat the wood with at least two layers of a liquid sealer or varnish.

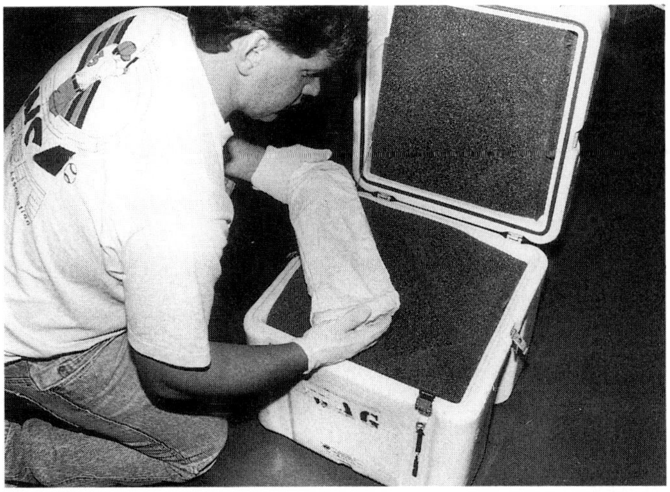

A fragile metal object is first wrapped in acid-free tissue, then placed in a cutout in soft foam within a gasketed, climate-controlled, molded polyethylene packing case for shipment. Courtesy The Walters Art Gallery, Baltimore

These sealers, as well as materials used to join, finish and decorate storage and display areas, should be approached cautiously. White glues such as polyvinylacetate emulsions release acid products over time, and sealers, varnishes, and paints may give off formaldehyde or other pollutants. Oil-based or alkyd paints, linseed oil, and oil-borne polyurethanes especially should be avoided. Latex paint is better than oil although not ideal; acrylic paints and primers tend to be safer. Some commercial water-borne polyurethane varnishes are currently being tested by conservators and have shown promise. Because products are constantly being "improved" by their manufacturers, one found to be safe by conservators today may have new additives making it unsafe tomorrow. It is worth calling a conservator for the most up-to-date information on products. Whatever the products ultimately used, let display or storage cases air out for at least two weeks before any objects are closed up inside in order to allow solvents, moisture, and plasticizers to escape.

Packing and Moving

When it becomes necessary for an object to be transported from one place to another, it should never be slipped into a pocket or purse or carried loose either on the seat or in the trunk of a car. To protect an object from accidents, the elements, and temperature and relative humidity changes, always use proper packing techniques, keeping in mind all of the previous cautions regarding selection of materials. If the object is large, complex, or if you are unsure of the best way to pack it, call a conservator for advice.

A metal object should be wrapped first in soft acid-free tissue to protect it from abrasion. Separate parts, such as lids, should be wrapped individually, although they may be included in the same packing box. It is a good idea to wrap antitarnish cloth or paper around the tissue-wrapped object for added protection from pollution. Washed cotton or nylon bags of a desiccating agent such as dry silica gel should be included within the packing materials to prevent condensation on the metal surfaces from temperature and relative-humidity changes during transport.

Packing materials should not give off gases or retain moisture and should provide cushioning and protection, as well as thermal insulation. The materials should be selected based on the specific object and the method of transport. Use only resilient materials so that voids caused by compression do not form in the packing container. After wrapping in acid-free tissue, a small lightweight object may be packed in a soft, stable polyethylene foam, while a large or heavy object may require a combination of soft and hard foams to absorb shock and provide cushioning. Never pack a fragile or lightweight object in the same container with a heavy one. A fragile object or one with projecting parts may be packed more safely by cutting a cavity into the foam in the shape of the object, providing enough space within the cavity to allow the tissue-wrapped object to be inserted and removed without stress.

Polyethylene and polystyrene foams are safe to use, although polystyrene may permanently compress when used with heavy objects, allowing movement of the object within the packing case. Both foams provide good thermal insulation and come in a variety of densities and forms. Do not use polyurethane foam with metals; it is unstable and can break down quickly under certain circumstances, giving off potentially damaging products. No excelsior or shredded-newspaper products should be used due to their acidity and their propensity to retain moisture and support mold growth. Avoid rubberized hair and other rubber products since they can give off sulfurous gases that can cause corrosion. Although liquid products that undergo chemical reactions to create expanding foams, such as polyurethane foam, are tempting to use since they can be made to conform exactly to the shape of the object, they can be extremely toxic, difficult to control, and can generate levels of heat great enough to cause damage as they set. The packing of complex, fragile, or heavy objects is best left to a professional since the choice and amounts of packing materials may be critical to the safety of the object.

The packing container should be strong and waterproof. If the object is traveling as checked baggage on a plane, the container must be built to withstand rough handling, vibration, and thermal changes. If the packing container itself is not waterproof, the inside should be lined with polyethylene plastic sheet. Within this waterproof package, silica gel conditioned to 35 to 45 percent RH should be placed in a washed cotton or nylon bag near the object to protect it from fluctuations in relative humidity. Keep the gel-filled bag in a sealable plastic bag until it is ready to be packed. Mark the packing container "fragile" and indicate which direction is up; however, always pack the object so that it is not damaged if it is turned in the wrong direction, since this may happen. To facilitate lifting, the container should have handles if it is too large to carry in one hand. Reusable molded double-wall polyethylene packing containers with water-tight gaskets are ideal for most metal objects.

Care of Specific Metals

Gold

Gold is one of the few metals found in a metallic rather than an ore state in nature; it is soft and malleable and does not corrode. However, the gold in objects is rarely pure. It has usually been mixed, or alloyed, naturally or intentionally, with other metals such as silver and copper. These additions to gold are what corrode, often covering the surface with their corrosion products and, through internal corrosion, causing the gold to become brittle.

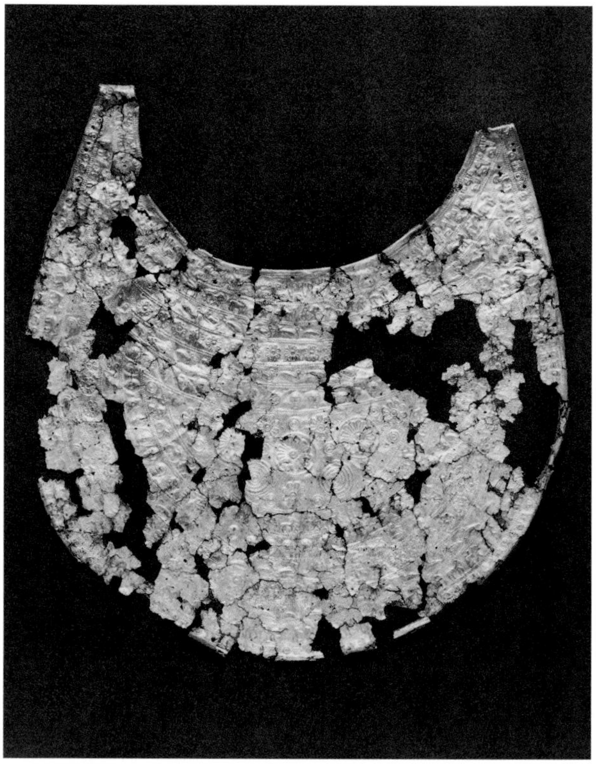

Ancient metal may be very brittle and easily cracked or broken. This Etruscan gold pectoral from the seventh century B.C. has suffered from internal brittleness. Courtesy The Walters Art Gallery, Baltimore

All gold objects must be handled carefully to prevent scratching and deformation of the metal. Ancient gold may be very brittle and need special care and support to prevent cracking and breaking. Materials that corrode the alloying elements silver and copper, which are discussed in the following sections, should be avoided with gold as well.

The beauty and luster of gold encourage us to remove accretions and corrosion that obscure its surface. However, when gold has been excavated from an archaeological site, it is not always wise to remove the corrosion. Sometimes the metal cannot be cleaned without the risk of damage. In addition, the corrosion and accretions may contain clues to the context and use of the object during ancient times, or may provide a key to the object's provenance or proof of its authenticity. All of this information may be lost through cleaning. If a

The sixth-century Byzantine silver chalice on the left was intended to be bright and polished, while the nineteenth-century Tiffany vase in the center was oxidized intentionally to a light gray. The covered vessel on the right was intended to be bright but is now heavily tarnished. Courtesy The Walters Art Gallery, Baltimore

decision has been made to remove corrosion, or if you are in doubt about what should be done, contact a professional with training in archaeological conservation.

While gold objects are on display or in storage, loose dirt and dust can be removed with a soft, dry watercolor brush. Apply ethyl alcohol, which can be obtained at most drugstores, with cotton swabs or a clean soft cloth to remove oily or greasy deposits, taking care to avoid scratching. If corrosion develops, do not polish the gold, since most polishes will scratch the surface and wear away surface detail. Contact a conservator to identify the cause of the corrosion and to remove the corrosion from the gold surface, if necessary. Repairs to gold objects should always be carried out by a professional.

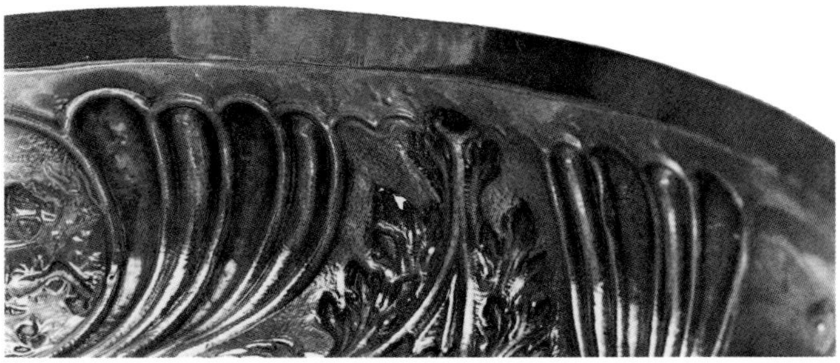

Not only have engraved lines been worn away by excessive polishing of this silver sugar box, but in one section the silver has worn away completely. Sugar box (detail) by Edward Winslow, 1702. Courtesy The Henry Francis du Pont Winterthur Museum

Silver

Silver is also a soft, malleable metal and is often alloyed with copper to lower its melting point and to make it harder. A common alloy is sterling, which is 92.5 percent silver. Like gold, silver objects must be handled carefully to prevent scratching and deformation of the metal. Silver

Removing Tarnish from Silver

Supplies:

- Precipitated chalk (precipitated calcium carbonate), *not* ground chalk or ground limestone
- Deionized or distilled water
- Mild nonionic detergent such as Igepal or Triton X-100, or anionic detergent Orvus WA Paste
  Commercially available substitutes: Ivory Liquid or Joy
- Diapers or other soft cotton cloths
- Cotton swabs with wood or cardboard sticks
  Surgical cotton (nonsterile is suitable and less expensive) or 100-percent cotton balls (no synthetics)
- Thin polyethylene or other plastic wrap
- Protective gloves such as latex or uncolored vinyl
- Soft, natural-bristle brush such as Chinese hog bristle

Note: If old coatings are present, a professional conservator must be consulted.

Mask water-sensitive areas of silver objects such as wood or ivory fittings with plastic wrap before attempting to remove tarnish. Make a slurry (a suspension of particles in liquid approximating the consistency of thick cream) of precipitated chalk in distilled or deionized water and apply in small quantities to tarnished silver with cotton and cotton swabs. Polish gently and in a circular manner, as excessive force results in scratching of the surface. Discard the cotton as soon as it is soiled to minimize scratching, as corrosion particles trapped in the cotton can be very abrasive. Cotton-swab sticks can also scratch silver surfaces. (Denatured alcohol may be used in place of or in conjunction with water to remove tarnish more quickly, but it produces more scratching of silver surfaces and requires ventilation via an exhaust system or fume hood.) A minimum of precipitated chalk should be used.

Remove residual chalk by washing surfaces with a very dilute solution of detergent in deionized or distilled water using a soft, natural-bristle brush of the type used for oil painting, followed by rinsing in deionized or distilled water. Dry wet surfaces with soft, absorbent cloths. Dry areas where water may be trapped with compressed air if available.

It is important that water not remain on the surface or in crevices for prolonged periods of time. Remaining traces of dry chalk may be removed with a soft-bristle brush.

Information courtesy Arthur Beale, Research Laboratory, Museum of Fine Arts, Boston

especially should not be touched with bare hands, since fingerprints can become etched into the surface.

Silver objects found in archaeological contexts are usually corroded and brittle. In fact, it is not unusual for these objects, or parts of them, to be completely converted to corrosion, with the shape retained in the corrosion products. Therefore, ancient silver should be handled with special care and should be supported to prevent cracking and breaking. As with gold, seek professional advice before removing burial corrosion and accretions.

Historical and modern silver objects, those which have not been found in an archaeological context, are generally malleable and seldom suffer from deep-seated corrosion. However, silver, whether it has been buried or not, is very susceptible to surface tarnishing, or blackening, from sulfurous gases. Therefore materials for display, storage, and packing should be selected carefully. In particular, avoid rubber and protein-based materials. Antitarnish papers and cloths containing activated carbon or silver salts give added protection in display and storage as well as in packing cases. Although light generally is not a problem for metal objects, it can heat the metal surface and increase the rate of tarnishing. Therefore, place display cases carefully—away from direct sunlight—to avoid this problem.

Dust, dirt, and greasy deposits may be removed from silver in the same fashion described for gold. Leave more complex cleaning of archaeological silver and repairs to all types of silver objects to the professional conservator. If historical or modern silver becomes tarnished, it is best to polish it with precipitated chalk mixed with distilled water, deionized water, or ethanol (see box for step-by-step instructions). Do not use polishing products that contain tarnish inhibitors; undesirable effects have been noted in some cases. After cleaning, all traces of polish must be removed from the surface; it is not only unsightly but also can promote new corrosion.

It is important to prevent further tarnishing of silver since polishing removes silver metal and repeated polishing can result in the loss of engraved lines and other details. During the manufacture of silver objects, areas of dark copper oxide—called *fire scale*—sometimes form beneath the surface. Repeated polishing may also uncover these dark patches, and additional polishing only makes them look worse. Silver-plated objects, such as Sheffield plate and electroplated silver, should be polished only sparingly, as the silver will be worn away, revealing the base metal beneath.

Keep in mind that some silver, especially from the late nineteenth century to the present, has been darkened intentionally by the artist. In order to preserve the maker's intent, this silver should never be polished. If in doubt, consult an art historian or museum curator for an opinion on whether or not your silver may have been darkened originally.

It is not a good idea to use commercial silver-dip solutions or chemical reduction techniques involving immersion in chemical salts, acids, or alkalis or metal granules or foils to remove tarnish. Silver-dip solutions are toxic and do not always give the desired results. Both silver-dip solutions and chemical reduction techniques can cause disfiguring plating on the silver surface and can result in the object looking overcleaned or pitted. If the silver is decorated with *niello*, a black material usually composed of metal sulfides, these treatments will damage it.

Tarnishing of silver may be inhibited by coating the object with a stable, reversible resin or lacquer. This should only be done by someone with experience because improper coating techniques can lead to severe corrosion problems. A good resin coating will protect a silver object for many years, if it is handled carefully and the object is never used for any purpose but display. The coating should be removed and replaced if it begins to look yellow or gray or if the silver appears to be tarnishing through the coating. If the coating becomes scratched or otherwise damaged, the object should be recoated immediately, since the newly exposed metal surface will corrode deeply and may become impossible to clean.

Lead and Pewter

Although lead objects are not commonly collected, many other metal objects contain lead as an alloying element. Old pewter, usually a mixture of lead and tin, and leaded bronze are two examples. The precautions for lead apply equally to other metals alloyed with lead.

Lead and leaded pewter are soft metals and are easily scratched or dented. With age, an even gray oxide film normally develops on their surfaces, a look most collectors consider desirable. This film is protective and should not be polished off. Do not handle lead and pewter with bare hands. If repairs are necessary, a professional conservator should carry out the treatment.

Lead and its alloys are particularly susceptible to attack by organic acids, which can be found in wood and paper products, paints, varnishes, fabrics, and many other materials. Since it is difficult to know in advance what materials will affect lead adversely, it is wise to carry out a preliminary test on the environment using a sacrificial piece of lead as described earlier in this chapter. Afterward, examine the objects on a regular basis for white, powdery spots, which may indicate contamination.

If evidence of corrosion is found, call in a professional conservator to examine the objects and to test the suspect material.

Britannia metal, a mixture of tin, antimony, and copper, came into use as a substitute for leaded pewter in the mid-eighteenth century. This nonleaded modern pewter often can be distinguished by its brighter, harder, and more corrosion-resistant surface, which rarely requires anything more than dusting with a clean soft brush and wiping with ethyl alcohol to remove greasy deposits.

Copper, Bronze, and Brass

Copper is a soft metal that can be easily scratched or deformed. Various metals have been added to copper throughout history to change its properties, for example, to lower its melting point so that it could be more easily cast, to increase its corrosion resistance, to make it harder, or to alter its color. When tin is the major additive to copper, the resulting alloy is called bronze. When zinc is the major additive, it is called brass. These three copper-based metals—copper, bronze, and brass—will be discussed together here as *copper alloys*.

Copper alloys are very susceptible to corrosion and are especially sensitive to ammonia, acids, strong alkalis, chlorides, and sulfide gases. Touching with bare hands can leave potentially corrosive deposits. On polished surfaces fingerprints may become etched in and be difficult or impossible to remove. Zinc in brass may be attacked by acidic and alkaline substances, leaving behind discolored, weakened metal. Heating brass even to relatively low temperatures can vaporize the zinc, changing the color of the surface from yellow to a coppery red. Other elements, that may have been added to copper alloys, lead, for example, may be vulnerable to organic acid vapors. It is especially important that the collection be examined on a regular basis in order to note any changes in a timely fashion.

Ancient copper alloys present special problems. During burial they can be converted relatively quickly to corrosion products, and often during archaeological excavations only green stains are found in the earth, indicating where the object had been. When copper alloys do survive burial, they are often brittle, covered with corrosion, and contaminated with chloride salts from the ground. These chloride salts can cause a type of corrosion so damaging and disfiguring that it is referred to as *bronze disease;* it is one of the major worries of the collector of archaeological copper-alloy objects.

Bronze disease, which is characterized by the eruption of powdery, light green spots, is activated when a particular copper-chloride corrosion product combines with oxygen and water. To prevent the reaction, the chloride, oxygen, or water must be eliminated or significantly reduced. Removal of the copper chloride is difficult, and removal of the oxygen is impractical; however, removal of enough water to inhibit the corrosion reaction is possible by lowering the relative humidity to below 35 percent. All ancient copper alloys should be displayed and stored at 35 percent relative humidity since it is easier to prevent bronze disease than to cure it. If the symptoms of bronze disease are observed, call an archaeological conservator at once; serious damage can be rapid.

In general the cleaning of copper alloys that once were buried should be limited to the removal of dust, dirt, and other modern deposits. Cleaning can be done with soft brushes, either dry or dampened with ethyl alcohol. Any removal of corrosion should be done by an archaeological conservator. If the corrosion is stable, it can be left alone or selectively removed to improve the object's appearance or to reveal hidden detail. If the corrosion contains remnants of textiles, textile impressions, or other information about the past history of the object, leave the evidence in place or document it before removal. It is important to note that removal of all corrosion from an ancient copper alloy may result in an aesthetically unpleasant surface, one that is pitted and eaten away, as well as the loss of original elements, such as gilding, enamel, inlays, niello, and decorative lines. Generally, smooth, even corrosion layers, or patinas, are considered more desirable than clean metal surfaces. Do not be lured into removing corrosion from your objects with home-style recipes. It is difficult to correct well-intentioned but misguided cleaning attempts, which often devalue an object.

This ancient bronze ring suffers from bronze disease, a light green powdery corrosion caused by contamination from chlorides in the soil during burial. Courtesy The Walters Art Gallery, Baltimore

Historical and modern copper-alloy objects do not pose some of the severe corrosion problems common to ancient objects. They are, however, just as susceptible to contaminants in the display and storage environments and to damage from improper handling.

It is unusual, but not impossible, for a historical copper-alloy object to develop bronze disease. The chloride contamination may come from a variety of sources, such as handling with bare hands, salt-laden air, and cleaning solutions. A correct diagnosis must be made by a professional conservator since similar symptoms can be caused by other phenomena. For example, a white or light green product on a copper alloy surface may be caused by salts migrating with moisture from a sculpture's internal ceramic core and may be incorrectly identified as bronze disease. Treating this problem as bronze disease would be inappropriate and unnecessary.

Cleaning of historical and modern copper alloys must be approached cautiously because artificial patinas and colored lacquers, waxes, or paints may have been applied by the maker to create special effects. These are usually thin layers on the metal surface and can be disturbed or removed by abrasives, chemicals, and some solvents. Dry cleaning may be done safely with a

This Japanese metalwork box exemplifies the use of metals, alloys, and colored patinas on the surface to create an imaginative design. Abrasive cleaning techniques would remove the thin patinas and destroy the intent of the artist. Courtesy The Walters Art Gallery, Baltimore

clean soft brush to remove loose dirt and dust. Use ethyl alcohol to remove fingerprints and greasy deposits, but only after the solvent has been tested with a cotton swab in an inconspicuous area to be certain that it does not remove original coatings.

In the case of most historical and modern copper-alloy objects, it is appropriate and aesthetically acceptable to let a natural patina or surface oxidation film develop. However, if polishing is necessary and no intentional patina or surface treatment is present, the metal may be cleaned with precipitated chalk in the same manner as for silver. All polish residues must be removed afterward. In order to keep the surface bright, the object should be professionally lacquered with a clear, reversible resin. If the lacquer film breaks or discolors, replace it with a new coating. If a coating is not applied, protect the object with antitarnish cloth or paper.

Special Categories of Metal

Coins

Most coins are composed of gold, silver, copper alloys, or are plated with gold or silver. The precautions and care techniques mentioned earlier for these metals apply equally to coins. Many coin collectors prefer to buy uncleaned coins since the value of a coin can be decreased by improper cleaning. If cleaning is necessary, seek the guidance of a conservator. Some collectors prefer to clean coins themselves; however, there are serious health hazards associated with some of the cleaning reagents used for coins and safety precautions should be taken seriously. Generally, collectors prefer to store coins in plastic envelopes so that the coins can be easily viewed without being handled. Avoid polyvinyl chloride (PVC) plastic for this purpose. DuPont Mylar Type D, a polyester plastic, is ideal due to its stability and transparency.

Japanese Metalwork

The Japanese are known for their mastery of metalworking and coloring techniques, resulting in beautiful and imaginative blades, armor, and decorative objects. The unique quality of this work is enhanced by the subtle variations on the surfaces achieved through the use of various metals and alloy compositions, etchants, chemical patinas, and lacquers. These subtleties may easily be lost through a lack of understanding of the intent of the maker combined with overzealous cleaning. Even mild polishing may alter forever the beauty and value of the original work. Never touch the metal with bare hands, and clean only with a soft, dry brush or cotton cloth to avoid damaging or scratching the surface. In addition, steel blades require special maintenance. For a demonstration of proper maintenance techniques, as well as any additional treatment, contact a conservator who has had extensive experience with Japanese metalwork.

Outdoor Bronze Sculpture

Collectors of outdoor bronze sculpture will find themselves in a constant battle with the natural elements, pollution, and vandalism. Some of these problems can be avoided by choosing carefully the site for installation.

Sculpture should be kept clear of any overhanging trees or shrubs. Vegetation can scratch a sculpture and can also be a source of moisture, sap, and droppings from nesting birds, which may disfigure and corrode the surface. The sculpture should not sit directly on the ground but should be separated from it by an impermeable material. Otherwise, salts from ground water, fertilizers, snow removal, and dog urine may attack the base of a sculpture, or the salts may migrate through a porous material to attack the bronze.

As soon as a sculpture is placed in an outdoor location, protect it from the elements by a stable, reversible coating. Otherwise, in a very short period of time, the surface of the sculpture, and any patina applied by the artist or foundry, will become disfigured through reactions with gases, salts, and acid rain. The choice of a coating should be determined by a conservator based on the particular problems and environment of the sculpture, as well as aesthetic considerations. The coatings most recommended by conservators are reversible synthetic resins and waxes. Often wax is applied over an initial resin coating. This combination gives greater protection because the wax protects the

This previously unmaintained bronze by nineteenth-century French sculptor Antoine-Louis Barye has been damaged by pollutants in the outdoor environment. Mount Vernon Square, Baltimore

This bronze statue of Harvard University's founder, John Harvard, by Daniel Chester French, is beautifully maintained. Gift of Samuel James Bridge

more easily broken resin coating—an important point since, once the coating is broken, corrosion in that area can be more severe than if no coating were present. Also, a wax coating can be easily and economically maintained.

Whatever coating is chosen, it must be diligently maintained. The initial coating should be selected and applied by a conservator who can then train you to maintain your sculpture. Inspect the sculpture periodically for breaks in the coating, corrosion, and other problems. At least once a year, preferably on a warm day, wash the sculpture with water containing a few drops of a nonionic detergent, rinse, and allow to dry. If a wax coating is present, recoat at this time using the mixture recommended by your conservator. Every five years (or immediately, if problems develop) a conservator should be called in to examine the sculpture and to determine whether the coating should be removed and reapplied or if other treatment is necessary.

If an outdoor bronze sculpture has already corroded, treatment may be required. It is wise to consult several conservators before deciding on a treatment, since opinions vary as to what is appropriate for outdoor sculpture, from simple washing and waxing to complete removal of corrosion by various techniques followed by coating. Once the bronze has been treated, maintain it by periodic inspection and annual coating as described above.

STONE OBJECTS

George Segan Wheeler

Nature always gets her way, and often it is a way of great beauty. Take the rock and mineral kingdom, whose splendor and variety never cease to astound the eye. A walk through the geology section of any major natural-history museum quickly reveals millions of years of nature's plenty. Across the much shorter expanse of man's history, virtually all of these geological materials have in one form or another found their way into art objects, ranging from the delicate soapstone of many ancient cylinder seals to the massive granite monolith of Mount Rushmore. In fact, some of our earliest records of man's creative impulse are preserved in stone, and these prehistoric periods are collected under the name Stone Age. The care of stone objects from these earliest times to the present day is the subject of this chapter.

Salt efflorescences—the white powder appearing on the surface of this brownstone—often appear in winter when the air is driest.

When we talk about stone as a material—not just as an art material—we often speak of its *mineralogy.* Nature has provided us with thousands of minerals with many different properties. It is an unfortunate coincidence, for example, that much of our cultural heritage has been carved in limestone or marble whose primary mineral component is *calcite*. Calcite is soluble in acid, and the acid rain produced by the burning of so-called fossil fuels is literally dissolving our visual history. Throughout history, stone has been used by poets and writers as a metaphor for permanence, yet our modern industrial environment has eroded much of our stone and sent poets in search of other metaphors. It would seem that indeed we live in a world where nothing is permanent.

Routine Care

Knowledge of a stone's mineralogy is important with respect to more than just acid rain. This information can support provenance or authentication studies, it can help guide conservators in establishing proper conservation treatments, and it can guide you as the collector in

Opposite:
The artist Barbara Segal has used nature's geological plenty and variety to great advantage in Smoking Jacket. 1989. *Marble and onyx, serpentine. 38 x 24 x 4"*
Collection the artist

The crystallization of salts can cause irreversible damage to stone objects. Sedimentary rocks such as the limestone shown above are susceptible to severe deterioration by salt action.

taking the necessary precautions in handling, storing, and displaying your stone objects. Soft materials like steatite (often called soapstone, which consists of the mineral talc), chlorites, alabaster, and marble can easily be scratched in handling. Fingernails and even some synthetic fibers also can scratch these stones. Such materials should be carried and examined in cotton-felted boxes or at least cotton-felted cloths. More durable materials should be handled similarly, but these softer minerals require "kid glove" treatment.

Speaking of gloves—clean white cotton gloves should be worn at all times when handling stone objects. Stones are more or less like sponges; frequent handling will allow hand oil to soak into and darken objects, and these oils can be difficult to remove. Gloves can also prevent fingernails from scratching softer stones. If gloves are not available, wash and dry your hands before picking up or touching stone objects.

The same spongelike quality—called *porosity*—that allows oils to penetrate also gives access to airborne dust and dirt, which eventually can become entrapped; these particles can be even more difficult to remove than hand oil. All stone objects are susceptible to such dirt and dust, but the more porous stones, such as lavas, tuffs, and some limestones and sandstones, are particularly susceptible. Routine feather dusting and vacuuming can reduce or prevent dust and dirt buildup: First, dust lightly with the wispy part of the feather, taking care not to scratch the object with the feather's hard backbone; then, vacuum with a soft-bristle attachment by moving the attachment lightly over the surface, being careful not to press the bristles into the surface. By all means avoid rubbing the surface of any stone object with dry cloths; rubbing creates static electricity, which captures yet more dust from the air. When kept in storage, large and small objects alike should be wrapped individually but loosely in polyethylene to prevent excessive buildup of dust and dirt.

Environmental Control

For display and storage, stone objects generally allow more latitude in temperature and relative humidity than most other mediums. Temperatures ranging from 60 to 75 degrees Fahrenheit and relative humidities from 35 to 60 percent *can* be acceptable. The two major risks to stone objects at the extremes of relative humidity are the drying of clays, which can cause cracking, at the low end and the promotion of biological growth at the high end.

In all cases, stability of relative humidity is of paramount importance, but it is even more crucial if salts are present. Objects of archaeological origin are the most likely to bear salts. Even small fluctuations in relative humidity can cause salts to alternately crystallize and go into solution, called *crystallization cycles*, and these cycles cause severe and continual damage. If salts are present—as evidenced by powdering of the stone surface or the appearance of tiny white crystals on the surface known as *efflorescence*—they should be identified by a conservator or scientist. Often salts cannot be removed without damage to the object; identification of the salts will help to establish the relative humidity conditions to produce the least damage. The underlying and important advice here is to have your objects carefully examined when you are considering purchase and to keep a sharp eye for the appearance of powdering surfaces or efflorescences once you own them. Efflorescences tend to occur during the winter when ambient air is often dry and is further dried by heating. With luck,

Sometimes referred to as the "Mobile Madonna," this Virgin and Child *is moved at least twice a year at The Metropolitan Museum of Art, New York, for the installation of the Baroque Christmas tree. It has its own base with wheels to facilitate moving without damage.*

no salts will be present and 50 percent will be a good ambient relative humidity to aim for.

Light presents few problems for stone objects, which are entirely inorganic and therefore do not suffer degradation by high-energy ultraviolet light. The paint of polychromed stonework is, however, susceptible to UV degradation (see also the chapter on the care of paintings), and care should be taken to filter the UV component of natural or fluorescent light. These paint coatings should not experience low or fluctuating relative humidity due to their tendency to embrittlement and consequent detachment.

Packing and Moving

We have touched upon the issue of how stone objects can be damaged: collecting hand oil, dust, or dirt, and scratching. By far the most damage to stone objects occurs during moving. This damage is the result of the failure to understand two material properties of stone: First, stone is very heavy—surprise! A cubic foot of water weighs about 62 pounds (136 kg) while the same volume of most stones weighs upwards of 160 pounds (352 kg). Second, stone does not bend (it breaks). Thus, stone objects should *never* be lifted by their extended parts, such as arms. In packing stone objects for transport, all parts—and again, particularly extended parts—must be supported by the packing materials. *Any* movement of these parts will cause breakage. The containers themselves must also not be flexible. Large flat objects such as tabletops (with or without a packing crate) should be moved on edge; the slightest flex in the container or stone will result in a complete fracture of the stone. Objects made of very porous stone such as lava (scoria) and tuff can be mechanically weak and quite difficult to move without damage. In general, don't move objects unnecessarily, and, if you must move large objects frequently, create a platform that itself can be moved with the object on it. Employ professional riggers for moving large objects, and not just any rigging company but one specializing in art objects. Experienced packers—even for small objects—will reduce breakage during transport.

Hazards to Outdoor Sculpture

Outdoor stone objects present a special set of problems. No longer can the environment be controlled at will; therefore, whenever possible, objects should remain indoors. It bears repeating that objects of limestone or marble, and even some sandstones, which contain calcite, are highly susceptible to acid rain. The telltale signs of acid-rain damage are loss of sharpness in carved details—letters carved into the stone by the sculptor are always a good barometer; granulation or "sugaring"—look for grains of the stone around the object's base; and the formation of black *gypsum* crusts. To physically shelter objects from direct rainfall will dramatically increase their lifetimes, but this kind of protection will not *entirely* eliminate the effects of acid rain.

Acid rain is but one problem faced by porous stone objects in temperate environments. Because freezing water can cause catastrophic damage to the more porous stones, a stone object should be physically isolated from its support environment upon installation in order to avoid drawing moisture from the ground or base into the stone. Support should consist of a concrete or granite base with lead spacers set between the base and the object. The lead spacers will distribute the weight evenly (remember, stones are heavy and don't bend) and prevent the transmission of water into the object. In general, granite is a better support material than concrete because it is less porous and concrete often contains or develops salts, which ultimately can be harmful to stone. For this reason, stone objects—be they indoors *or* outdoors—should never be placed directly in contact with concrete or cementitious materials. When outdoors, the support stone or concrete should itself be surrounded by gravel to encourage the drainage of water away from the base.

You may begin to see a pattern developing: for outdoor environments, *water* is the key functionary in deterioration. Precautions taken to prevent the ingress of water will also help to prevent deterioration from crystallizing salts. Soils can inherently carry salts, but we often use salts such as *halite* and *antarcite* to melt ice that has formed on roads and sidewalks. When salting porches, walkways, and driveways, take care not to bring the salts too near your stone objects.

Stone urns and fountains should have drains to prevent the pooling of water. These drains can be simple holes, or the water can be conducted away with plastic tubing. (Copper and even stainless-steel tubing will eventually oxidize and stain the surrounding stonework.) The plastic tubing will need to be replaced from time to time.

Stones that remain wet for long periods of time are candidates for biological growths such as algae, lichens, and mosses. At best, these growths are visually disfiguring and, at worst, cause damage by both physical and chemical processes. Objects that have areas that can easily hold soil and water are great places for plant growth to begin. The best preventive is to brush down your sculpture with a nylon or natural bristle brush once a season. This process can be done either dry or with deionized water.

The heat from sunlight can cause damage to large-grained marbles. Because of the special thermal properties of calcite, excessive heating of the surface causes cracking, and this tendency is even greater for dark-colored marbles. For this reason it is not advisable to dry the surface of a marble object with a heat gun or hair dryer. Other stone types—with the exception of some stones with high clay contents—are not as susceptible to heat damage. As was said at the outset of this chapter, it is important to know the mineralogy of your object to have a sense of the best way to preserve and maintain it.

To the question of whether or not a "protective" coating should be used on stone objects outdoors, the answer is *almost always* no. Waxes, acrylics, and urethanes are all unsuitable coatings because they will degrade and may cause damage to the stone in the process. (By the way, even the adhesive from stick-on labels, which employ similar materials as these coatings, can degrade and become impossible to remove from a stone object without damage.) Only coating materials based on silicone resins are safe, and the need for such a coating should be decided on a case-by-case basis by a professional conservator because these (and other coatings) may have undesirable visual effects.

I hope you are beginning to get the picture—don't put stone objects outdoors if it can be avoided. But indoors or outdoors, *you* are the real monitor of your collection; you know it better than anyone and see it every day. Be vigilant and don't let new and unusual appearances go unexamined. Do not, however, try to be your own conservator. Home remedies in conservation are often much less successful or indeed much more harmful than their medical analogues. Find a conservator whom you are comfortable speaking with and who may also become familiar with your collection. But most of all, good luck with your collection.

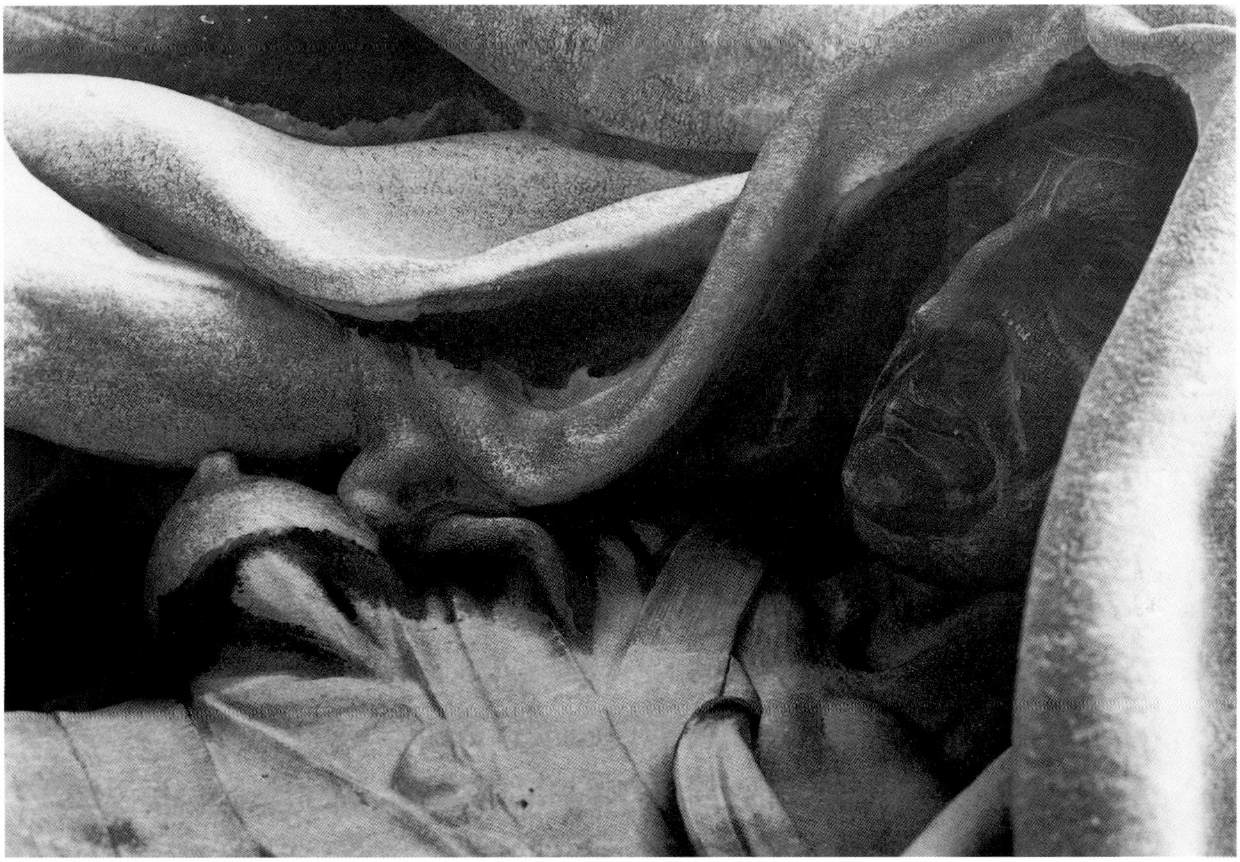

Black gypsum crusts, which form on limestones and marbles, are not only disfiguring but also an indication that the stone object is being damaged by acid rain.

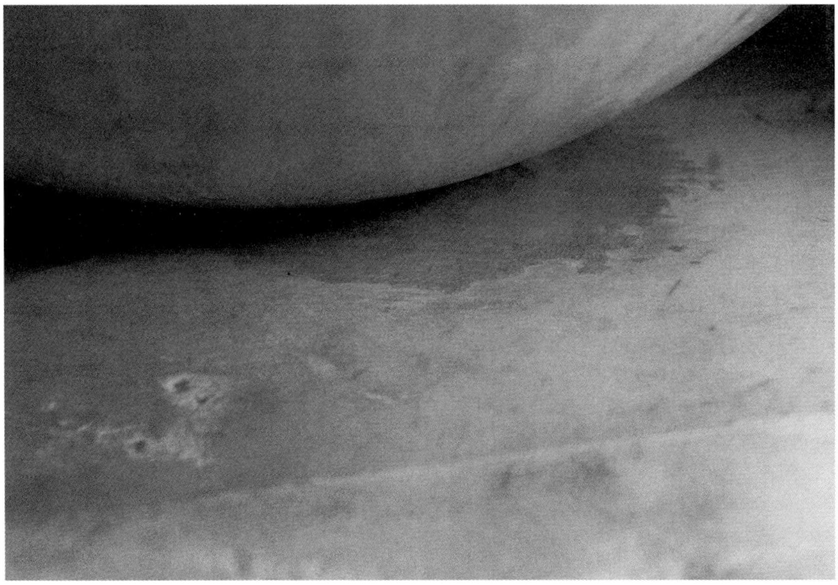

This marble sculpture's protective polyurethane coating has degraded in sunlight. As the film detaches, it removes the surface of the marble with it.

MUSICAL INSTRUMENTS

J. Scott Odell

Musical instruments come from all the world's cultures in an astonishing variety of shapes, sizes, and materials. Even among instruments of one type, pianos, for example, there are enormous differences in materials and construction methods. One may be lavishly decorated with mother-of-pearl inlay, another finished in plain black lacquer. An eighteenth-century piano of the sort Mozart played has delicate leather-covered hammers and a frame made entirely of wood, while the 1892 Steinway of Ignacy Paderewski has heavy hammers of compressed felt and a massive cast-iron frame. A collection of flutes may contain examples made of silver, gold, platinum, ebony, maple, ivory, ceramic, bamboo, and even glass. There are some broad similarities in the requirements for safe care of musical instruments, but the details are as different as the materials, physical structure, manner of use, and also their function in your collection. We can first consider these general principles before looking at the special needs of particular instruments.

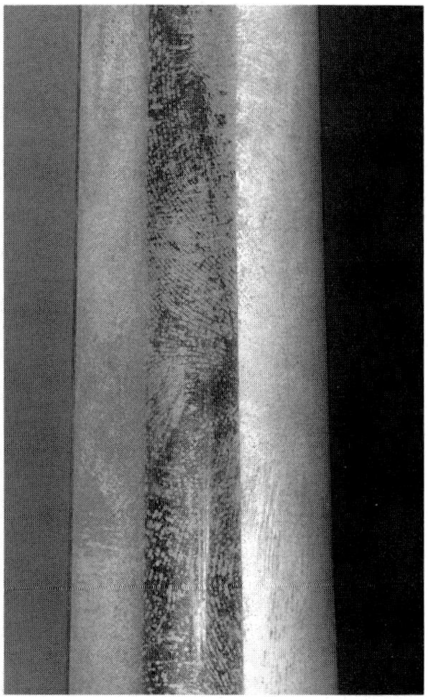

In this detail of a modern reproduction of a seventeenth-century trombone (seen on top of the cabinet in the photograph on page 133), one can see corrosion and etched fingerprints caused by handling unlacquered polished brass without protective gloves. Courtesy National Museum of American History, Smithsonian Institution

General Precautions

Artifact versus Playable Instrument

A visitor to a collection who would never walk up to an Old Master painting and touch it will casually set a briefcase on top of the closed lid of an antique piano, or pick up a wooden flute and try to play a few notes. Instruments and music are such a familiar part of our everyday life that such casual reflexes are hard to overcome or even recognize.

Although museums are professionally and legally required to give a high standard of care to objects that have been accepted into their collections, you as a private collector are not necessarily bound by the same requirements. Nevertheless, it is a useful approach to keep in mind. You might ask yourself these questions of

Opposite:
For this concert of mid-nineteenth-century band music using museum instruments of the period, the musicians wear cotton gloves to protect the polished metal from fingerprints and corrosion. Courtesy National Museum of American History, Smithsonian Institution

each instrument in your possession: Is this instrument of more than personal significance? Will it someday be valued by another family member, or collector, or a museum? Is it unique? Does it still possess interesting original features that would be lost in a restoration, or is it common, easily replaced, and of value principally as an instrument to make music? If the latter is true, perhaps you need only give it the routine maintenance and care appropriate to any other valuable but functional personal possession. But if you consider it to be of museum quality, its long-term value will be enhanced if you treat it like a museum artifact and guard against overly familiar handling and use.

The Issue of Restoration

Although a harpsichord may have a fine painting on its lid or a mandolin be embellished with intricate inlay and engraving, these visually splendid objects were originally created to make music, not just to be appreciated at arm's length for their visual beauty. A desire to use functional artifacts is not unique to musical instrument collectors, as anyone who has ever attended an antique-car meet or a gathering of tall ships will understand. The educational and aesthetic value of such use is often compelling, but the potential for wear and tear during rehearsal and performance, and loss of original substance during the restoration, is very great. As a private collector, you should be aware that such restoration for use may be inconsistent with standards of care considered normal for other kinds of museum collections such as paintings and fine arts.

Although it was once taken for granted that old musical instruments would whenever possible be restored to playing condition, today many museums and private collectors prefer to use copies. This protects the original from loss of historical value and avoids the painstaking, expensive, and continuing documentation, restoration, and maintenance work required to put and keep an historical instrument in playing condition. This change in attitudes is also reflected in sales prices, with original and unaltered instruments often bringing a premium over restored ones. Given a choice, many collectors prefer the violin with its original bass bar, fingerboard, and neck over one that has had all of its worn and warped parts replaced to suit the demands of modern performance. An original, unaltered, well-documented instrument will always be of much more interest to the scholar, or to a future craftsman looking for models on which to base his or her work.

In particular, historically significant instruments in unrestored, original condition should seldom, if ever, be put into playing condition. In the process of restoring and maintaining them so that they function reliably and well, strings, action padding, dampers, action clearances, and the like all must be replaced or adjusted, and unique documentary information is lost. From the standpoint of authenticity and scholarship there can be little rationale for a restoration unless you are confident that the finished result will stand fair comparison with the quality and reliability of the original when it was new. A good copy may more closely approximate the original sound and mechanical reliability of its historical model than will even a careful restoration of a badly deteriorated or much-altered original instrument. Another approach is to make a copy of the parts most susceptible to damage and wear, such as piano actions, and exchange these for the original when the instrument is played. Wear and tear on the original, easily damaged parts is avoided and performance quality improved.

Storage and Display

Whether in storage or on exhibit, instruments are subject to many risks, including high or low humidity, excessive light, dust, air pollution, water leaks, insect pests, strain caused by improper supports, and damage from careless handling.

Relative Humidity and Temperature

Pianos, harpsichords, banjos, drums, guitars, violins, bassoons—these are just a sampling of the many instruments made entirely or partly of wood, leather or skin, textiles, ivory, and other organic

When wooden instruments are exposed to excessive changes in relative humidity, rigid inlays such as this mother-of-pearl decoration can break or be dislodged when the surrounding wood shrinks, swells, or splits in response. Antonius Vinaccia, Naples. Mandola. 1790. Courtesy National Museum of American History, Smithsonian Institution

materials that are particularly sensitive to changes in relative humidity. If the atmosphere is too moist, necks will warp and joints become unglued and mildew will flourish; if too dry, woodwinds will crack, veneer will loosen, and the heads of banjos and drums will tear.

As a general rule, instruments do best in surroundings that you would be comfortable in yourself—neither too hot, too cold, too dry, nor too moist. Therefore, do not display or store them against a cold exterior wall or over a heating vent or next to a radiator, as the resulting extremes of temperature and humidity will surely cause trouble. Hot attics, dank basements, and uninsulated outbuildings are particularly dangerous storage locations, even for short periods.

Moisture-sensitive instruments should stay at about the same relative humidity year-round. Some changes are inevitable, but they should be small and gradual so that the instrument can adapt to them. A slow drift of relative humidity from 55 percent in the summer to 40 or 45 percent in the winter, while not ideal, may do little or no harm to your harpsichord, but if the same change occurs over a few hours or days, soundboard cracks, lifting veneer, or flaking paint are likely.

Temperature and relative humidity are interrelated, but for musical instruments humidity control usually takes precedence. Temperature within a range of 65 to 75 degrees Fahrenheit, allowed to drift higher in summer and lower in winter, coupled with a relative humidity of about 50 percent, should be safe for most musical instruments kept in average conditions in the United States so long as daily changes do not exceed a degree or two, and seasonal changes are gradual. Keep in mind however, that an instrument adapted to arid Arizona conditions will require a lower relative humidity than one from muggy south Florida. Instruments or furniture transported from a minimally heated English manor to a steam-heated New York apartment will shrink and crack unless humidification and a long period of acclimatization are provided. In such cases, where adherence to the conventional 50 percent RH recommendation may cause problems, you must first determine to what RH the instrument is acclimated and then provide appropriate conditions in its new home. In extreme climates, air conditioning, with humidification in the heating season and dehumidification during the cooling season, may be necessary.

If you decide to provide humidification for a collection housed in northern latitudes, thought and effort are needed to prevent wintertime condensation on windows and within exterior walls. If a room with exterior windows and walls is humidified, insulation and vapor barriers must be installed. Although theoretically possible and often attempted, this is hard to accomplish effectively in an older structure. Any defect in the insulation and vapor barrier will be penetrated by the moisture-laden interior air, and condensation will accumulate within the wall, possibly causing rot and other forms of water damage. A more elegant and cost-effective solution, building layout permitting, is to bypass the condensation problem entirely by placing sensitive objects in a humidity-controlled interior room isolated from cold exterior walls and roof by hallways or other rooms.

Light

Light damage is common, irreversible, and insidious because it happens so gradually that it often goes unnoticed until it is far too late to do anything about it. The problem is treated more fully elsewhere, but it is worth noting that many instruments are made entirely or partly of light-sensitive materials. Some are obvious—embroidered bagpipe covers, dyed wood inlay in guitar rosettes, or painted gouache decoration on harpsichord soundboards. The light-colored spruce of a soundboard will darken and the red mahogany of a piano lid will bleach when exposed to light. Even the protective lacquer on a brass instrument will deteriorate more rapidly if exposed to too much light.

To protect instruments from light and dust, avoid permanent display, as well as the common practice of hanging smaller instruments on walls. It is best to keep lids of keyboard instruments closed and smaller instruments safely put away in individually fitted instrument cases or protective cabinetry.

Storage and Exhibit Cabinetry

Whether you use storage cabinets or individually fitted instrument cases, all should be made of materials that do not release harmful gases such as volatile organic acids or hydrogen sulphide. Interior-grade plywood, particle board, oak, and wool felt are commonly used but likely to give trouble. Metal cabinets are often recommended over those made of wood, but there are many pitfalls in the choice of paint and padding materials for the shelves, so a conservator should be consulted before a major investment is made in cabinetry or instrument cases.

Safe Handling

Even experienced musicians and instrument makers often need some guidance in the handling of antique instruments. Wear cotton gloves for handling polished brasswinds; avoid damage from sharp measuring instruments such as calipers and steel tapes; keep hot photographic lights at a safe distance; pick up flutes, oboes, and recorders with two hands lest loose joints and ivory rings fall to the floor. The dangers are too many and too diverse to enumerate for every sort of instrument but are similar to those of other historical objects made of similar materials. Required is a cautious and thoughtful approach, which takes into account the particular susceptibilities of each instrument, plus an understanding that instruments in a collection cannot be handled as casually as modern instruments in regular use.

Special Handling

WOODWINDS

Wooden flutes, oboes, and other woodwinds kept in museum and private collections are very likely to crack if they are played after a long period of disuse. While an instrument owned and used by a musician who plays it frequently is never allowed to completely dry out, the sudden influx of moisture into an unused collection instrument causes the inside surface of the dry bore to swell, and the

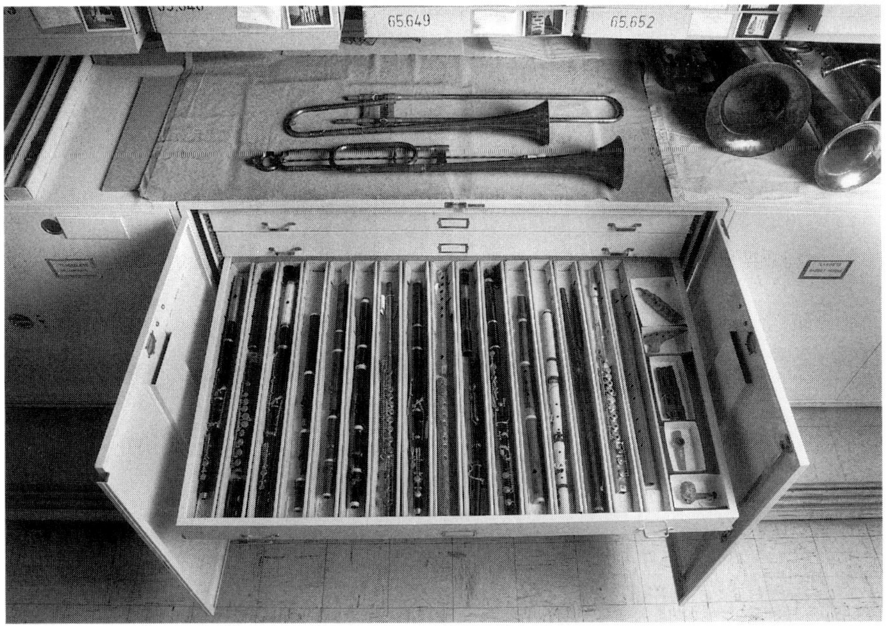

The conservation needs of the flutes and whistles in this drawer are as varied as the many different materials—including ebony, maple, cane, metal, ivory, plastics, ceramics, and paint—used to make them. All instruments will benefit from proper storage cabinets fitted with acid-free trays and padding to prevent damage from accidents, dust, light, and changes in relative humidity. Courtesy National Museum of American History, Smithsonian Institution

resulting pressure can easily split the wood. With an old instrument this can happen even if care is taken to break it in gradually. Playing of irreplaceable or unique instruments should never be permitted except for thoroughly justified reasons (such as to determine approximate pitch) and then only for very brief periods, measured in seconds rather than minutes. The bores of many antique woodwinds have shrunk and deformed with time, causing inevitable alterations to their original pitch and intonation, which is another reason to consider using a good copy in place of the original.

If you decide the benefits of playing an old instrument of no great historical value outweigh the risks, it should be "played-in" very gradually just like a new instrument, carefully swabbed out after each use, and the bore periodically recoated with a nondrying mineral oil or wax. Obtain expert advice from a conservator or musical-instrument specialist familiar with the care of historical instruments regarding appropriate materials and safe means of application. Moisture-proofing tricks-of-the-trade, such as soaking a commercial furniture polish into the wood or coating the bore with epoxy, are sometimes suggested by contemporary instrument repairers, but these methods are likely to be ineffective and, worse, are irreversible and will interfere with later treatments. Such nostrums have no place in the care of historical artifacts and should be avoided. Similarly, the original method of thread lapping for joint tenons should be respected and not replaced with modern sheet cork; finger holes and bore shapes should never be recut or reamed in an attempt to correct intonation problems.

BRASSWIND INSTRUMENTS

Valves and keys are subject to damage if they are depressed without first making sure that they will move freely and that they are clean and properly lubricated. Extreme care must be taken to protect polished metal surfaces from acidic fingerprints. Instruments in collections are more at risk than those in regular use by musicians, for an experienced musician will have a regular routine for cleaning, polishing, and oiling his instrument, while an instrument in a collection is likely to be casually picked up and set down by an enthusiastic visitor who gives no thought to the danger of bending a balky key or the ease with which fingerprints can be etched into polished brass. Keep inexpensive white cotton gloves or a clean cloth available for visitors to use when handling metal instruments. A coating of protective lacquer is sometimes sprayed onto instruments that are frequently handled or used in performance. This can be very effective if properly applied and maintained, but be aware that an old or damaged lacquer coating will cause etching of the metal wherever the coating is chipped, worn, or too thin. The application, examination, and removal of lacquer coatings is best left to a specialist, with advice from a qualified conservator.

Consult a metals conservator to help select safe materials and methods prior to any cleaning, polishing, or lacquering of badly tarnished or corroded brasswinds. Metal polishes containing ammonia can be damaging to brass instruments and should be avoided.

Historical brasswind instruments in good condition may sometimes safely be played, but additional warnings are in order. Instruments with valves are subject to wear of the moving parts; take care that they are clean and free of old abrasive polish residues and that they are properly oiled. Players of valveless natural horns (hand horns) must place a hand within the bell to manipulate the notes that fall outside the natural harmonic series, but the bells of such instruments often contain decorative paintings that can easily be damaged. Consult a painting conservator to determine the condition of the paint and perhaps apply a protective coating.

Even normal handling can damage the decorative paintings found on many musical instruments. Their care and treatment may require both a painting conservator and a musical instrument specialist. D. Jahn, Paris. Orchestral horn. c. 1825. R. E. Sheldon Collection, Library of Congress Music Division

KEYBOARD INSTRUMENTS

Most keyboard instruments are also major pieces of furniture, perhaps veneered, inlaid with marquetry, or more or less elaborately decorated with paintings. Therefore, one must distinguish between musical, structural, and decorative concerns. Many decorative and some structural treatments can be entrusted to a furniture or painting conservator, depending upon the manner of case and stand construction and decoration. However, any work involving strings, action, soundboard, or organ pipes will require consultation with a musical-instrument specialist, who must be chosen with great care. The skills and experience required to treat pianos, harpsichords, clavichords, and pipe organs are quite distinct, and experience with modern instruments and copies is only partially relevant to the problems of properly restoring and maintaining historical instruments. Before you restore a historical instrument to playing condition, seek professional advice from one of the major institutional instrument collections.

Pianos

Square, upright, and grand pianos are among the most common instruments found in public and private collections. A distinction can be made between early instruments with wooden frames and those dating from the end of the first quarter of the nineteenth century. The earlier instruments are very susceptible to warping of the frame, case, and soundboard caused by the unrelenting pull of the strings. Although some attempt it, relatively few collections have the resources to restore and maintain these historical wooden-frame instruments in good playing condition. Early square pianos are particularly hard to maintain; keyboard and action regulation and tuning are quickly affected by humidity changes and warping of the wooden frame. There are few, if any, commercial suppliers of some materials used in their construction, such as baleen damper springs and obsolete tannages of leather for hammer coverings. Most modern piano technicians have neither the proper experience nor ready access to the esoteric materials needed to properly restore and maintain these instruments.

Later nineteenth-century pianos usually have a cast-iron frame, which provides good support against the tension of the strings so that warping of frame and soundboard is not likely to be a major problem. Modern piano technicians often can make such an instrument play satisfactorily, but achievement of an accurate historical sound may still be elusive due to the difficulty of obtaining the right kind of leather or felt to replace deteriorated hammer coverings. One should always retain samples of any original materials removed during the course of such restorations.

Harpsichords and Virginals

What has been said of other early wooden-frame keyboard instruments is even more true of these lightly built instruments in which the strings are plucked with quills, rather than struck with hammers as in a piano. There are some contemporary makers of excellent copies and, once again, a good copy will usually be the least expensive and most musically satisfactory choice for most collectors wanting a playable harpsichord or clavichord.

Pitch Levels

Many historical instruments were designed for pitch levels and temperament systems quite different from those of today. Pitch, string diameter, and string density have a profound effect on both sound and tension; if an instrument is restored with heavier strings or tuned to a higher pitch than it was designed for, unauthentic sound is certain and structural disaster is likely. Guitar necks may warp, harpsichord and piano frames collapse, violins distort.

If a stringed keyboard instrument is not going to be maintained in playing condition, you can reduce harmful stress on the case and soundboard by lowering the tension on the strings to the minimum needed to keep them neatly aligned on the bridge pins. Changes of more than a semitone

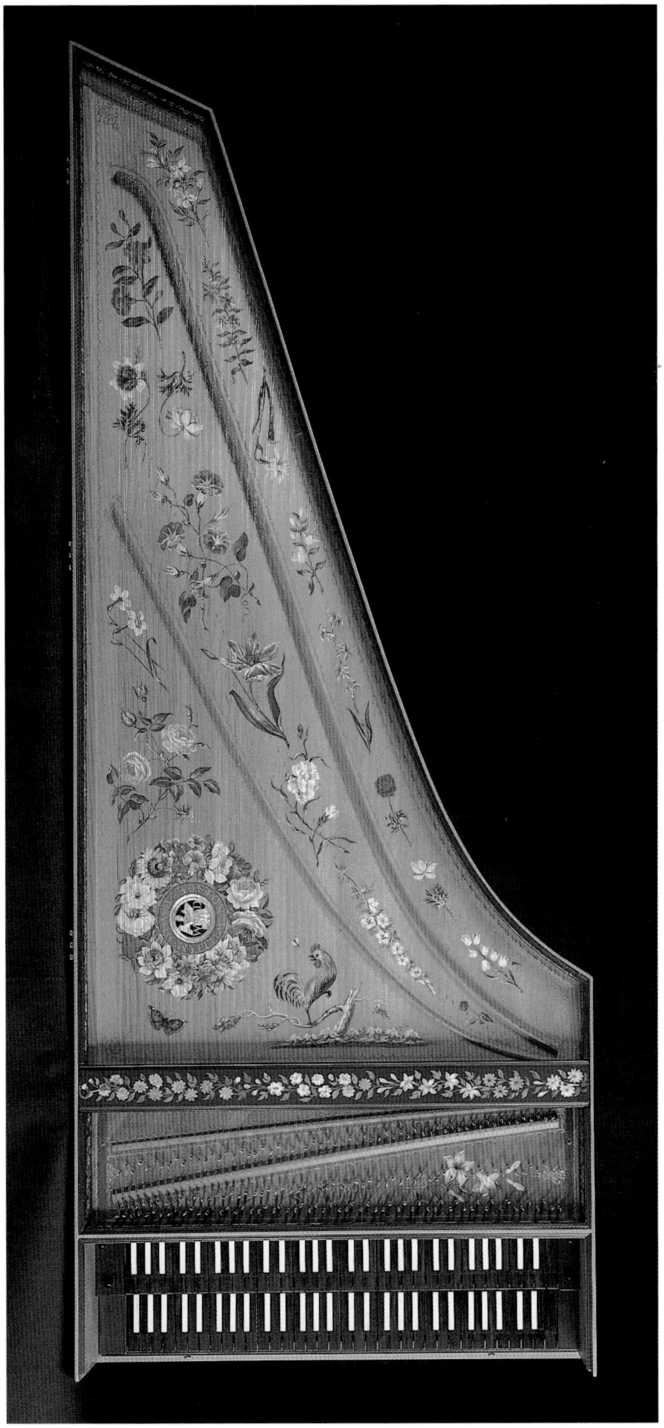

Careful copies of historical instruments can provide a musically satisfactory alternative to the difficult and sometimes harmful restoration and maintenance of original instruments for use in performance. William Dowd, Boston. 1980 copy of a harpsicord after N. and F. E. Blanchet, Paris, 1730. Courtesy National Museum of American History, Smithsonian Institution

in the pitch of pianos should be made carefully, with tensions raised or lowered gradually and evenly from bass to treble. The forces involved can be great enough to break the cast-iron plate of a piano if the tension on one group of strings is radically different from that of the others.

Most early guitars, banjos, mandolins, violins, and other fretted and bowed instruments were designed for light gut strings (made of twisted sheep's intestine) that placed a relatively low stress on the instrument. Such instruments will be severely damaged if tuned up to modern pitch and fitted with steel strings. Seek professional advice on pitch levels and stringing materials before putting such instruments into playing condition.

Cleaning and Polishing

So much damage can be done by improper cleaning and polishing of the wood of instruments such as pianos and violins and the fretted and bowed strings that a special warning is in order. Homemade furniture-polish mixtures of linseed oil and turpentine, perhaps with some vinegar added, are often recommended in newspaper "hints to the homeowner" columns and old recipe books. Even if one follows the usual prescription to "rub off more than you put on" the eventual result will be an impenetrable film of sticky, semiopaque goo. There are also widely available commercial violin polishes, which have similar ill effects, and all such polishes should be avoided by the amateur. Violin varnishes vary so much from maker to maker that it is unwise to generalize about safe cleaning and polishing methods. A soft dry cloth can be used to gently wipe off dust or loosely adhered rosin, but any cleaning beyond this should only be undertaken by a professional.

The soundboards of some harpsichords and clavichords have painted gouache decorations that were originally left unvarnished and can easily be damaged by spills or overenergetic dusting and cleaning. Undecorated soundboards can sometimes be dusted safely with a soft brush, brushing toward the nozzle of a vacuum cleaner, but a decorated soundboard should first be examined by a conservator who may suggest safer methods of routine cleaning.

Because routine polishing causes significant wear over a long period of time and always leads to unsightly polish stains on the surrounding wood, brass hinges and stop knobs are probably best left unpolished.

Moving

Although most pianos and many harpsichords have casters on their legs, these should be regarded as delicate and venerable decorative accessories and not as an invitation to move the instrument around by pushing it. A piano or harpsichord should always be moved on a dolly or, for short distances, by lifting and carrying it in order to avoid vibration and almost certain damage to the legs or stand. Before lifting a keyboard instrument lid, always check to make sure that hinge pins and screws are in place.

Metal organ pipes may be surprisingly soft and are very easily dented and distorted if mishandled. If an instrument is to be moved, an organ maker should be consulted on the proper way to dismantle, label, and pack the parts.

Ethnographic and "Folk" Instruments

Instruments that fall outside the mainstream traditions of European-derived "classical" music present special problems of care and conservation. Many instruments from non-European cultural traditions, such as Indonesian gamelans or Native American drums, represent well-developed traditions that continue today. Information useful to their conservation usually can be found by seeking advice not only from ethnomusicologists, but also from musicians still active within the living tradition. Instruments from obscure or unfamiliar traditions should be given only the minimum treatment needed to stabilize them against deterioration. In the absence of solid information about crucial details of performance style and normal adjustment techniques, nothing useful can be gained by attempts to make such instruments playable. It is wiser to preserve them intact, unaltered, and unimpaired for future research and interpretation.

Drum heads are likely to tear if relative humidity falls too low and the head tension is not reduced. The leather tensioning "ears" seen here are typical of many old drums in that they are so deteriorated that even a gentle pull would rip them off. Blair and Baldwin, Boston. Snare drum. Early twentieth century. Courtesy National Museum of American History, Smithsonian Institution

Records and Tape Recordings

Disk and tape recordings should be kept in the same stable relative humidity and temperature conditions as other moisture-sensitive materials. A paper conservator can advise on the care of original jackets, sleeves, and boxes, which are often made of poor-quality paper and will deteriorate, damaging themselves and their contents. To prevent warping, records are best stored vertically, placed close together on edge on a shelf or in a box without undue pressure.

Valuable master copies of original tape recordings should never be played routinely; make a preservation copy plus one or more working copies for use instead of the original. Because of the many kinds of magnetic recordings and the variety of materials used in their manufacture, the long-term care of unique tape recordings is not a simple matter. In some cases, the magnetic coating becomes brittle and falls off the tape into a pile of powdery flakes alongside the playback head; in others, the magnetic signal is "printed through" from one layer of tape to the next, causing a faint echo. The management of recorded-sound collections should be planned in consultation with an archival specialist, but the basics of care are covered in publications cited in the bibliography.

Finding Professional Assistance

Relatively few conservators specialize in musical instruments, so finding the right person may require considerable effort and persistence on your part. Musical instruments take so many forms, span so many cultures, and embody such an array of arcane materials that it is unreasonable to suppose that any one individual might deal with all the problems of all instruments. A local musical-instrument maker or technician may be trained and highly competent to deal with modern pianos, band instruments, or orchestral bowed strings, but to possess the experience and skills needed to properly treat unique or historical instruments is quite another matter. Understandably, most such craftspeople are by training and inclination predisposed to make an instrument function well by modern standards and look as good as possible, an approach that is dangerous and inappropriate when dealing with historical artifacts.

The best care and treatment of your instruments may require consultation and cooperation among several experts, much as is the norm for medical treatments. You should not hesitate to look beyond your immediate geographic area to find the right consultants for a particular instrument. It may be wisest to pair the craft skills and specialized knowledge of a musical-instrument maker with those of an experienced object conservator in order to come up with a well-justified proposal and a final written report that thoroughly documents the materials and methods actually used in the treatment. Curatorial advice, and referrals to conservators and skilled craftspeople sympathetic to the problems of particular historical instruments, usually can be found by asking staff at major institutional collections of musical instruments.

ETHNOGRAPHIC MATERIALS

Carolyn L. Rose

Our fascination with places and cultures different from our own has contributed to the creation of a huge industry of tourism throughout the world. Each year new travel adventures are offered to even more exotic sites. From these travels, we often bring back reminders of the countries we have visited and the new experiences we have enjoyed. The collecting of such mementos is an ancient pastime; many early explorers gathered objects for scientific studies, as treasures, or simply as examples of curiosities from faraway lands. These objects, collected directly or indirectly from indigenous cultures, make up the ethnographic collections found in museums and in our homes. From them, we learn about other societies and customs and gain insight concerning differing technologies and aesthetic values.

Many anthropology museums and university departments continue to collect ethnographic objects to aid in research concerning the cultural diversity of mankind. Art museums also have acquired ethnographic objects as examples of nonwestern art, and institutions dedicated to specific regions or cultures have been created. In each case, ethnographic objects may be used for differing purposes, resulting in various interpretations and representations.

Regardless of whether your collections have been acquired for your pleasure or as an investment, you should keep a record of the circumstances under which each object was collected and, if possible, how, where, and when it was made and by whom. The source of this information, the date, and any conservation records should be kept with the object as an important part of its history. Proof that your object has been legally acquired or exported also can contribute to its value. In addition, some objects may be sacred to the culture that made and used them. Your collections should be evaluated in light of this documentation when determining their monetary

The Kachina doll on the left has been damaged by the application of a fixative to the surface. Note the color change and staining as compared to the untreated doll on the right.

The fish-oil deposits on this Eskimo food dish relate to the use of the object and should not be removed. Courtesy Smithsonian Institution

value and their research and cultural importance. Even recently collected items may be significant, as technologies and cultures are modified and changed through time.

In order to care for ethnographic collections and to protect their future value, their association with the culture of origin should remain intact. In addition to documentation, this may mean not removing surface deposits, remnants of food, or other associated materials that demonstrate how the object may have been used. In fact, the major value of an object in future years may depend upon the fact that it has *not* been cleaned or modified in any way. The preservation of many ethnographic objects therefore requires an approach less intrusive than that used for many traditional art objects. Usually, only minimal cleaning and stabilization treatments are recommended. Recognizing those factors that lead to an increased rate of deterioration and mitigating their effects is considered the best approach to preserving ethnographic objects. In addition, such care prevents the need for costly remedial treatments at a later date.

Examination and Documentation

A complete record of the condition of each object, through both written and photographic documentation, is a basic step in registering your holdings and in planning for future treatments. For ethnographic collections, a thorough examination of each item is critical, not only to record its condition for insurance purposes, but also to become well acquainted with each of your objects so that you can identify any changes that may occur. An awareness of the preservation needs of each material component also will enable you to provide the exhibition and storage conditions and maintenance programs that will best ensure the object's survival for the future. In addition, a basic understanding of your object will contribute to your ability to recognize problems with similar objects you may wish to obtain in the future and to communicate more effectively and knowledgeably about your objects with a conservator, insurer, dealer, or other collectors.

Examination sheets for each object (see samples provided) will help you in identifying the materials comprising your object and recording their condition. The materials checklist is divided into two major categories: *organic* materials, which include those derived from plants and animals, and *inorganic* materials, such as metals and other mineral-based substances. Some materials, such as bone and ivory, are composed of both organic and inorganic substances and can exhibit problems associated with the deterioration of both component materials. Most of the natural resins and other adhesives, such as gums and starches, that you may find on your object are obtained from plants. Some resins, such as shellac, are produced by insects, and skins and bones are commonly processed to form protein glues. Your object also may contain synthetic (man-made) materials, either in the form of a repair or restoration or because of the more recent fabrication of the object. Examples of synthetic materials include textiles such as nylon or rayon and more modern polymer fibers, plastic fills, and paints such as acrylics and polyesters. The presence of these synthetic materials may provide clues to the age of the object or may indicate that it has been repaired. Therefore, if you have made any repairs to the object in the past, be sure to note and date them on the form.

To aid in identifying various materials, it may be helpful to read about the technologies and materials of the cultures from which your objects

OBJECT EXAMINATION SHEET

(Description, to include clear photograph or drawing of the object)

Date
Object Name ______________________ **Collector's Number** ______________________
Origin ______________________ **Location** ______________________
Description ____

Organic Components

PLANT (CELLULOSE-BASED)
____ bark
____ cotton
____ linen
____ paper
____ plant fiber
____ textile (unknown)
____ wood
____ other ______________

ANIMAL (PROTEIN-BASED)
____ claws, beaks, hooves
____ feathers
____ fur (skin + hair)
____ hair
____ horn
____ intestine (gut)
____ quill
____ silk
____ sinew (thread from tendon)
____ skin
____ textile (unknown)
____ wool
____ other ______________

NATURAL PRODUCTS
____ dye
____ oil
____ resin
____ wax
____ other ______________

Inorganic Components

METALS
____ copper (+ brass and bronze)
____ gold
____ iron (+ steel)
____ lead
____ silver
____ tin
____ other ______________

NONMETALS
____ ceramic
    ____ glazed
    ____ unglazed
____ clay
____ glass
____ pigment/paint
____ plaster
____ mineral
____ stone
____ other ______________

Inorganic/Organic Components

____ antler
____ bone
____ shell, mother-of-pearl
____ teeth and ivory
____ other ______________

Synthetic Components

____ adhesives
    ____ white glue
    ____ model glue
    ____ other ______________
____ dye
____ fibers
____ fillers (i.e., restoration)
____ textile
____ other ______________

OBJECT EXAMINATION SHEET
(Condition of object)

Date
Object Name ______________________ **Collector's Number** ______________________

Problems	**List Material(s) Affected**
STRUCTURAL	
____ broken	______________________
____ corroded (extensive)	______________________
____ cracked	______________________
____ hairline crack	______________________
____ open crack (dimensions)	______________________
____ dented	______________________
____ frayed	______________________
____ holes	______________________
____ torn	______________________
____ other ____________	______________________
SURFACE	
____ abraded	______________________
____ corroded (light rust/tarnish)	______________________
____ deposits	______________________
____ dusty or dirty	______________________
____ flaking	______________________
____ gouged or nicked	______________________
____ salts	______________________
____ scratched	______________________
____ stained	______________________
____ other ____________	______________________
COLOR CHANGE	
____ darkened	______________________
____ faded	______________________
____ yellowed	______________________
____ other ____________	______________________
BIOLOGICAL ACTIVITY	
____ insects, spiders, etc. (+ remains)	______________________
____ mildew/mold	______________________
____ rodents	______________________
____ other ____________	______________________
MENDS/REPAIRS/RESTORATIONS	
____ stable	______________________
____ unstable	______________________

Conservation Treatment (including cleaning) By Whom ____________ Date

(Append conservation examination and treatment report with specific materials and methods used, analysis conducted, and photographic documentation.)

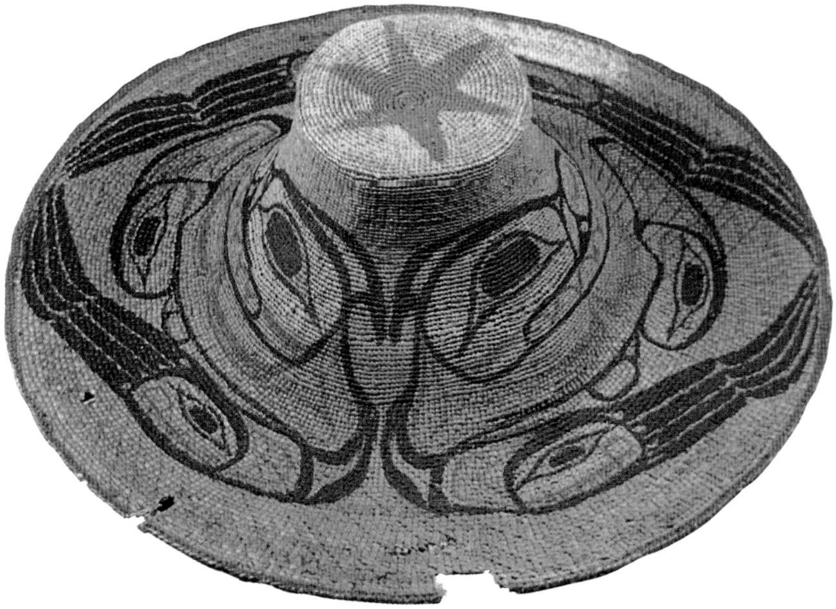

This (Tlingit?) basketry hat has been damaged as a result of lifting it by its rim. Courtesy Smithsonian Institution

originate. Many museum shops sell books on the fabrication of different objects, especially those pertaining to local cultural groups. In reviewing the information contained in these books, it is important to note the time period that the author is addressing because modern technologies may be different from earlier, traditional ones. Also, some nontraditional materials may have been used even though the object is old. In addition, some objects specifically produced for the tourist trade may have been artificially aged through burial or chemical treatment. They also may be spattered with paint or mud to make them look old. Information about materials used can assist further in determining the origin and authenticity of each object.

While examining each object, check off the material components to the best of your knowledge. A conservator, scientist, or material-culture specialist can assist you at a later time in making a more specific identification.

Guidelines for Examination and Handling

A good area for examining objects can be created on a large table by covering it with padding, then a light-colored bed sheet. The padding should provide cushioning under the sheet but should not be lumpy or irregular, or else the object may tip over. A new bed pad, without fitted corners, or several layers of towels could be used. This setup also could serve as your photography area for documenting the condition of your objects with a still or video camera.

Assemble the materials you need for examination. These include your checklists; a magnifying glass; a shallow box for moving objects with dangling parts; a towel and pillowcase for padding the box; and a sturdy, smooth sheet of cardboard for lifting and moving flat, fragile objects. Wear cotton or surgical gloves when handling your objects, especially those made of metals and those with lacquered surfaces. For measuring your objects, use a cloth tape rather than a retractable metal one, which can rewind easily, tearing across delicate surfaces. Use a pencil to record information about the object. Too often, irremovable marks have been left on objects from pens or felt-tip markers.

In preparation for examination, remove all articles of jewelry, including neck chains and bands for glasses, to prevent accidental scratching or entanglement in the object. Loose sleeves and bulky sweaters also can cause accidents.

Lift each object with both hands below the center of gravity. Objects should not be lifted by handles, spouts, or other protrusions, and dangling portions should be supported carefully during movement. It is useful to carry and examine objects with fragile appendages or attachments in a shallow padded box so that the box rather than the object can be turned during inspection. A smooth padding

The deterioration of these shells on a Somali milk container was caused by interaction with the fatty acids in the underlying skin. Courtesy Smithsonian Institution

for the box can be made by placing a pillowcase over a small folded towel or foam sheet. As fingerprints can cause damage, gloves should be worn while handling objects, and no eating, drinking, or smoking should be permitted at the examination table.

If an accident does occur and a small segment breaks off the object, it should be placed in a self-closing plastic bag or small archival box, or it should be wrapped in acid-free paper until a conservator can be consulted. In addition, it is important to place the broken section in a box or container with the object so that the pieces are not misplaced or accidentally thrown out. Unless the box is made of acid-free materials, storage in such a container should be temporary. Under no circumstances should newspaper, cardboard, or excelsior be used for wrapping or padding the object. These wood-based materials can produce an acid environment that can accelerate the deterioration of materials. Cotton is a poor padding material as well because it can become entangled in the object, causing the breakage of delicate parts. In addition, cotton can hold moisture next to the artifact, which is especially harmful for metal. If the items must be stored for longer than a few weeks, follow the storage recommendations in this or related chapters. If a serious accident should happen, such as dropping and breaking the object into a number of pieces, or if wetting or staining should occur, call a conservator immediately. The longer you wait, the more difficult it may be to contend with the damage.

As a note of caution, in the past organic objects may have been treated with insecticides and other poisons, including arsenic and mercury compounds, strychnine, and DDT. These compounds, applied as liquids or powders, may be embedded in fibers or lodged in porous surfaces, making their removal difficult or not possible. Sometimes poison residues are in the form of powders or white crystals on the surface, as in the case of arsenic. Darkening or black spots may signal that mercury compounds are present. In many cases, however, no residues may be seen even though poisons are present. Therefore, it is recommended that disposable gloves be used when handling all older organic materials. Discard the gloves after handling each object to avoid contaminating other artifacts. Alternatively, hands can be covered with plastic wrap. Keep the disposable gloves or contaminated plastics out of the reach of children and pets and seal in a plastic bag before discarding.

General Problems

As has been explained in earlier chapters, inappropriate levels of light, relative humidity, and temperature, especially broad fluctuations in the latter two, can rapidly increase the rate of deterioration of your collections. In fact, adverse environmental conditions already may have dramatically altered your ethnographic artifact because it is a composite object, meaning that it is constructed of a variety of different materials. Each component material may have responded to changes in relative humidity and temperature in a dissimilar manner, exerting stress on other component parts and on the object as a whole. Even with mild stresses, aged adhesives and paint mediums may give way, causing your object to be unstable. The organic components of your objects also may be stiff and/or brittle and falling apart.

In some cases, one component material may accelerate the deterioration of an adjacent one. For example, metal beads may be affected by the woolen textile to which they are attached. The textile may hold moisture, causing increased corrosion of the metal. Acidic dyes also may exacerbate the corrosion. In turn, corrosion of the metal may cause deterioration of the textile. Similar problems exist with metal-cellulose combinations, metal-metal combinations, and with some protein-cellulose combinations.

A number of ethnographic objects are composed of light-sensitive organic materials or are colored with natural, light-reactive dyes. Evidence of fading of colors may be determined by comparing areas hidden from light with those which have been exposed to the light. Look carefully for unexposed areas, but do not pull apart or stress the object in the process. Note the materials which are faded on your checklist under materials affected.

Pollutants in the atmosphere and particles of dirt and dust can react with your object and can catalyze other chemical reactions, especially in the presence of light. Harmful pollutants can be produced from cooking, and oils and grease can be deposited on objects as they are on kitchen cabinets. Abrasive dust particles introduced through open windows and from poorly filtered heating, ventilation, and air-conditioning systems can damage objects through abrasion. They also can work their way into crevices and between woven structures, damaging fragile materials. In your observations, note whether dust and dirt may be covering all or only parts of your object. A general accumulation of dust on the surface probably was caused by poor display and storage conditions and not as a result of cultural use.

Many ethnographic objects are extremely susceptible to pest infestations, both because they are often composed of organic materials and because some have been collected from tropical countries where insect problems are abundant. Carefully examine your object for signs of pests. Objects containing remnants of insects, insect carcasses, droppings, frass, or those with pin-size or larger holes on the surface may have an insect problem. If you think that insects may be a problem, consult the section on care and maintenance and take immediate action.

Fungal growth can occur on a number of different materials and surfaces, resulting in permanent staining and structural damage to the material. The development of mildew and mold is a sign of high relative humidity, indicating that the object is stored in a poorly controlled and often poorly ventilated area. If mold is observed on your objects, or if a musty odor is present, move the objects to drier and more stable environment as described under care and maintenance.

Other problems to note include unstable mends or the presence of inappropriate materials or devices such as rubber bands or pressure-sensitive tapes that have been used to repair the object. Tapes may pull off fragile surfaces or stain and cause embrittlement of organic materials. Further, the deterioration of tapes and rubber bands may make their removal extremely difficult. The presence of these mending and fastening materials should be noted but no attempt should be made to remove them yourself. One exception would be if you put a rubber band around a broken object during the last few months. Cut the rubber band to release it, holding broken pieces securely in place. Bag the broken portion and keep it with the object.

Specific Problems

Most of the specific problems you will encounter with individual materials composing your objects are discussed in previous chapters. Please refer to these sections as you complete your examination form. (The index can help you in finding appropriate references to materials.) Not discussed in other chapters are problems related to animal-based (protein) materials such as skins, feathers, fur, and bone, which will be detailed in this section. Also explained are special problems associated with ethnographic objects. Materials are discussed according to the basic categories of organic, inorganic, and inorganic/organic combination materials as listed on your examination form.

Organic Materials

WOOD AND PLANT MATERIALS

Wooden objects are found in most ethnographic collections and have been used for utilitarian, decorative, and ritual purposes. Some cultural objects, such as furniture or musical instruments, are functional. One of the characteristics that sets some ethnographic objects apart, however, is that the wood may have no coating or surface treatment to aid in its protection. Untreated surfaces can respond more quickly to changes in relative humidity than coated ones. Objects newly collected in tropical countries can crack rapidly when they are brought to residences in arid or temperate climates, especially during dry winter months. Depending upon the way in which the object has been constructed and the type of wood employed, your object may exhibit checks or cracks throughout the surfaces or may have split apart. Because it is difficult to remember whether a crack has increased or decreased in size over time, its length and width should be measured at specific positions and recorded on your checklist for later comparison.

This painted wooden Lega mask (Zaire) has been infested with insects; however, the insect casings are under some of the painted layers and therefore should not be removed. Courtesy Department of Anthropology (cat. no. 399.747), Smithsonian Institution

Although light is generally more damaging to surface coatings or decorative attachments on wood, uncoated woods, especially those that are yellow or red, also can show signs of fading. Wooden objects are prone to insect infestations and should be examined carefully for pinholes or any other signs of insect activity. Fungal growth and subsequent rotting also may be apparent, especially if wooden objects have been dampened or are resting on a moisture-absorbent surface, such as a basement floor. Therefore, although seemingly stable, wooden objects may be very fragile because of structural damage caused by desiccation, insect infestation, or from fungal attack. Additionally, attached portions may be loosened because of failure of the adhesive or differential shrinkage of appended parts. Careful handling and support should be afforded to these objects during examination.

Bamboo and gourd artifacts exhibit problems similar to wood and should be examined as such. A special problem to note is that they grow under considerable tension, and rapid environmental changes can lead to severe cracking and distortions.

Painted wood, bamboo, and gourd objects can exhibit special problems, especially if the coating is thick and poorly adhered to the surface. Some objects contain a ground layer between the substrate and the paint. One of the basic problems with these objects, therefore, is that the dissimilar substances expand and contract disparately with fluctuations in relative humidity and temperature. This phenomenon produces stress in the object, resulting in the loosening and separation of component parts. Such losses often are difficult to readhere to the surface without changing the visual characteristics of the artifact. The original adhesives that bind other decorative materials to wooden objects also may give way with environmental changes and with the deterioration of the adhesive.

Objects made from plant fibers, including baskets, mats, and bark cloth, as well as strings, cord, and other fasteners, are common among most cultures. Older fiber objects, those that have been used as utilitarian objects or that have been stored under adverse conditions in an attic or basement, are probably in a fragile state. Even if these objects appear to be in a sound condition, extra care should be taken to avoid additional structural damage. Fiber wrappings can be extremely brittle and should not be handled while moving an object to which they are attached. Fiber fringes, such as those found on grass skirts and cedar bark attachments on masks, must be supported to avoid continual loss.

Plant fibers will undergo deterioration processes similar to those described for paper materials. In fact, unprocessed plant fibers are inherently more susceptible to deterioration because they are not refined (as good-quality paper is) to remove resins and other noncellulose plant substances. Their deterioration, therefore, may be more analogous to problems inherent with newsprint and some textiles. Look for broken and detached fibers, brittle and cracking surfaces, and fading and discoloration from light or from contact with acidic materials.

The fabrication technique of some fiber objects can create internal stress in the object from twisting, coiling, and wrapping in a wet state and then drying under tension. Fibers may be broken, barkcloth may be separated into layers, and bark paintings may be curled to the original shape of the tree. Dyes may be faded or paints and resins may be flaking from flexing or from changes in relative humidity and temperature. Other decorative elements may be loose. Insects and mold growth are also common problems for fiber objects.

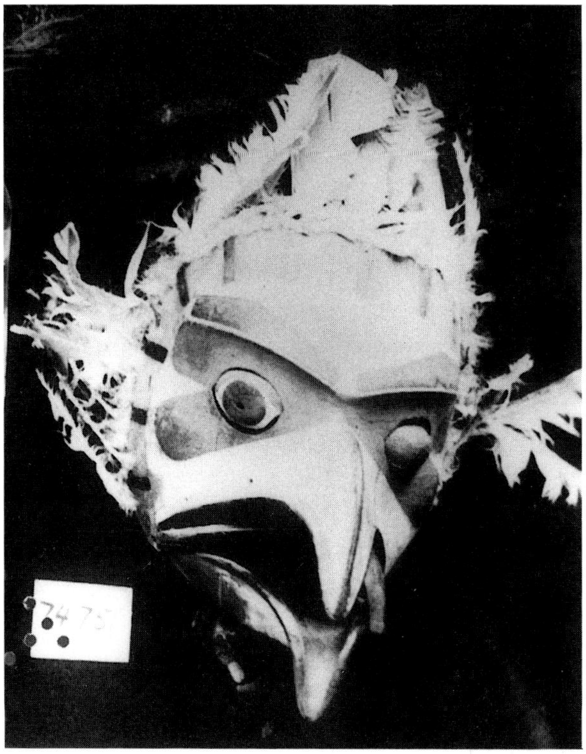

The feathers on this Haida mask have been damaged by exposure to light and fluctuations in relative humidity and temperature. Courtesy Smithsonian Institution

SKINS, FURS, FEATHERS, AND OTHER ANIMAL MATERIALS

Objects comprised of animal parts are frequently found in ethnographic collections. Some cultures, such as those in the far north where vegetation is more scarce, have used almost every available part of local animals for functional objects. It is not unusual to find parkas made of intestine, or fishing floats made of seal bladders or materials from other aquatic animals. Sewing thread made of sinew (fabricated from tendons) has been used by many cultures. In addition to internal parts, external animal parts such as feathers, porcupine quills, hair (such as wool), horns, and claws also have been used. Probably the most conventional portions of animals used, however, are the skins, which, like wood, have been employed by almost every culture.

Because many protein materials can become very brittle with time, they should be handled with care and fully supported on a flat surface during movement to prevent cracking. Objects made with appended parts, such as claws and feathers, should be positioned so that feathers, for example, are not crushed from the weight of the object. Because these attachments often are joined to the structure with fragile threads and ties, it is important to support these sections adequately so that they do not break off of the main structure. Layers of tissue, internal cushions, or other padding materials may be needed to support these objects during examination, transport, exhibition, and storage.

Protein-based materials readily respond to changes in relative humidity and temperature, causing movement, stress, and sometimes irreparable distortion of the object. Painted surfaces will crack and flake as the object expands and contracts. Protein materials that are held under tension, such as drumheads and portions of other musical instruments, can easily split apart when drying occurs. High relative humidity also can lead to deterioration. At levels above 65 percent RH, fungal activity can occur, causing staining and damage to protein structures. Additionally, bacterial action can produce protein decay. Loose hair, for example, can be a sign of microbial or fungal activity. In fact, recent studies have shown that fungal growth may continue even after an object containing hair is removed from conditions of high relative humidity. With the addition of moisture and heat, untreated skin materials can denature, turning into gelatin or glue.

The stability of skin objects depends to a large extent on the way in which they were prepared and whether the skin has been tanned and what tanning agent was used. Semitanned, tawed, or untanned skins, such as buckskin, parchment (or vellum), and rawhide, are less resistant to deterioration than skins that have been treated with a vegetable or mineral tanning compound (leathers). Vegetable-tanned skins, however, are very susceptible to damage from sulfur in the air. The resulting irreversible reaction produces a powdery red compound called *red rot*, which easily rubs off the leather surface.

Insects are a problem for protein materials. Moths commonly attack wool (hair) and feathers and can infest other animal materials. Dermestid beetles can destroy most protein-based materials. Objects containing animal parts should be examined thoroughly for signs of insects and isolated as described above. Some signs of infestation include broken and chewed hairs, quills that look as though the surface layer has been removed, and holes or abraded surfaces on wool.

Light is detrimental to protein materials. Semitanned skins are more easily damaged than tanned skins, and vegetable tanning is more susceptible than the mineral process. Colored surfaces, especially those colored with natural dyes, fade quickly, as do some colors in feathers and dark hairs.

As these organic materials age, they often become brittle and lose their original physical properties. Horn objects, as well as bird beaks, hooves, claws, and other decorative attachments on objects, may crack, split, or delaminate, separating into layers. Feathers and quills can undergo similar physical deterioration and breakage. It is important to note, however, that some types of "damage," such as the clipping or breaking of feathers, may have been performed by the culture as a symbol of some ritual and are not a result of poor environmental conditions.

Inorganic Materials

METALS

Some ethnographic objects, such as African and Asian brass objects and Native American Indian copper and silver ornaments, are composed entirely of metal. All-metal jewelry also is found in many cultures. Although these objects may have been worn in the past, always use gloves when handling and examining metal objects; even one fingerprint can be etched indelibly into the surface. These metal objects may be colored or lacquered, as in Japanese metalwork; *blue* and *blackened* iron also can be found on African objects and Native American Indian pieces. Sometimes the metal is so heavily corroded or tarnished that such metal treatments may not be obvious immediately. Metal objects also may be brittle from fabrication or use. If severely corroded, they could easily fracture from flexing or from contacting a flat surface too abruptly. If metal decorative attachments are loose or bent, do not attempt to straighten out or reattach loose pieces. In addition, never scratch or abrade metals for identification. This action only provides a clean surface for further corrosion.

Many ethnographic objects have only decorations or parts that are composed of metals, which can make their preservation more difficult. For example, weapons are commonly composed of metals and organic substances such as wood and may be tied or wrapped with fibers and adhered with resins. These attached organic materials often are acidic and hold moisture close to the metal, thus contributing to the corrosion problem. Beaded

The right-hand portion of this ceramic was improperly restored. The original missing section is pictured at the far right.

objects should be examined carefully for metal beads, which may be blackened from corrosion and difficult to identify. Signs of deterioration should be detailed for later comparison and changes in the extent of corrosion noted since changes signal an unstable condition.

Sometimes corrosion problems are exacerbated when a weapon is stored in its sheath. Be careful when handling blades and do not force them in or out of a sheath. Metal tools and weapons can be extremely sharp and additional protection around a pointed blade or barb may be required. In addition, fatal poisons have been used on the tips of some weapons; for example, curare was used on South American arrows. Recent analysis of older museum pieces has shown that remnants of the poisons are still present. A thick washcloth or small hand towel folded over a blade offers some extra protection during lifting. The use of a padded tray, however, is better.

Other special problems to look for include the formation of green waxy deposits around copper-based pieces that are attached to skin materials. An example would be brass tacks on a leather belt, garment, or box. Some brass objects may show similar problems if they have been coated with certain waxes or oils. You may have observed such green deposits if you wear glasses with brass parts; the areas in which your skin touches the metal may be corroding. Residues from cleaning and polishing preparations also may be embedded in crevices or decorations, causing corrosion.

Corrosion also may occur because two metals are in contact with one another. In some instances, their contact is a result of the way the object was manufactured; in others, it is because metal objects are resting on one another or because a metal bracket or wire has been added to the artifact.

STONE, CERAMICS, AND GLASS

Ceramics are an important part of most cultures and have been used for a variety of utilitarian and ritual functions. Although ceramic objects are generally more durable than the organic materials previously discussed, they are not immune from deterioration processes. Salts are especially problematic for ethnographic ceramics. Some modern Acoma ceramics, for example, have a high salt content. Also, salts may have been added to a ceramic during use or repair. Another problem affecting these collections is that some ethnographic clay objects have not been fired to increase their stability. These objects often are cracked and crumbly, and they respond negatively to changes in relative humidity and temperature. Ceramic objects also may be coated with slips and paints after firing. These surface applications may be cracked, flaking, or may have been partially removed during use. In addition, they may be water soluble.

Resins may have been used to repair ceramics that have been cracked or broken. Sometimes these native repairs are brittle, cracked, and flaking. In the past, some ceramics were mended by lashing them together with skin thongs and metal wires. Skin ties and covers and cellulose fiber cords and wrappings may be present, posing the greater preservation problem.

Also important to note are mends that appear very weak and in danger of collapsing, as well as extensively restored areas. In fact, a number of early restorations have been found to be incorrectly executed, leading to misinterpretations about the shape and design of various artifacts.

Ceramic, glass, and/or stone beads frequently are found on ethnographic objects. These beaded objects usually fall apart because of the decay of the strings that hold them together. Improperly supported, the beads can cause these weakened fibers or strands to break more quickly, so careful handling and adequate support is extremely important. White crystals or deposits on the outside of glass beads or a slippery feeling to the surface are telltale signs that the glass is deteriorating and that a conservator should be contacted. Reducing the relative humidity, as one might recommend for deteriorating glass objects, may only lead to further embrittlement of the other organic materials.

Variations in relative humidity and temperature may affect the structural stability of some stones and decorative minerals. Argellite, a black stone carved in northwest America, for example, can crack with desiccation. Some minerals are sensitive to moisture and can change in structure and appearance as a result. Additionally, photosensitive minerals may be changed in color by light.

Inorganic/Organic Materials

As mentioned previously, some materials are composed of both inorganic and organic components. Examples include bone, outgrowths of bone such as antlers and teeth (including ivory), and the shells of mollusks such as snails and oysters. Mother-of-pearl and pearls also fall into this category. These inorganic/organic combination materials can be found as decoration on other base materials and as carved figures or designs. In small segments, it is often difficult to distinguish ivory from bone. In a larger piece, the more porous sections of bone can be seen, as compared to the denser "whorled" structure of ivory. Size and shape are a good indication as to whether the object is of bone or ivory. Although seemingly strong, these materials can be cracked easily or chipped from mishandling.

Because these materials are composed of both inorganic and organic portions, they can easily be stained, abraded, and eroded by acids. Like other organic materials, they are affected by changes in relative humidity and temperature, and splitting and cracking are common problems. Delamination can occur and often is seen on shell and mother-of-pearl. Materials with porous surfaces, such as antler and unpolished bone, may have dirt embedded in their surfaces. Yellowing, darkening, or discoloration may be evident because of surface oxidation and deterioration of the organic components. Bleaching from light also can occur. In some cases these objects, especially ivories, have been decorated with inks and colored with paints and dyes. These colorants may be faded, abraded, or flaking, especially from movement of the ivory with changes in relative humidity.

Care and Maintenance of Your Ethnographic Objects

As discussed in the preceding section, ethnographic objects are composed of many of the same materials reviewed in other chapters; therefore, methods of caring for them are similar to those detailed earlier. What follows are recommendations specific to the delicate nature of ethnographic objects.

In general, the temperature should be kept as low as is practical for all objects; the higher the temperature, the more rapid the rate of deterioration. When controlled properly, temperature can also be used to equalize some of the fluctuations in relative humidity.

The high salt content of this Southwestern Acoma ceramic contributed to its breaking into pieces when it was moved to a location with a higher relative humidity. Courtesy Smithsonian Institution

Light levels should be reduced for most organic objects, especially those with light-sensitive dyes. Daylight and ultraviolet radiation from fluorescent lights generally should be excluded or filtered and exposure time to light should be kept to the minimum. In other words, keep room lights off and shades or curtains drawn when the room is not in use. Another option would be to cover light-sensitive objects kept in a room that is frequently used by the family, exposing them only for your special enjoyment or as a display for others. Rotation of these objects to darker rooms or to storage is another option.

Ideally, relative humidity should be maintained between 45 and 55 percent for most organic objects. Recent studies suggest that even lower levels may be appropriate for certain objects. And, in some cases, materials may have become acclimated to a drier environment and are stable under those conditions. For combination materials such as ivory and bone, it is recommended that the relative humidity remain above 40 percent to prevent cracking. Mold growth also can occur on these materials at above 65 percent RH. Generally more important than achieving these precise levels, however, is that the relative humidity remain as stable as possible. For example, turning the air conditioner on and off during the day and night in humid climates can create more damage than not using an air conditioner at all.

For composite objects, a well-controlled environment is the key to maintaining the integrity of the piece. Because these objects consist of a variety of materials, 50 percent RH, plus or minus 10 percent, generally is recommended as a level to achieve. In some instances, newly acquired ethnographic objects may need to be acclimated to your local environment. This is especially true of objects acquired from climates markedly different from your own. In these instances, house the object in a plastic bag or stable packing materials for several weeks, and monitor and inspect it periodically. If the relative humidity levels between the two locations are very different (greater than 15 percent), then humidity buffering materials should be included in the package and the acclimatization period should be lengthened. This precaution should reduce the stress in your object in adjusting from one climate to another; however, it will not guarantee that the object will not crack or undergo some other physical change. Similar precautions should be taken with sensitive objects when the enviromental systems are shut down for repair or if dramatic environmental changes occur between seasons. In addition, broken steam pipes, basement flooding, and roof leaks can greatly increase the relative humidity, even if the object is not wetted. Do not place a damp or wet object in a plastic bag. Such types of enclosure can lead to the corrosion of metals and mold growth.

Gradually acclimate objects with mold growth to a drier environment with a dehumidifier or by moving the object to a slightly drier room. Dispose of damp and wet packing materials. Fans also can be used to increase air circulation, but do not place the fans so they are blowing directly on the object. If the surface of the object is stable and undecorated, it should be vacuumed when it is dry to remove mold as described later. In any case, an expert should be consulted as soon as possible concerning the mold problem associated with your specific object.

Inspect objects periodically for signs of insect infestations. Seal suspect objects in a plastic bag and watch for new signs of insect activity. Often it is helpful to put a white sheet of paper under the object to make insect droppings and remnants more visible. This practice of bagging and isolating objects also should be adopted for all recently collected artifacts from tropical countries, regardless of whether there are any signs of insects or not. Failure to take these precautions could result in the infestation of organic materials throughout your house. One way of determining which insects are active in your home is to set up sticky traps from the hardware store in corners and near food sources. These traps can give a good basic indication of where problems exist and what housekeeping habits or environmental storage conditions may need to be changed to better protect objects.

If you see any signs of insect activity on your objects, keep the objects encased and call a conservator immediately for advice. Remove objects infested with silverfish, which can be an indicator of high humidity, from packing materials, which should be discarded outside, and store in a drier location. Do not apply poisons or other chemicals to your objects because they may cause irreparable damage.

Also important in preserving ethnographic objects is good housekeeping; surface dust and dirt can be difficult to clean and can foster insect activity. In addition, although some ethnographic objects should not be cleaned because they contain culturally significant deposits as described earlier, or because the structures are unstable, superficial dust and dirt should be removed from the surfaces of sturdy cultural objects to prevent further deterioration. Modern textiles; undecorated baskets and mats; wooden objects with sound structures and nonfriable, unpainted surfaces; stone, bone, and ivory artifacts; and many all-metal objects can be cleaned.

Stable textiles and mats can be cleaned by low-powered vacuuming through nylon or polyester window screening. Another useful vacuuming apparatus can be constructed by taping a long, thin plastic or rubber hose to the nozzle of your canister vacuum cleaner. An aquarium hose is about the right size. This setup provides a low-powered, controlled method of cleaning most stable objects. However, the exhaust from the vacuum should be filtered or directed through a hose to the outside so that mold spores are not blown throughout the room. Brushes should not be used because they have a tendency to work the dirt and dust further into the surface.

In general, insect remains should be removed from all objects so that new infestations can be identified. For sturdy objects as described above, careful vacuuming will remove some of the debris. In other cases, tweezers can be used to pick insect remains from the surface. This procedure should be carried out very carefully to avoid damaging the object. In instances where the insect materials are firmly adhered, when hairs are broken, or when the removal may cause loss of surface decoration or structural materials, it is best to leave the insect remains in place. Moreover, some insect parts may be integral to the object.

Under no circumstances should any cleaning compounds, solutions, or abrasive substances be used on ethnographic objects. In addition, avoid dressings such as saddle soap, oils, or furniture or floor waxes. Such preparations may only exacerbate previous problems and irreparably damage the piece. Recent studies, for example, have shown that some leather dressings can actually cause desiccation of skin objects, and the oils sometimes suggested for use on ivories and shell can lead to further deterioration. Even fine waxes and polishes that are safe for some furniture and wooden floors can easily damage ethnographic wooden objects.

Solvents such as water, alcohol, and other cleaning fluids can remove color and protective surfaces and may cause organic materials to dry out. Actions based on old wives' tales, such as "regularly misting baskets with water" and "feeding fibers with oil," should be avoided altogether. The temporary cosmetic effect that these treatments render can cause problems at a later time. Similarly, do not try to clean portions of complex composite objects, such as glass beads, metal ornaments, or textiles, with treatments that are recommended for single-material objects.

Remember that minimal intervention is the best approach for most ethnographic objects. When further treatment is warranted, choose a conservator who is well acquainted with your ethnographic collections and support him or her in undertaking the minimum treatment that is necessary. Finally, do not forget to update your documentation with the specifics of any cleaning or other treatments that are used on your object.

Displaying Your Ethnographic Collections

Choosing a location that will highlight your ethnographic collections and protect them at the same time often can be difficult because of the sensitive nature of many of the materials. Ideally, we should store our objects in archival boxes out of the light and under very controlled conditions to preserve them for posterity. In practice, however, we would like to enjoy our collections and share them with others.

The exhibition of your object is, in fact, a compromise between the reason that you acquire and save each object and those conditions that will preserve your object for the longest period of time. You must determine how to make this compromise based on the importance of each object and its individual stability requirements. The examination process can assist you in determining the latter criteria. If your goal is to give each object the best possible care, then you should evaluate a potential location for each item according to its positive and negative impact on the artifact. Locations near

Three-dimensional objects can be supported in polyethylene foam blocks with cutout areas slightly larger than the base of the object. The objects should be protected from the rough edges of the cut foam with acid-free tissue or a thin layer of polyethylene foam sheeting. Courtesy Smithsonian Institution

sources of heat—sunlight and windows, for example—should be used only for dispensable objects. In some instances you may need to create special microenvironments to provide adequate protection. Sometimes this can be accomplished by simply covering an object with a Plexiglas box or bell jar. A range of shapes and sizes are available at large hardware or department stores. If you are handy, you can make a box yourself with Plexiglas sheets. In other cases, you may need to include a humidity-buffering material such as silica gel or Artsorb® and purchase or construct tightly enclosed cases.

After selecting a proper location for your object, you must consider adequate support. Some objects have flat surfaces or a base that can support their weight; however, check to make sure they are not top heavy and prone to tipping over. Many wooden sculptures need auxiliary support for this reason. Consider also the overall weight of the material. Unstable shelving and wobbly furniture can give way under the pressure of heavy objects.

The mounting of unstable objects or those without a flat surface can be an art in itself, and museums often employ special bracket makers to create appropriate designs in Plexiglas and metal. The goal is to provide supports that alleviate stress without detracting from the object or causing additional deterioration problems. For special objects, these custom-designed mounts should be considered.

Many objects can be mounted on less expensive padded forms and supports made of polyethylene foam, polyester batting, and stable textiles. Most ethnographic conservators are well versed in creating such supports, and a number are easy to construct yourself. An example would be a padded ring support for ceramics or baskets with rounded bottoms.

In creating any mount, it is important to use stable materials in the construction. Unstable substances or those that produce harmful vapors, such as styrofoam, polyurethane foam, wood, cardboard, and textiles such as wool, may only compound your preservation problems. In creating any support, it is equally critical that the stress be alleviated rather than concentrated by forcing the object over or into an inappropriate mount. The object should dictate the type of support to be used, not vice versa. Do not display objects so that they rub against one another or rest on top of each other. Pad rigid mounts to absorb shock from normal vibrations, and always coat or cover metal brackets.

Objects to be mounted on the wall also require some type of support system, which may include textile mounts or more three-dimensional mounts fabricated as some variation of those described above. Some objects, such as heavy, beaded garments, may not lend themselves to vertical suspension and should be displayed on a padded mannequin or custom-built form. To develop methods of display that have a visual impact yet also protect your objects, visit a museum, note the possibilities, then get an expert to assist you in determining an appropriate and protective method for displaying each of your objects.

A variety of supports can be constructed with polyethylene foam, acid-free board, cotton-knit fabric, and polyester fiberfill (batting). Courtesy of the University of California, Davis

Storing Your Ethnographic Collections

To insure their long-term preservation, store your objects using stable archival materials, such as acid-free papers, boards, and boxes; washed, unbleached muslin; and certain synthetic products. Objects like mats and small textiles should be stored flat in shallow boxes lined with acid-free paper or tied with cotton twill-tape to acid-free cardboard. Many objects with a flat side can be stored in a similar manner. Use acid-free papers for padding-out garments, baskets, and other flexible three-dimensional objects. Generally it is less expensive to purchase unbuffered papers in quantity to use with all your organic objects; remember that buffered papers can be used for cellulosic substances but may cause problems in association with protein-based materials.

Some ethnographic objects may require sturdier supports during storage to avoid stress and damage. Although these mounts need not be as decorative and finely made, their construction must be equally supportive and stable. Polyethylene foams are generally stable and can be obtained in a variety of densities and thicknesses. Foam blocks

can be cut to shape to make both internal and external supports. A protective layer of tissue should be used between the foam and the object because the cut edges of the foam can be abrasive and can catch on fragile or rough surfaces. Other creative forms can be constructed by padding polyethylene or polypropylene food containers to conform to the shape of the object. Less preferable are polyethylene bubble packing materials. If they are used, be sure to cover them with paper or muslin so that they are not in direct contact with the object. Never use styrofoam or shredded polyurethane foam around your objects. Not only can the dust and small particles from these materials work their way into crevices and become difficult to remove, but also unstable foams can deteriorate in time, sometimes sticking to the object. Do not make any constructions with polyvinyl chloride (PVC) tubing or other questionable vinyl or chloride containing plastics. If your storage mount or container is complicated, it is helpful to sketch a diagram of how you have packed or mounted your object for storage so that objects are not damaged in the unpacking or dismounting process.

Ideally, objects should be stored in separate containers in museum-quality metal cabinets. The next best solution would be to store objects on padded shelves in metal cabinets or in individual containers on metal shelving. If cabinets and acid-free containers are not available, objects can be stored on padded metal shelving with a dust cover of polyethylene sheeting or muslin. One also could create a dust cover by attaching a window shade to the top of the shelving unit and carefully pulling it down over the face of the shelves.

Sometimes objects are enclosed in good-quality polyethylene (not vinyl or common dry-cleaning plastic) bags for protection from dust and rapid environmental changes. If polyethylene bags are used, however, it should be with caution because of possible problems with condensation, mold, or static electricity. In the latter case, fur, feathers, and other delicate fibers can be attracted to the plastic surface; therefore, take care when moving these materials in and out of plastic bags. Regardless, it is almost always better to provide some covering for an object than to leave it in the open.

Although some light objects such as small mats and textiles could be housed in the same box with adequate padding between layers, it is otherwise best to avoid stacking objects on top of one another in a container. Baskets and ceramics, for example, should not be nested one within the other.

Although private collectors rarely have many options for ideal storage locations, the storage of collections in uncontrolled damp basements or open attics is usually the worst choice. Dark closets with poor ventilation can cause problems as well. More central locations in your house are often more stable. Wherever the storage location, collections should be inspected routinely to check for insect activity and mold growth from unexpected dampness. A periodic comparison with your examination sheet will aid in detecting problems before extensive damage has occurred.

SECURITY FOR CULTURAL OBJECTS IN THE HOME

Wilbur Faulk

The possibility of theft of artistic and cultural objects is of increasing concern to collectors today. It has been estimated by *U.S. News and World Report* that "art theft is now second only to drug trafficking among international crimes."[1] Over the past decade the United States has seen a dramatic increase in art theft from museums, galleries, corporate collections, and especially from private homes. Worse still, recent law enforcement reports suggest that less than 10 percent of those art objects stolen are ever recovered.[2] And crime is not the only threat. Fire and natural disasters such as earthquakes, tornadoes, and floods pose further risks. As a result, collectors of cultural objects have a responsibility to develop a comprehensive protection plan for their collections.

The purpose of this chapter is to assist the private collector in developing an effective security program within the constraints of philosophy, needs, and budget. Whether your present security program is extensive, minimal, or nonexistent, whether it is antiquated or incorporates the most modern technology, the information here will help you to evaluate the security and safety of your collection. It is a basic guide to understanding the nature of the threats you face, how to minimize risks, and where to find more detailed information.

Conducting a Security Survey

Assessing the security requirements for your collection begins by conducting a security survey—this simply means a systematic evaluation of the strengths and weaknesses of your current situation, from your neighborhood to the interior details of your home. The principles for protecting a collection from theft in a home are not

Even without the resources of a large institution, private individuals can do much to safeguard their homes and collections. The J. Paul Getty Museum, Malibu, California

fundamentally different from those that apply to protecting the home itself. Good security, reduced to its essence, is a matter of finding the vulnerabilities and eliminating them.

As a first step, you may want to conduct this survey yourself. By all means, do so. You will find useful information in the references at the end of this chapter and the book. You may also find that you need additional assistance. If so, contact the crime-prevention unit of your local police department, your insurance broker, or a reliable security consultant. Regardless of who conducts the survey, the following guide should be helpful.

Assessing the Perimeter, the Building, and the Interior

The security survey begins not inside your home but outside, in the surrounding neighborhood. Your community is your first line of defense. Unfortunately, there are few places today that could be considered immune from the threat of crime. However, if your collection is located in a high-crime area, the threat of attempted break-in is correspondingly greater and more extensive protection may be needed.

Attempt to view your neighborhood through the eyes of a potential burglar. Is it busy or secluded, high crime or low, well-lighted or dark at night? Do strangers stand out or go unnoticed? Are there frequent police patrols or private guard companies active in the area? Is there a neighborhood watch program?

Next, consider the overall property. Providing security for objects inside the building begins by controlling access to the grounds. The most basic of these measures are obvious. The grounds should be securely fenced and gated, if possible. The exterior of the building should be well lighted at night and clear of shrubbery or obstructions that could provide cover for an intruder. Ideally, there should be frequent (but irregular) patterns of activity at all times, including weekends and holidays, to convey the impression that the building is inhabited and protected around the clock. An outdoor watchdog may also be helpful.

The final stage of the physical survey requires scrutinizing the outside and inside of the building itself to discover its weaknesses—which is exactly what a burglar would do. Two-thirds of the time, a burglar's mode of entry and exit is a door, often an infrequently used side or rear door. Windows and skylights are targets the remainder of the time, except for the small percentage of break-ins that involve cutting through roofs, walls, or floors.

Once you have completed your survey, you should have identified your vulnerabilities. While you won't yet have all the answers, you will be able to determine your priorities and establish a plan of action. The next step is to solicit itemized proposals from security firms in order to estimate the costs and evaluate the feasibility of your plans. Be certain to consult with more than one company, and ask for references and check them out. During this process, as always, be cautious about displaying your collection or discussing its value with people you don't know. Compare products and services with care. At this point, you may decide to proceed in phases.

Elements of Physical Security

There is no such thing as "perfect" security; it is axiomatic that any building can be entered and robbed, given enough inside information, ingenuity, privacy, and time. The goal of your physical security program must be to make it too difficult to attack your collection. A would-be intruder must be too unsure of your defenses, and they must be too visible and too loud or it must take too long to make it worthwhile to circumvent them.

Hardware

Both the architectural design and quality of construction of your home will have a significant effect upon your ability to provide adequate physical security. For example, a secluded terrace with French doors is inherently more difficult to protect than a front door of solid oak. The more vulnerable the exterior shell of your building, the more you must rely on supplementary electronic devices. First, however, you should make every effort to bolster your home's conventional security hardware.

High-security deadbolt locks with restricted keyways offer the best all-around protection. Use them for all exterior doors and any sensitive indoor areas. The bolt must have at least a one-inch travel and should be supported by a strong door frame with a reinforced strike plate. Exposed lock cylinders should have sturdy cylinder guards. All exterior hinge pins should be protected as well. A substantial slide bolt should be added to the inside of any door that is seldom used.

One further caveat: even the most sophisticated locking system is useless without assured key control. It makes sense, for this and other reasons, to form a good working relationship with a full-service, bonded locksmith.

Skylights, ground-floor windows, and other accessible glassed-in areas require protection. Modern innovations include unbreakable polycarbonate glass and security films (tough transparent coatings that also offer ultraviolet filtering). These may offer alternatives to the traditional security bars, where aesthetic considerations or local fire regulations restrict their use.

A well-lighted building is a far less inviting target for burglary. A recent innovation, rapidly growing in popularity, is a floodlight connected to a motion detector that turns on the light whenever anyone moves into the protected area. These devices are inexpensive and easy to install; a few of them, strategically placed, can cover the exterior of a typical home. Placing selected interior lights on random timers can also be helpful.

Electronic Security and Fire Systems

According to *Consumer Reports*, "Police in a wealthy New York City suburb found that during a six-year period 90 percent of the burglaries it recorded occurred in houses without burglar alarms."[3] Many insurance companies will reduce your insurance premiums by 5 to 15 percent when you install deadbolt locks, burglar alarms, and a smoke-and-fire-detection system.

Having an alarm system may demand modifications in your daily routine. This should be given serious consideration. You should design a system you can live with comfortably rather than buy a system you won't use. Here is where a qualified security consultant may be extremely helpful—particularly one with special expertise in museum, library, or historic-house security. In most situations, the more simple the system, the more likely it is to be used and maintained.

No specific brand names for security or fire detection devices are recommended in this chapter. There are too many from which to choose, and the technology evolves rapidly. Some items considered "state-of-the-art" only a few years ago have already been supplanted by newer, improved designs. A welcome trend is toward less obtrusive devices that are aesthetically acceptable in nearly any interior decor. Remember, however, that it is not imperative that you be on the cutting edge of security technology. In fact, it is generally a better idea to stick to proven designs and manufacturers.

A complete electronic security/fire detection system has four principal components. First are sensors, which detect a specific type of activity. Second is a means of communicating the alarm, either via low-voltage wiring (hardwired) or by radio transmission (wireless). Third is an annunciator/control panel, which constantly monitors all activity and instantly reports the location of an alarm to a reliable source. Finally, there must be an outside agency, such as the police or fire department, or a private security company, that responds to the alarm and investigates its cause.

TYPES OF SENSORS

Among the various models of detectors on the market today, four principal types will meet the majority of your requirements: motion detectors, magnetic door contacts, break-glass detectors, and duress alarms.

The *motion detector*, particularly the passive infrared detector (PIR), has gained wide acceptance in recent years. Motion detectors are usually mounted unobtrusively on the ceiling or high on a wall. They can cover wide areas, such as an entire room or corridor, or focus on a critical spot. They also can be used to provide "interior traps," either to detect an intruder who has circumvented the perimeter defenses or as a deterrent to employees who might otherwise enter sensitive or private areas. In a home, the use of dual-technology motion detectors (such as a combination of infrared and ultrasonic sensors) can virtually eliminate the inconvenience of false alarms.

Magnetic door contacts are most often used to monitor doors and windows. They can also be installed in cases and on cabinet and storage drawers. The device is activated when the door or window is opened. Door contacts are popular because they are reliable, easy to install, small, and inexpensive.

Break-glass detectors may be used to protect windows, skylights, and glass showcases. The *shock-sensor* type is mounted on the glass or frame and reacts to the physical vibration of breaking glass, while the *audio-discriminator* type is an electronic device located anywhere within a room; it is activated by the sound of shattering glass.

Duress alarms can be added easily to an electronic alarm system for additional personal protection. The preferred type of duress alarm, like the teller's alarm in a bank, is silent and concealed. Its purpose is to summon outside help without the knowledge of the intruder.

ALARM COMMUNICATION

To communicate alarms to the control panel within your house, a hardwired low-voltage system remains preferable. Over the past ten years, however, major strides have been made in the development of wireless alarm systems, and in some situations—particularly in retrofitting an existing home—this may be the method of choice. A wireless alarm uses a battery-powered radio transmitter to send its signal to a concealed nearby receiver. The receiver communicates with the control panel via conventional low-voltage wiring. Whichever means of transmission is used, it must be "supervised"—that is, designed to signal if any part of the communication system has been interrupted, tampered with, or compromised.

CONTROL PANEL

The annunciator/control panel constantly monitors the status of the entire system and instantly reports all alarms to the off-site central station. It should be versatile enough to accommodate all of the owner's requirements (for example, fire and water detection in addition to security alarms) and offer maximum flexibility in programming options. It should have separate alarm zones and the capability to activate specific zones as needed—for example, in order to allow freedom of movement inside the building with only the perimeter security turned on. The control panel should be placed in a secure and convenient location and alarmed against tampering. A back-up battery power supply is essential.

OUTSIDE RESPONSE

The final essential element in the system is communication of any alarms to a reliable off-site agency, often the central station of a commercial security firm. They in turn will initiate a response by your local police or fire department or security patrol. The central station may be located many miles away, but proximity is not critical, as your alarm system automatically communicates with them by telephone. The serious collector may wish to consider installing a dedicated phone line exclusively for this purpose. A cellular telephone as a backup further protects the system, by maintaining a channel of communication when regular phone lines are disrupted.

You should consider installing local alarm bells on the inside and/or outside of the house. The noise they make is primarily intended to let the intruder know that he or she has been detected and encourage flight.

Closed-Circuit Television

In recent years the popularity of closed-circuit television (CCTV) has grown rapidly, in private homes as well as in industry. Today CCTV has become both reliable and affordable, and a properly designed CCTV system is a valuable adjunct to an electronic alarm system, useful for monitoring grounds and entrances as well as building interiors. Visible CCTV monitors at gates and entrances give an impression of high-level security and may be a significant deterrent to intruders.

A CCTV system, even when not monitored around the clock, can be equipped with time-lapse video recorders to provide a record of activity that could be used later as part of an investigation. If used, the video recorder should be installed in an extremely secure, well-concealed location in order to prevent a thief from removing the tape.

Household Security Practices

Commonsense procedures can offer low cost and valuable protection. It is prudent for the collector to periodically review basic security routines with all family members and household staff. These begin with the simplest of habits, such as not hiding keys under the doormat or anywhere else on the premises, and removing all house keys from the key ring when leaving the car with a parking-lot attendant or garage mechanic.

It is also basic, but nevertheless important, to ensure that some sort of routine continues when you are gone: that lawns are mown, leaves raked, snow shoveled. Note that contrary to past advice, law enforcement officials currently suggest that one should avoid canceling newspapers and mail when traveling, since this information may get into the wrong hands. Instead, they should be picked up daily by a trusted person. A reliable house sitter may prove valuable (but see the comments about domestic employees below).

Documentation and Inventory

It is absolutely essential that you maintain an accurate inventory of your entire collection. The inventory must include both comprehensive written documentation and high-quality photographs—black-and-white and color—of every object in the collection. The records should include size, material, weight (if a factor), and a unique description. At least one complete set of this information should be stored in a safety-deposit box or another secure off-site location.

Detailed photographs of any flaws or distinctive features in the object are also very helpful for identification. This is especially important for antiques or prints that are rare but not one of a kind.

Should any part of your collection be stolen, these photographs will be indispensable to the police as they alert other law-enforcement agencies and dealers to whom the objects might be offered for sale. Without them, the authorities will not be able to conduct as effective an investigation and the chance of recovery is correspondingly lessened. Video inventories, which have become increasingly popular, do have their value, particularly for insurance purposes, but are no substitute for good photographs in a theft investigation.

Domestic Employees and Business Strangers

Detective William Martin, head of the Art Theft Detail of the Los Angeles Police Department, states that "in 80 to 90 percent of the private homes burglarized in Los Angeles where art is the target, the thief himself, or the person who planned the crime, has previously been inside the house for one reason or another. This is one of the most likely ways for a potential thief to become aware of the existence of the objects and to decide how to steal them."[4]

Obviously, we all need to invite strangers into our homes. Friends and relatives, business associates, party guests, and full- or part-time domestic help would head a list that also includes mail carriers, dry cleaners, decorators, baby-sitters, house sitters, pest controllers, remodelers, and salespersons. Not only guests and employees, but also their friends, whose character may be unknown to you, pose a risk when allowed into your home.

In fact, anyone who has access to your house could have the opportunity to study your security measures or to unlock a door or window or steal a key ring. Some of these people can learn much about your habits just by being observant. All domestic employees, including baby-sitters and house sitters, should be investigated thoroughly before being hired, and this background information should be stored securely. Whenever domestic staff leave your employ, inventory your collection and change your alarm combination and your locks. The cost is minimal compared to the risk.

Do not provide service and delivery people with detailed information about your personal schedule. Anytime work is done in your home, arrange to have someone you trust accompany the workers, and inventory your collection at the end of each day. Again, change your locks at the end of the project if any worker had access to your keys.

Safes

Safes have always been popular devices to protect personal valuables in the home. The most effective type is a floor safe mounted in concrete in an obscure corner of your house. The objects and the safe are reasonably secure from theft and fire. Obviously, there are many kinds of safes. Some people, for example, store important papers and documents in fire safes, but remember that they are built primarily to protect against fire, not theft.

Thieves have been known to steal portable safes, even when they are very heavy, and to force them open once away from the victim's house. Regardless of whether you have a security or fire safe, see that it is securely fastened to the structure.

Fire Protection

Fire is probably the greatest threat to your collection. Even a small fire can destroy it completely in a matter of minutes. And, as compared to a theft, objects destroyed by fire can never be recovered. The risk of fire can be minimized by the development of a fire-prevention program.

Your program should begin with good housekeeping. Conduct a fire-prevention survey—like your security survey—to identify and eliminate fire hazards. Maintain an adequate number of fire extinguishers, not only where the objects are displayed, but also in all areas of the house, and periodically train your family and employees in their use. Establish a no-smoking policy, at least in the areas where you display or store your collection. Smoking greatly increases the risk of fire and creates other hazards for your collection as well.

Special care should be taken anytime there is construction in your building. More fires start during construction projects than at any other time.

Possibly the single most important step you can take to minimize the risk of fire is to install an automatic smoke-detection system throughout the house. Most fire codes throughout the United States require each dwelling to have one smoke detector—often merely a battery-powered one—which sounds only locally. It is strongly recommended, however, that you consider hard-wiring the detectors and integrating them into your electronic security system. This ensures that any fire or smoke alarm will be reported automatically to your local fire department.

It is important to understand that smoke-detection systems do not extinguish fires. The system only notifies you and the central station that there may be a fire. You should be aware that automatic fire-sprinkler systems are an option for residential fire protection and are even beginning to be required for new homes in some parts of the country.

Your local fire-prevention bureau can provide guidance in developing a fire-prevention system. More detailed information about fire protection of collections is also available in the National Fire Protection Association's *Recommended Practices for the Protection of Museums* (see the bibliography at the back of the book).

Water Detection

Water poses a serious threat to many cultural objects, but major improvements in water detection technology make this problem more preventable. There are several water-detection systems on the market that provide early detection of leaks in sensitive areas and that can be designed as part of your overall electronic system. Your local museum or library may be able to give you references and suggestions.

Emergency Preparedness

Cultural institutions around the world face the devastation of natural disasters and try to prepare for them. The International Council of Museums, in cooperation with UNESCO, has declared the

1990s the Decade of Natural Hazard Reduction. The Council's goal is to identify the risks and minimize the damage that cultural objects may face in the event of a natural disaster. Private collectors should also take reasonable steps to protect their collections from the types of emergencies or natural disasters that may be anticipated in their geographical area. Contact the conservation or security staff at a local museum for advice.

Avoid the temptation to assume that you will be able to handle any emergency personally. As a simple first step, prepare a list of people you need to reach in the event of the most likely emergencies: law enforcement and fire agencies, utilities companies, locksmith, insurance agent, etc. Keep copies handy, take the list with you when you travel, and review and update it regularly. Some people find it helpful to reduce the list to a plasticized wallet-size card.

Thinking the Unthinkable: If a Theft Occurs

1. Notify your local law-enforcement agency. You should know in advance who is assigned to the art-theft detail.
2. Do not allow anyone to disturb the crime area until the police have arrived.
3. Be prepared to provide detailed information about exactly what was stolen. The photo documentation mentioned earlier will greatly enhance the ability of law-enforcement personnel to conduct a successful investigation.
4. Notify your insurance company.
5. Law-enforcement officials may favor immediately publicizing the theft in the hope of eliciting information that helps them to solve the crime. Be prepared to make this difficult decision based on the likelihood of recovery, insurance considerations, your feelings about personal privacy, et cetera.
6. The following agencies may assist local law enforcement:

Federal Bureau of Investigation (FBI)
National Stolen Art File
9th and Pennsylvania Avenue, N.W.,
Washington, D.C. 20535
(202) 324–4434

International Foundation for Art Research, Inc. (IFAR)
46 East 70th Street
New York, N.Y. 10021
(212) 879–1780

Interpol/United States National Central Bureau
U.S. Department of Justice
Washington, D.C. 20530
(202) 272–8383

Los Angeles Police Department
Art Theft Detail
150 North Los Angeles Street
Los Angeles, Calif. 90012
(213) 485–2524

New York Police Department
Art and Antique Investigation
Special Fraud Squad
One Police Plaza, Room 1108
New York, N.Y. 10038
(212) 374–6850

NOTES

1. "Heisting Buyers on their Own Petards." *U.S. News and World Report* (May 15, 1989): 16.
2. Ibid.
3. "Burglar Alarms." *Consumer Reports* (October 1984): 568–71.
4. Detective William Martin, Art Theft Detail, Los Angeles Police Department. Interview, September 1990.

Acknowledgments

The author wishes to thank Will Royston, Bob Combs, Barbara Whitney, and Laurie Sowd of the J. Paul Getty Museum for their contributions to this chapter.

THE INCREASING VALUE OF ART AND HISTORICAL ARTIFACTS

John L. Marion

"How fascinating the price of pictures has become in this humdrum world."

—Gerald Reitlinger
The Economics of Taste: The Rise and Fall of Picture Prices, 1760–1960

On May 17, 1990, at Sotheby's New York, John Marion auctioned Wassily Kandinsky's 1914 oil painting Fugue, *from the collection of the Solomon R. Guggenheim Museum, for $20,900,000, a record price for the artist's work.*

Every collector, whether he thinks much about the subject or not, likes imagining that the works of art he has assembled, either bought cheaply or at great expense, are increasing in monetary value. After all, everyone cares about value. One is always delighted to learn that an Art Deco lamp passed down from Grandmother and used as an everyday object has been appraised by an expert at many thousands of dollars; or that a favorite painting on the living room wall done by an artist once out of favor, and now favorably reappraised by the critics, has shot up wildly in value. Experiences like these are bound to make a collector sit up and take notice of the works in his possession and, one hopes, to take all necessary steps to preserve and protect them.

Opposite:
On December 16, 1988, the piano and bench from the Paris scene in the film Casablanca *(Warner Bros., 1942–43) sold at Sotheby's New York for $154,000. At the same sale of Hollywood memorabilia, the original hat worn by the Wicked Witch of the West in* The Wizard of Oz *(MGM, 1939) sold for $33,000, and Clark Gable's leather-bound copy of the script for* Gone with the Wind *(MGM/David O. Selznick, 1939) brought $77,000.*

Recognizing the value of paintings, furniture, collectibles, and other works of art is a skill every serious collector should strive to master. This can be done rather easily, and even enjoyably, by keeping in mind a few practical guidelines. I have prepared a list of these and will be discussing them later in this essay. First, however, I would like to relate a couple of stories that help to illustrate the dramatic changes that have taken place in the art market in recent years. The first story is about connoisseurship, about how a knowledge of a specific collecting field can occasionally lead to an extraordinary discovery. The second is about value, about how the price of an art work in recent years has shot up like a rocket.

The Fourth Tea Table

The renowned American furniture dealer Israel Sack was a master of unearthing treasures in New England farmhouses and other remote but promising locales. His son Harold, in his charming memoir *American Treasure Hunt*, recalls Saturday afternoons back in the 1920s spent motoring with his father through the back roads of Vermont and Massachusetts in an open Buick touring car, calling on farmers and local dealers who were often to be found down some rutted and nearly impenetrable backwoods dirt road. While these trips often proved fruitless, occasionally something extraordinary would happen: quite unexpectedly father and son would come upon a piece of furniture of surprising beauty, rarity, and value, and one whose price was still manageable. Harold Sack describes this as "The Remarkable Discovery Syndrome," and he provides an example that took place a few years ago, not in rural New England, but in the Sack showrooms on East Fifty-seventh Street.

An attractive, gray-haired woman from Connecticut came into the showrooms one day with a photograph of a tea table she had bought some thirty years earlier from a decorator, who had found the piece in Seattle. That was the table's entire provenance; nothing else was known about it. Yet to the experienced eyes of the Sacks, the table looked tantalizingly familiar. With its intricate open ball-and-claw feet, it bore a resemblance to a Goddard-Townsend tea table dating from the period 1750 to 1760, the golden age of American furniture. However, only three such tables were known to exist, and all three were accounted for. The Sacks began to hold their breath. Could this possibly be a fourth?

A visit to the lady's home for inspection of the table proved it to be authentic, making it a very rare find indeed. The owner was thrilled with the news but was not about to part with the table until exploring whether an auction or a private sale would yield the highest price. Eventually the Sacks were able to buy it for $350,000 and then sell it to a collector in Virginia for $675,000. It should be added that the lady from Connecticut had originally purchased this historic piece of American furniture for the modest sum of $180.

The Two Auctioneers

Having spent thirty years in the auction business and stood at the auctioneer's podium for countless sales in every major field of collecting, I have witnessed firsthand an extraordinary evolution in the art world, one in which the value of works of art and the stature of artists have reached stratospheric levels. When I began my career in the auction business, art news was not considered headline material; few artists enjoyed superstar stature, and art auctions were not attended by film crews eager to record multimillion-dollar bidding wars. But all of that has changed, which brings me to another story, one with a personal twist.

My father, Louis J. Marion, started out in the auction business at the age of sixteen in the mail room at the firm that would become Parke-Bernet and later merge with Sotheby's. He became chief auctioneer of the firm in 1947 and presided over many record-breaking auctions. I, too, began my tenure at the firm in a modest way—working in the basement on an inventory of works that had been auctioned but remained unclaimed. My first turn at the podium came in 1961, and the first lot I auctioned, a book from the Auchincloss Collection, went for a breathtaking $75. The gentleman who bought it was David Kirschenbaum of the Carnegie Bookshop, who is still active today at the age of ninety-seven. Over the years I have had the honor of selling several major works, paintings in particular, that my father had sold before me. I can think of two such examples that illustrate how the value of art has increased dramatically.

In October 1952, my father sold Jacques-Louis David's *Farewell of Telemachus and Eucharis*, which David had painted after his exile to Brussels following the fall of Napoleon. The work fetched $3,950, which was a good price at the time. When the painting reappeared at auction more than three decades later, in February of 1987, it stirred tremendous enthusiasm among collectors and dealers. When the bidding ended I had sold the painting for $4,070,000, a new record for a nineteenth-century European painting. This price was more than a thousand times higher than the price my father had sold it for some thirty years before.

Another example concerns a sculpture by Constantin Brancusi entitled *M'lle. Pogany.* Executed in 1913, this stunning work of polished bronze depicts a Hungarian artist named Margit Pogany, who met Brancusi while studying art in Paris. She posed for the sculptor in 1910 and 1911, and *M'lle. Pogany* was completed two years later. According to the scholar Sidney Geist, four casts of the work were struck. Three eventually went to museums.

In 1950 my father auctioned the "fourth" cast of *M'lle. Pogany* at a sale of paintings and sculpture from the collection of Walter P. Chrysler, Jr. A noted American collector bought it for $1,700. Flash forward to November 1984. This same cast of *M'lle. Pogany* was consigned to Sotheby's for sale and I was able to auction it for $1,650,000, a new record for Brancusi.

Once again, the value of an object, sold first by my father and then by me, had increased a thousand times in just a little more than thirty years. As a postscript, I should like to add that prices for major works by Brancusi have, since that sale in 1984, been pushed much higher. In May 1990 I auctioned Brancusi's *La Negresse Blonde* from the collection of Lydia Winston Malbin for $8,800,000, establishing another new record for the artist.

Supply and Demand

There is one very compelling reason for this phenomenon, which can be summarized in two words: supply and demand. The art market, like any other, is governed by the law of supply and demand. There are more buyers than ever before but only a finite number of objects to be offered. This is especially true in the field of American furniture. To understand why, we need to consider a bit of history.

Consider the thirteen original colonies and the population of the United States in the eighteenth century. A tiny fraction of the people in that time were employed in making, by hand, the finest furniture, such as the Goddard-Townsend tea table, and very little of their output survives today. By comparison, think of the population explosion in the United States since Colonial days. Then think of the corresponding increases in the number of collectors, dealers, curators, and others eager to acquire the very best pieces of early American furniture.

With the number of buyers increasing so rapidly, and the number of pieces available shrinking, having gone into private collections and museums or been lost or destroyed, it is hardly surprising to see prices for the rarest pieces of American furniture being pushed beyond the million-dollar barrier. How else to explain the extraordinary price which Sotheby's achieved in January 1987 for the Chippendale "hairy-paw-foot" wing armchair that was made for General John Cadwalader of Philadelphia in 1770 by Thomas Affleck. This magnificent chair, which had been in use in the Children's Library at the Upland Country Day School in Chester County, Pennsylvania, was part of a celebrated suite made for General Cadwalader. It sold for $2,750,000. This was the highest price every paid for a piece of furniture at auction, and more than double the previous record for American furniture. This is a good example of what we might call the Manifest Destiny of the art world: that the rise in value of rare works of art is more or less inevitable because there simply aren't enough of them to meet the growing demand worldwide.

I would stress the word *worldwide* here because another very important reason for the

On January 31, 1987, this Chippendale serpentine-front mahogany "hairy-paw-foot" wing chair, made in 1770 for General John Cadwalader, brought $2,750,000 at auction at Sotheby's New York. Thomas Affleck, Philadelphia. Carving attributed to James Reynolds

This Philadelphia Queen Anne shell-carved walnut wing chair sold for $85,000 at Sotheby's New York in 1977.

increased value of art is the internationalization of the art world. Thanks to vastly improved communications systems, information about works of art, and about their sale, can be shared on a global basis, bringing together private collectors and dealers from the four corners of the earth in a manner that has greatly broadened the art market beyond national barriers. And, just as people travel more than ever before, so does art: Exhibitions tour everywhere, heightening our awareness of different artists and the cultures that have nurtured them like never before. Today, art truly is an international language.

On a related topic, the art world has become more service oriented. Auction houses and museums, in particular, have expanded the public's awareness of art through a dizzying array of seminars, symposiums, exhibits, publications, and films. Such programs at New York's Metropolitan Museum of Art each year, for example, typically are sold out. The public's appetite for books and magazines about art, in every conceivable field of collecting, is almost insatiable. These services and publications have made the art world a more open and inviting realm to the general public while helping to educate the potential collector's eye.

In short, this increased awareness of the art world has helped increase the demand for works of art and further helped prices rise. Information has been the key. I believe it is also the key to increasing your own awareness of your collection.

The Biggest Little Secret

"Collecting is a world habit," someone once wrote. "Collectors practice it consciously and with a definite, recognized aim. The rest of us practice it more or less unconsciously." Whether you practice collecting consciously or unconsciously, you'll find that although acquiring an eye for quality takes time and commitment, if you are disciplined about collecting in a particular field you will, over time, acquire knowledge that can be put to very sound use. You will also discover what I like to call the "biggest little secret" in the collecting world: that there are extraordinary, affordable finds out there. One hardly needs formal training to pursue collecting. In fact, the self-educated collector is in a position to see what others often don't.

I like to cite the example of a woman who bought a "sweetmeat" dish at a garage sale for $4. It was not an impressive-looking dish, yet the woman had seen some quality in it that riveted her attention. She had spent considerable time reading about American porcelain and studying pieces in museums and had a pretty good idea what this modest little garage-sale dish was really worth. She brought it to Sotheby's, and our experts correctly identified it as one of the few remaining pieces of porcelain made by Bonin and Morris of Philadelphia, America's only eighteenth-century porcelain factory. It sold for a breathtaking $66,000. At the time this was a record for American porcelain.

A Practical Guide for the Collector

Let us now talk about how to educate your eye. There are a number of important considerations one should take into account when assessing the value of a work of art. With this in mind, I have compiled the following practical guide for the collector.

Authenticity

There is a delightfully informative book called *Lock, Stock and Barrel*, by Douglas and Elizabeth Rigby, which takes an encyclopedic view of collecting since the days of the pharaohs. One of the more fascinating chapters discusses how to determine values in a collection and contains this insight about authenticity:

> The amateur . . . wants his possessions to be the best of their kind available, and in establishing this criterion of value he takes into consideration *quality* and *authenticity.* Alone among all these considerations, the question of authenticity is one which probably did not come into being until the collecting custom was sufficiently developed to be worth exploiting, and even this criterion to our certain knowledge has been in existence for several thousand years.

This is one area where the help of an expert is most important. Apart from examining certificates of authenticity, seeking the opinion of an expert is probably the safest route to assuring yourself that a work of art is not a reproduction or a fake. You can perform a certain amount of sleuthing yourself—as the woman with the sweetmeat dish did—by comparing the piece in question with documented examples illustrated in books and magazines or on display in museums. Experts at major auction houses are always available to lend their advice and opinion, and getting more than one such opinion will go far in confirming whether a work is authentic or not. My feeling here is that it is always better to know the truth, even if it hurts, than to assume it.

Condition

The rule of thumb is that any condition less than perfect makes a difference in the value of an art object. I'll quote the Rigbys once more: "Objects which have endured the buffeting of time and have survived relatively intact are preferred to damaged items, which are acceptable only when perfect examples are very rare or nonexistent."

We have probably all read stories about paintings of great value (the Mark Rothko that hung in the sunwashed dining room at Harvard, for example) that, because of careless treatment, have faded and lost considerable value. Condition is crucial. An almost microscopic hairline crack or scratch on a tabletop can be disastrous. A careful examination of a work being considered for purchase is absolutely necessary. Auction houses will provide a condition report for every lot offered, and it is a service well worth using. Such an examination should be supplemented by a condition report provided by the seller.

Keep in mind that restoration is not always a desirable solution to a flaw in a piece, for such "improvements" can often diminish an item's integrity. A few years ago, a chair from an estate in New Jersey arrived at Sotheby's looking like a wreck because the upholstery was so shredded. Most people would have consigned this chair to a junkyard rather than to an auction house; on examining it, however, our experts discovered that it was a Philadelphia Queen Anne shell-carved walnut wing chair of great value. In American furniture the frame is of primary importance, not the upholstery, and the frame on this chair was in nearly perfect condition. Fortunately, no one had tampered with the chair and we sold it for $85,000.

Rarity

Rarity can sometimes overshadow all other considerations of value, and it seems to be one quality every collector likes to emphasize when praising the virtues of a particular object. Rarity, of course, has many meanings. A stamp may be rare because of an imperfection in its printing; a book because it is an early edition of an obscure work by a famous (and perhaps dead) author; a painting because of its unusual subject or style within the artist's oeuvre; a table because every other one like it is in a major museum; an old baseball card because Babe Ruth or Lou Gehrig signed it. Of course, this rarity adds value to an object only if a sufficient number of people want it. A signed print in a limited edition of fifteen, for example, will be in much greater demand than one in an edition of fifteen hundred.

With some research you should be able to assess the rarity of any work of art in your collection, although, once again, getting an expert's opinion will also prove helpful.

Historical Importance and Provenance

Fame plays an unusually powerful role in the value of art. I am thinking here of a piano, a rather battered, cheap-looking upright. It had been painted crudely in green and blue, possessed only fifty-eight keys, and stood a mere forty-two inches high. If you were to have spotted this piano in a junk shop you would probably have snickered at its dwarf dimensions and splotchy paint job. But at a recent auction this piano and its bench, on which Dooley Wilson played "As Time Goes By" in the 1942 MGM film *Casablanca*, commanded a winning bid of $154,000.

I cite this as an example of how an object's appeal and monetary value can rest almost entirely on its historical or nostalgic value. A few years ago World War II veterans began bringing their Japanese sword trophies to our auction house in New York after learning that the Japanese government was seeking swords thought missing in this country and which were of national treasure status. One such sword that came to us was identified by a Japanese art expert as one listed in a sixteenth-century Japanese sword manual as one of the hundred-best swords in Japan. It was signed Aoe Suketsugu and dated 1312, and in May 1973 it brought $70,000, then a world auction record for Japanese art. This is perhaps another good example of why a collector should take an interest in researching, as much as possible, the history of any object in his collection.

Provenance is the history of ownership: who possessed an object and when. Just as the provenance of a work establishes its pedigree, so to speak, it also attaches value, and sometimes extraordinarily so. The lofty prices fetched for Andy Warhol's cookie jars when they were sold at auction in 1988 are a case in point. The Warhol sale also illustrates why single-owner sales at auction of property from a renowned collector—such as French furniture and Impressionist paintings of Florence Gould, the jewels of the Duchess of Windsor, and the paintings and furniture of Greta Garbo—are so appealing. Where the provenance is noteworthy, the value in a work of art is greatly enhanced.

Size

The most important thing to consider about the size of a work of art is that one should probably stay away from extremes. A ten-foot-high breakfront, for example, will require a room with a very lofty ceiling. While its size might be majestic, it might also affect the breakfront's resale value.

In comparing paintings by the same artist, a rule of thumb is that a very small work will probably be less valuable than a more standard-sized work (the paintings of Renoir being an excellent example). This is, of course, simplifying things a bit, for one has to take into consideration other factors, such as what period the painting comes from in the artist's career, as well as its artistic merits. But size is also a factor to consider.

Medium

As you delve deeper into a particular collecting field, you will find that the quality and composition of material that make up a work of art must be carefully assessed in determining value. The material used to create a work of art or an antique will have an effect, and possibly a substantial one, on value. Douglas and Elizabeth Rigby provide an interesting example from the field of porcelain. They write: "Modern collectors treasure the early 'soft-paste' Sèvres porcelain (manufactured between 1753 and 1804) far more than they do the later 'hard-paste' pieces, partly because the soft-paste examples are older, partly because they are actually finer, and partly because, due to the destruction in 1804 of the secret formula by which they were made, the early pieces are rarer and will become progressively so."

As a rule you will find that oils are more valuable than watercolors in the valuation of a painting, and pastels deemed least desirable. This is so because oil painting is generally regarded as a more difficult medium for the artist and is less affected by light, heat, and moisture. Unlike works on canvas, works on paper may suffer from fading spots and mildew, and works on panel may be affected by drying and splitting. As for sculpture, bronze is usually more valuable than wood. In jewelry, sapphires are less prized by collectors than rubies, and a platinum setting is deemed more valuable than one made of gold.

Subject Matter

Subject matter may not be decisive in determining the value of a work of art, but, taken in combination with other factors, it can be important. This may pertain more to paintings than to other fields of collecting, but the subject of a work should be considered when determining value. Landscapes, for example, are usually more valuable than portraits, except when the artist or subject is very desirable—a good example being Vincent van Gogh's record-breaking *Portrait of Dr. Gachet*. The delightful gaiety and charm of the Sunday afternoon dance depicted in Renoir's famous oil *Au Moulin de la Galette*, with the figures awash in bright colors filtered through the overhanging acacia trees, makes this painting irresistible. The same painting without the crowd would be far less engaging.

Fashion

This is perhaps the most subjective factor of all, for it depends so much on perceived taste. Some examples, like Queen Anne and Chippendale furniture, American silver, fine Old Master paintings, and precious jewels, never seem to go out of fashion.

Art Deco lamps, vases, and furniture, on the other hand, have been on a roller coaster of popularity. People who inherited Tiffany lamps and Gallé vases that once were consigned to the attic by their forebears are seeing record prices being paid for these works in the current art market. Who is to say whether this will last? Paintings of the nineteenth-century French Barbizon School have also gone in and out of fashion, although they are currently enjoying a resurgence of popularity.

It is not a bad idea, therefore, to consider the matter of fashion in terms of your own collection. Objects that have withstood the test of time clearly will have an advantage here in terms of increasing value.

The art market is driven by passion. Just as Israel Sack took to the back roads of New England in search of hidden treasures, you may find yourself on the same quest, whether in the major auction rooms here and abroad, in galleries, or at country-house sales. What we have examined here is the need to pursue this quest with a knowledge of how works of art should be evaluated for potential value. The best place to begin, of course, is not on the road but at home, with your own collection. Using the guidelines I have suggested, you should begin by evaluating each piece in your collection, studying and researching its characteristics, and determining its value in the current market. You may well be surprised by what you learn.

AUTHENTICATING YOUR COLLECTIONS

Richard Newman

In describing works of art, the word *authentic* can be used in more than one sense. In the broadest sense, an artifact is authentic if there is no doubt about its general time and place of origin; for some types of artifacts, more detailed information on its origins, such as the artist who created it, may also be crucial. In a more narrow sense, authenticity relates to the condition and current appearance of the artifact. Has the object been restored or conserved in the past, and, if so, how extensive has this restoration been? It is not unusual for comparatively old artifacts to have been restored at some time in the past; thus, determining the current condition of the artifact is usually a part of most general authentication studies. In some instances, where the general authenticity is not in question, an assessment of condition may be the entire purpose of an authentication study.

As the reader will imagine, the specific approach to authentication of different categories of artifacts can vary considerably, and in a chapter of this scope few details can be given. No matter what the specific type of artifact, however, there are some generalizations regarding the authentication process that can be made, as shown in the flow chart that follows.

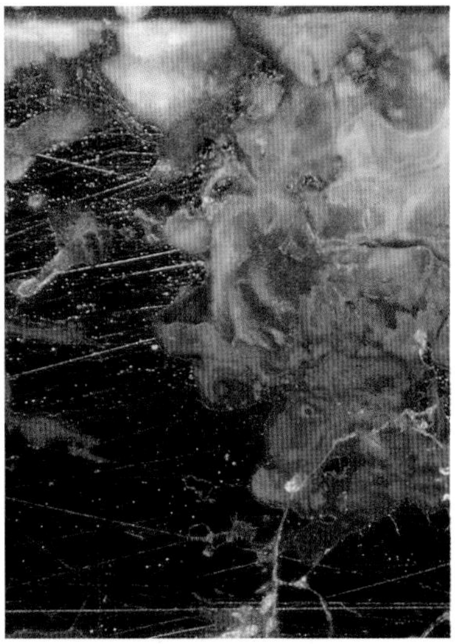

Another test on the Cambodian female deity produced this photomicrograph of a polished cross section of metal and corrosion products (width of the area shown is about .05 millimeters). The thick greenish gray and red corrosion products extending along the grain boundaries into the uncorroded bronze metal at the bottom indicate that the patina on the sculpture is a result of natural, long-term corrosion.

Stylistic Analysis

The first avenue of approach should always be *stylistic analysis*. There may be anomalies of iconography or style that present a very strong case against the authenticity of an artifact. Art-historical research is also important because it can serve to formulate specific questions or point to problematic aspects of an artifact that technical examination or scientific analysis—the next level in the flow chart—could help to resolve. It is this level upon which this chapter will concentrate.

Opposite:
The authenticity of this bronze, hollow-cast statue was supported by thermoluminescence dating of a sample of the remaining ceramic core. Female deity. Cambodian, tenth century. Museum of Fine Arts, Boston

FLOW CHART FOR AUTHENTICATION PROCEDURES

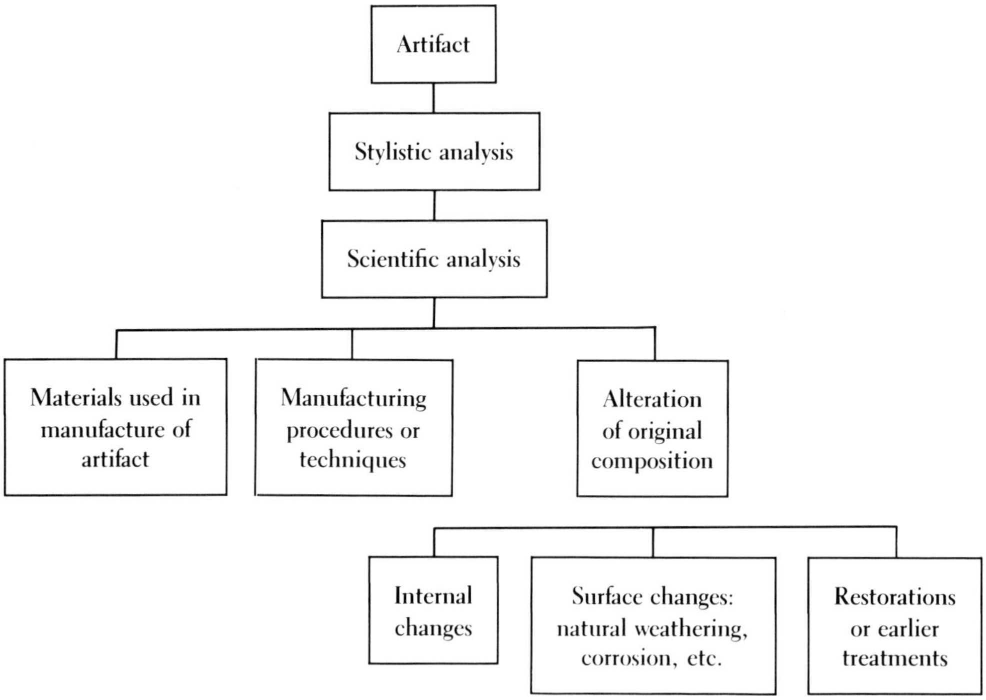

Scientific Analysis

Technical examination and *scientific analysis* are phrases that are more or less interchangeable, at least as we shall use them. They indicate examinations that concentrate on the material aspects of the artifact; the particular examination techniques involved can be as simple as observation under a low-magnification microscope or may involve analysis of a sample or samples from the artifact using an expensive piece of scientific equipment. Technical study of a given artifact typically involves a combination of several different examination or analytical procedures.

Materials

The material aspects of an artifact can be divided into three broad categories, as shown on the flow chart. The first category of scientific analysis involves identification of the materials of which the artifact is composed. In the case of a painting, these would include the pigments and binding mediums that have been combined to create the painted image and the support on which the painting was carried out (such as wood or fabric). In the case of a print, one would analyze the paper (or other support) on which the print was made and the ink with which it was printed (the ink itself is a combination of coloring materials and adhesives). For many types of artifacts, a complete list of the materials that went into their creation could be quite lengthy.

The manner in which information on materials could be useful in authentication studies is self-evident. If a painting that is supposed to date to the seventeenth century contains a pigment that was not invented until the nineteenth century, and the suspicious pigment is not part of a restoration on the painting, then the painting cannot be authentic. Among famous historical examples are Hans van Meegeren's Vermeer forgeries, carried out about the time of World War II. For the most part, Van Meegeren actually utilized pigments Vermeer would have been expected to use, including a valuable blue pigment made from the semiprecious stone lapis lazuli. Unbeknownst to Van Meegeren, however, was the fact that his supply of lapis lazuli had been adulterated with a small amount of another blue pigment that had not been invented until well over a century after Vermeer's lifetime.

Another example could be seventeenth- and eighteenth-century American and British silver objects. As a consequence of the manner in which silver metal was manufactured from ores prior to the late nineteenth century, silver of these periods almost invariably contains small amounts of gold and lead (usually not more than a few tenths of a percent by weight). If such trace impurities are not present in a silver object purported to be from the seventeenth or eighteenth century, then it probably is not authentic. Other examples of this kind for all categories of artifacts included in this book could be mentioned. All are dependent on knowledge of the history of materials, and not simply a general knowledge, but sometimes (as in the case of the trace impurities in early silver metal) quite specific knowledge of some aspect of a given material.

Manufacturing Techniques

The second category of scientific analysis involves methods of manufacture. For a print, one would study the printmaking technique. For a painting, one would trace the way different pigments were combined and layered to create certain passages; also involved could be the genesis of the painted image from drawing or underpainting stages to painted image, to possible adjustments or changes made during the course of painting, to final touches of paint and possibly application of varnish.

The potential applications of information on manufacturing techniques are probably somewhat more limited than those of materials themselves, but once again many examples could be cited. From a technical point of view, one of the most exhaustively studied ancient artifacts is a small bronze horse in the collection of the Metropolitan Museum of Art. An early examination condemned the sculpture since there seemed to be evidence that it had been manufactured by a casting process not available in classical antiquity. If the evidence had been incontrovertible, the sculpture certainly could not have originated in ancient Greece. However, it was later proved that the rather tenuous evidence was not reliable. Other analyses, mentioned below, further supported the attribution to classical antiquity.

INFERENTIAL AUTHENTICATION BY MATERIALS AND MANUFACTURING TECHNIQUES

Although some information on materials and manufacturing techniques occasionally provides unambiguous answers in authentication studies, it is more commonly the case that analyses of these material aspects of an artifact will not provide a definitive answer. There are several reasons why this is true. A major reason is simply that many materials and manufacturing techniques have very long histories, sometimes extending to the present through hundreds or thousands of years. For example, consider a small metal statue that scholarly research suggests could have been produced during Roman times in the second century A.D. Examination may prove that it was cast by the lost-wax process in bronze to which some lead was added. Suppose the alloy composition was analyzed in detail, so that we know the exact amount of each element in the alloy, not only the major elements (copper, tin, and lead) but also a number of elements present only at very low (trace) levels. As both the casting technique (lost-wax) and alloy (leaded bronze) are still commonly used today, there is nothing in the results that proves the object inauthentic or authentic. Even the pattern of trace elements in leaded bronze alloys can be quite similar in ancient and modern alloys. At most, on the basis of these analyses, it could be stated that the materials and manufacturing technique are consistent with an ancient Roman origin, but such an origin is not proved.

As time goes by, the wealth of detailed information on the materials and techniques employed by cultures and artists of the past continues to grow. And, as analytical procedures brought to bear on cultural artifacts become more sophisticated, new types of information on materials can become available that could have a bearing on authentication studies. Current research on materials often focuses on discovering a material "fingerprint" that is as specific as possible to certain classes of artifacts produced in certain regions over a restricted period of time. While such fingerprints are rarely if ever as unique to an artifact as are human fingerprints to an individual person, this area of research has produced much valuable information that can have a bearing on authentication studies. Lead isotopes are one such "fingerprinting" method.

To return to the classical statue, although the alloy composition (including trace elements) was not very useful in resolving its authenticity, since the alloy contained some lead, the isotopic composition of the lead could be determined. Isotopes are different forms of a particular element; all lead in nature consists of four different isotopes. Different lead-ore deposits can have varying isotopic compositions. Information on the compositions of the lead ores used in the ancient world is beginning to accumulate, primarily from analysis of samples from artifacts such as coins and statuary. A modern forgery could well have utilized a lead ore with a different isotopic signature, and if a reliable body of data on the lead in genuine Roman artifacts were available, it could be used to help authenticate problematic pieces. Once again, however, a "correct" isotopic signature (that is, a signature like that found in genuine Roman artifacts) would not prove directly that the object was authentic; a similar ore could conceivably have been employed in a forgery, or a forger fortuitously could have used a lead from a different source from that employed in Roman times but that happened to have the same isotopic signature.

Continuity and commonality in many types of materials and techniques of manufacture will always pose a limit on how specific a date or even region of manufacture can be attached to a problematic artifact through scientific research. Broad either/or questions are answered more easily than highly specific ones. Let us consider one example. Suppose the object being studied is a canvas painting that has been attributed to Rembrandt. If the question is whether the painting is a nineteenth-century canvas in the style of Rembrandt or a seventeenth-century painting, an answer quite possibly could be provided by analysis of the painting materials. A nineteenth-century painting would be likely to contain some pigments that were not available to seventeenth-century painters. Suppose the painting is found to have been carried out with materials that were available in Rembrandt's time, and suppose further that the actual structure of the painting and general painting technique are similar to those of Rembrandt. Can it be proved that the painting is by Rembrandt? The answer, from a scientific point of view, is no. Even the most exhaustive series of analyses and examinations could at best show that the materials are those that a seventeenth-century Dutch painter would have used; however, quite possibly there would be nothing in the materials that could rule out the possibility that the painting was done after Rembrandt's lifetime. Rembrandt, Rembrandt's students and followers, and even other painters who worked around the same time in the same region would have used the same range of materials, and examinations suggest that even many aspects of the overall structural layers of these many different artists' works could be quite similar. This question is simply too specific to be answered by scientific analysis, at least at the moment. Questions of this kind are enormously important, obviously, but the ultimate answers continue to be based on connoisseurship, as shown by the three volumes (to date) of the Rembrandt corpus, produced beginning in the early 1980s by the Rembrandt Research Project in the Netherlands. Most authentication studies involving technical or scientific examination incorporate identification of materials and manufacturing techniques. Even if not definitive in and of itself, this information is very useful to accumulate, as our knowledge of the material aspects, both genuine and false, for the most part grows out of analytical research. As this body of knowledge grows, we may be able to make more confident judgments on the authenticity of problematic pieces.

DIRECT DATING BY MATERIALS

The earlier example of the metal statue is one whose authentication only involved inferential information. In other words, the tests made could not provide a definite or even approximate date of manufacture. As in the examples of paintings and silver noted above, however, there are cases where such technical information will definitely rule out certain attributions. This is the type of information that studies of materials and manufacturing techniques provide for many artifacts.

Within the broad categories of original materials and manufacturing techniques, there exists one important analytical procedure capable of directly dating a material. *Dendrochronology* is a method of dating wood by counting and measuring the thicknesses of tree rings and comparing the resulting pattern with a master chart of rings for the particular type of wood and geographical region in which it grew. Among the results useful for authentication purposes are studies of Rembrandt's panel paintings, in which dendrochronology has refined the traditional art-historical chronology and even proved that false dates were painted on the panels in some instances. In order to date a piece of wood by dendrochronology, it is necessary that a complete sequence of the most recent rings for the tree be visible; fortunately, wood panels for painting and other purposes were usually cut so that the sequence is exposed on two of the edges of the panel. Actual measurement of the rings can be carried out without damaging the image area of the painting.

Alteration of the Original Composition of Materials

DIRECT DATING OF INTERNAL CHANGES

While we are more aware of external or surface changes to material, subtle internal changes—often the result of natural processes—also occur in some materials and can be used in authenticating objects made from them. In addition to dendrochronology, two other major direct-dating techniques are routinely applied to artifacts in collections. The other two techniques draw on what we may call internal changes in composition of a material that take place after the material has been shaped into an artifact. The first of these techniques, *radiocarbon dating*, can be applied potentially to any organic material in an artifact, that is, any material that has once been living, such as wood or fabric. The technique recently was used to prove that the fabric of the Shroud of Turin is medieval in origin and cannot date to the time of Christ. In part due to sample size requirements, radiocarbon dating is not often employed in the study of museum artifacts; however, with recent advances in instrumentation that have decreased sample sizes, it may come to be used more frequently. The sample size for a textile (such as the shroud) using the more modern instrumental technique is about that of a postage stamp; for a wooden object, a fraction of a gram. Sample sizes for the traditional technique are typically more than a hundred times as large. The dating technique involves careful measurement of the amount of radioactive carbon in an object relative to the total amount of carbon (most carbon in nature consists of two isotopes that are not radioactive, but a very minute fraction is made of a third isotope that is radioactive). Like all radioactive elements, radioactive carbon decays as time goes by. All living things contain a roughly constant amount of radioactive carbon while they are living, but once they die that amount begins to decrease. Knowing the ratio of radioactive to total carbon allows the time since the living thing died to be at least approximately calculated. This, of course, is the same as the time of manufacture for the artifact.

The other direct-dating technique is *thermoluminescence*, which can determine an approximate firing date for a ceramic object and is now widely applied to ceramics in museums and private collections. It can also be applied to the ceramic cores of hollow-cast metal objects to determine the approximate date of casting: this technique was used to prove the ancient origin of the small bronze horse in the Metropolitan mentioned earlier. The sample size is about 100 milligrams, which is taken by drilling; for most ceramics, if a one-eighth-inch-diameter drill were being used, the required hole would be around a quarter- to a half-inch deep. Like radiocarbon dating, thermoluminescence is based on determination of a property of a material that has changed since the object was manufactured. In this case, the property is the slow buildup of a certain type of stored energy within the crystal structure of minerals in the ceramic. This energy is removed by heating to the temperatures used to fire ceramic objects but will accumulate in a regular fashion after firing due to the interaction of small amounts of some naturally occurring radioactive isotopes with minerals in the clays.

Both radiocarbon dating and thermoluminescence dating, as well as dendrochronology, obviously have limited potential applications, and unfortunately there are many types of artifacts to which none of the so-called direct dating techniques can be applied. For these, only inferential techniques are applicable.

Further, even though dendochronology, radiocarbon, and thermoluminescence are truly "direct"-dating techniques, there are limitations to the specificity of information they can provide. In ideal cases (where a complete sequence of the most recent rings in a panel is preserved) dendrochronology can provide a date that will be within a few years of the felling date of the tree; the actual date of a painting (or other object made from the tree) would likely be within five to ten years of this date (wood panels were usually allowed to stabilize for a period before they were actually used). Thermoluminescence and radiocarbon dates are not this precise. Typically, dates from these techniques will have quoted errors of plus or minus 10 to 20 percent of the determined age. These errors arise from many causes, such as analytical uncertainties. As with the situation with artist's materials, if the dating question is a fairly broad one, a radiocarbon or thermoluminescence date with this amount of uncertainty could be quite adequate. For example, suppose a terra-cotta object purported to have been made in Italy during the sixteenth century is being dated by thermoluminescence. If, based on other evidence, the earliest date that a copy or forgery of the piece would have been carried out is the late nineteenth century, the thermoluminescent date will likely be definitive. However, if there is a question as to whether or not the piece was carried out in the mid-sixteenth century or during the following century, the thermoluminescent date may not be definitive.

SURFACE ALTERATIONS

As you have learned no doubt from earlier chapters in this book, virtually all materials of which artifacts have been and are made deteriorate over time. Sometimes such deterioration may be very slow, either because the material is quite stable or its environment has been mild and nonaggressive. Other times deterioration is extensive. Among the products of deterioration that are now valued as an important part of ancient artifacts are the corrosion layers that develop on metal objects in burial environments. While it is not a complicated matter to copy genuine corrosion products in a laboratory, the manner in which corrosion proceeds to eat into the underlying metal cannot be duplicated. For this reason, cross sections of metal objects that include unaltered metal and corrosion products are valuable in the study of ancient metal artifacts. Evidence of extensive intergranular corrosion is indicative that the object has been buried for an extended period of time. This is not a direct-dating technique, and no very specific definition of "extended period of time" can be given, but it is a valuable piece of information for authentication questions.

As before, however, the absence of this phenomenon does not necessarily prove that the object is not authentic. Layers of deterioration or weathering products also occur on other materials, such as stone or glass. Current research is focusing on the weathering layers that build up on ancient marble artifacts in burial environments. While at the moment there are few common applications of layers of surface alteration for authentication, more may be developed in the future. Hence, conservation treatments of artifacts should take into consideration the fact that such surface-alteration layers may be crucial for research purposes. It has been all too common in the past for surface-alteration layers to be stripped from artifacts during restorations, although this is becoming a far less frequent practice today.

RESTORATION OR EARLIER TREATMENTS

This brings us to an important point. All of the foregoing alterations described are the result of natural processes. However, internal changes or, much more commonly, surface changes can also be the result of restorations or earlier treatments. Because at least some restoration will have been carried out on most old artifacts, examination of the overall condition of an object is a common part of most authentication studies. There are many instances where there may be no question about the general authenticity of an artifact: what may be in question is its overall condition, and the extent to which it may have been restored. In extreme cases, restorations can involve replacing of lost parts, considerable cosmetic work on the surface of the object, or other extensive interventions. Such extensive interventions add an element of "inauthenticity," at least to the outward appearance, and can cause the overall authenticity of some artifacts to be questioned.

Consulting an Expert

For advice on how to proceed in a scientific authentication study and what information or tests would be appropriate to include in a study, consult an art conservator or museum scientist. Most major museums have conservation departments; private conservators are often listed in the yellow pages of telephone directories. For a list of conservators or museum scientists in a given city or region, the American Institute for Conservation of Historic and Artistic Works can be contacted. If you wish to have an elaborate authentication carried out on an artifact and your local resource is unable to do it, the International Foundation for Art Research (IFAR) has an authentication service. On projects they undertake, staff members consult appropriate experts, whether art historians, conservators, or scientists.

In authentication studies, the actual information or data accumulated is obviously important, but just as critical is the interpretation of that data or information. For this reason, it is strongly advised that collectors follow the suggestions given above in beginning and pursuing authentication projects. Conservators and museum scientists are well versed in the material aspects of artifacts and works of art, and they can offer the necessary advice on planning, executing, and properly interpreting the results of that research.

Collectors should realize that, while some common examinations techniques (X-radiography, for example) do not require samples, samples *are* required for virtually all detailed analyses of artifacts that are part of authentication studies. Sample sizes vary from relatively large—as in the case of a sample for thermoluminescent or radiocarbon dating—to minute, barely visible specks of material. Although some tests simply cannot be carried out on all artifacts because the appropriate samples cannot be taken, in general, given the range of analytical procedures available today, some sampling can be carried out on most artifacts. The prospect of sampling artifacts is one that may make many collectors and art historians uneasy, but it should be realized that conservators or scientists are skilled in carefully removing such samples without posing a danger to the artifact.

No chapter of this type could be complete without some mention of costs. Actual costs for an analytical examination will vary considerably, from hundreds to thousands of dollars, depending on the tests that have been proposed and the facilities at which the research will be carried out. The standard appraisal procedure, as discussed elsewhere in this book, would typically include "authentication," but this authentication generally would be mostly based on stylistic criteria and perhaps some technical information. Scientific analysis, as discussed in this chapter, has much to offer in the study of artifacts and occupies an increasingly important role overall in the authentication of many types of artifacts.

To the general public, scientific authentication of works of art may conjure up visions of magical computerized black boxes, into which one can put the artifact or a sample from it and some short time later receive an answer proving or disproving its authenticity. While this chapter has mentioned a few techniques that could be said to approach such a degree of "magic," in general there are no such black boxes, and the answers that come out of the boxes that are available are not as immediately enlightening. Collectors should have realistic expectations of scientific authentication studies, and hopefully this chapter has been able to give a glimpse of these.

Magritte

APPRAISING AND INSURING YOUR COLLECTIONS

Huntington T. Block

There comes a time in the lives of many collectors when they realize that the objects in their home may be worth more than the home itself. It is a daunting thought indeed.

While it is true that works of art of real quality have become one of the best investments one could have made in the years following World War II, it is also true that most serious collectors have not acquired art because it was, or is, such a good investment, but simply because they enjoyed doing it. Important collections have been assembled by good eyes and great passion.

However, in the contemporary world in which we live one cannot overlook the economics of art, and many collectors are asking themselves if they can afford to keep what they have, if they can afford to protect what they have, and if they indeed can afford to insure what they have. Meanwhile, reports of art thefts become front-page news, and the press treats us to long discourses about how easy it is to spirit a picture out of the country to another part of the world where extradition even of stolen art is difficult if not impossible.

The panic button has indeed been pushed, so perhaps it might be helpful to look at the record. Insurance companies will tell you that their experience in insuring private art collections has been excellent. The same could be said for their experience in insuring museum collections. Most men and women who own or care for art are careful by nature, and museums by definition are places where art normally should be safe and secure.

Furthermore, contrary to what one reads in the papers and hears on television, there is still a good chance that important works of art that are stolen may be recovered eventually. It is difficult if not impossible to fence a Van Gogh that, at the time of its theft, may have been reproduced on the front pages of every major newspaper in the world. Also, it should be noted that there is no honor among thieves, and since substantial rewards are

In the course of cataloguing their collection, the owners of the painting Sans Famille *by Surrealist artist René Magritte were horrified to discover that it had been replaced by this forgery* (opposite). *To make matters worse, because the painting had not been appraised for some time, its insured value was much less than the estimated current value. Fortunately for the owners, the original painting was recovered.*

usually offered, it is often difficult for even the cleverest of criminals to keep such a secret.

Of course, theft is but one of the concerns a collector must consider. An object can be defaced, broken, damaged by water, or destroyed by fire. In fact, statistics show that insurance companies pay out more dollars for damage claims than they do for theft claims, and there are usually two parts to a damage claim. The first is the cost of restoring the object to the best of a conservator's ability, and the second is the loss of value it may have suffered as a result of the damage.

The Appraisal

How do collectors cope with the problem of knowing what their possessions are really worth and of seeing to it that they are properly insured? An appraisal is a valuable document. Not only does it provide the collector with a professional description of each object he owns, it also tells him what each is worth. It is not unusual for an appraisal to be enhanced by photographs of each object or by a videotape record of the entire collection.

How does one find a reliable appraiser? No government body regulates the appraisal profession; however, there have been court decisions in recent years that have held appraisers personally liable for gross errors of judgment. There are a number of organizations to which appraisers may belong that require some proven expertise before an applicant may be considered for membership. Two of these are the American Society of Appraisers and the International Federation of Appraisers. The Art Dealers Association of America provides a highly regarded appraisal service, as do the major auction houses like Sotheby's and Christie's.

There was a time when appraisers charged a percentage of the value of the objects they appraised as the fee for their services. For obvious reasons, this method led to a good many allegations of impropriety, and it has largely been abandoned. Today appraisers charge by the hour, plus transportation expenses. It is important to specify the reason an appraisal is being requested. An appraisal for estate-tax purposes will be a good deal different from an appraisal for insurance purposes.

Some appraisers can be eclectic in their abilities, but these days it is almost impossible to keep up with value trends in all the different art disciplines, and it is not unusual for an appraiser to call in a colleague or two when a collection ranges from Pre-Columbian to Ash Can.

Besides becoming the basis for proper and responsive insurance policies, appraisals can be invaluable in other ways. It is not unusual for someone to discover that the objects promised to one child turn out, after appraisal, to be a good deal more valuable than those promised to another. An appraisal therefore helps someone writing a will to make equitable distributions. An appraisal sometimes makes a joyful discovery, for example a family heirloom that turns out to be quite valuable. Unfortunately, the opposite can happen as well, and those requesting appraisals should be prepared to learn that an object treasured within a family for generations can turn out to be virtually worthless. For many practical reasons, therefore, it is good to know what a collection is really worth.

There was a time when our tax laws were such that people of means could eschew insurance on collectibles altogether. A loss or damage to a valuable work of art could be treated as a loss on an individual's annual income-tax report. No more. Today a collector may only deduct as a property loss the amount he originally paid for a work of art. Hence, although a Matisse may be worth millions today, if it is destroyed or stolen, the owner can only take as a deduction that which he paid for it thirty-five years ago.

For obvious reasons, therefore, insurance has become an ever more significant factor in asset protection. Traditionally, a collector obtains an appraisal, hands it to an insurer, and the appraisal becomes the basis of the resulting insurance policy. Most fine-art policies will pay losses on the basis of the values set opposite each object on the schedule that appears on the policy. Insurance policies covering art are considered "valued" policies, different from those that cover furs and jewelry, where insurers usually reserve the option to either replace the lost object themselves or pay out its real value at the time of loss, which with a fur coat can be a good deal less than the value stated on the policy. Valued policies generally include words like "insured for and valued at," which guarantee that the insurer will pay the stated value.

The real difficulty, certainly during the past several years, has been the problem of keeping values current. It is not an exaggeration to say that prices bid at an auction in New York on a Tuesday could directly affect the value of an object lost or damaged in San Diego on a Thursday. It is true that once an original appraisal has been made, it is a much simpler process for a professional appraiser to bring the documentation up to date every two years, or even more often, and the cost of an update is usually quite reasonable. However, in a market that seems to change almost monthly, and often quite significantly, biannual or even annual updates sometimes are not enough. Some insurers have recognized this and have been willing to issue policies covering distinguished collections that agree to pay claims on the basis of the current market value of the object(s) as of the day a loss occurs, even if the last stated value is lower. These insurers recognize that most collectors maintain elaborate security, or at least sufficient security so that the maximum loss a collection might suffer is probably something less than the total value of the collection. In fact, they know also that it is not unusual for a collection to be disbursed between a principal home, a second home, and an office, which is a form of insurance in and of itself. These insurers are willing to offer a collector a blanket limit of art insurance at a level below his total value. The key, of course, is that these blanket-limit insurance policies will cover every object in a collection up to the blanket limit selected, and will pay losses on the basis of current market value.

This is exactly the manner in which museums have been buying their insurance for years, and it is very similar to the method commercial art dealers use for their insurance, so it is nothing especially new or revolutionary. It is just a method that has not been offered to private collectors until recently.

The Fine-Art Insurance Policy

Modern insurance policies for art collections often contain special features that need to be understood. For example, if a lost object is one of a pair or set, traditional insurance policies will pay the value of the lost piece and will not recognize that the loss of one piece may render the pair or the set virtually worthless. A properly written art insurance policy will afford the collector the option to surrender the remaining piece or pieces to the insurance company and be paid for the entire pair or set.

In addition, art insurers recognize that a picture stolen today and recovered nine years hence could be worth a good deal more then than it is now. Accordingly, they are making it possible for a claimant to buy back a recovered object at the price paid at the time of the loss. Anyone who has followed the rapid rise in the value of Impressionist paintings over the past decade will understand the value of what is known as a "loss buy back" clause.

It is not unusual for a collector eventually to be asked to loan a work of art to a special exhibition, perhaps one that will travel to more than one museum, and sometimes to museums in other countries. Invariably, the borrowing institution asks the lender to sign a loan agreement form. These forms ask the lender to stipulate the values of the objects being loaned, and it is important to understand that these values immediately become agreed values, especially if the lender also agrees to allow the borrowing institution to arrange the insurance. The lender also has the option to arrange the insurance and to bill the borrower for it, but if the borrower is allowed to insure, the lender should know that the value placed on the loan agreement is sacrosanct. If there is a loss, the borrower's insurer will pay the claim on the basis of what the loan agreement says—no more, no less. It is therefore just as important not to understate as it is not to overstate the value of a loaned object.

Important/Standard Clauses

It is helpful to examine exactly what an art-insurance policy says and what it is prepared to do. It starts quite appropriately by specifying exactly whom it insures. This could be one individual or organization, or perhaps several, each to be insured "as their respective interests may appear." Next the policy should explain what property it is insuring and where that property is. A statement such as "all fine arts of whatsoever nature, the property of the Insured, all of which shall be covered while at the premises of the Insured, in transit, or otherwise within the states of the United States, the District of Columbia, and the Provinces of Canada" is not unusual. Some fine-art policies have no territorial limitation. A phrase in the last quoted wording—"the property of the Insured"—deserves attention. The meaning is clear—if the Insured does not own the property, or if the title to it is obviously clouded, the Insured has no "insurable interest." Quite simply, one cannot insure what one does not own.

Following a description of the property insured is a section that lists the limits of the insurer's liability. The policy might state how much is insured at the Insured's residence, how much at an office, and how much in transit or at any other location within the policy's aforementioned territorial limits. These limits are important to understand, because if a collector sends a million-dollar picture to a conservator's studio, and the insurance policy contains only a $500,000 transit limit, there is an obvious problem.

There is also, quite naturally, a paragraph that tells you what the premium is and when coverage begins and when it ends. For example, it is customary for a policy to commence at 12:01 A.M. Standard Time at the place of issuance and end a year later. Insurance on objects of art is not necessarily expensive. In fact, most collectors are pleasantly surprised at how modestly it is priced when compared to insurance on jewelry or furs. An annual rate should certainly be less than half of 1 percent, and more like a fifth of 1 percent. Before changing insurers, it is important to determine when your existing coverage will cease and the new coverage commence. Gaps between policies can be dangerous, because accidents can be very fickle about when they choose to happen.

Many policies contain a *deductible* or a *franchise clause*. A deductible simply means that from every claim settlement a stipulated amount will be deducted. It is not unusual for a fine-art policy to contain a $1,000 deductible. A franchise clause, on the other hand, works just like a deductible until the loss exceeds the amount stipulated, at which time the entire claim is paid. Under a $1,000 franchise arrangement, a loss of $999 would not be paid, but a loss of $1,001 would be paid in full.

Perhaps the most important clause in any insurance policy is that which tells exactly what is to be paid when a loss occurs. Aptly called the *valuation clause*, it directs the claims adjuster, and if properly written, reassures the policy owner. As mentioned earlier, art policies agree to pay either on the basis of a predetermined schedule of values or on the basis of "the current market value of the property at the time any loss or damage occurs." An insurance buyer should read the valuation clause carefully and make certain it is prepared to do exactly what the buyer intends it to do.

Exclusions

A fine-art insurance policy is often described as an "all risks" policy. These are two very comfortable words, but they are not quite accurate. The phraseology normally employed says that "the policy insures against all risks of physical loss or damage from any external cause, except as hereinafter excluded." The key word of course is "except." Happily, the exceptions, or exclusions, are relatively few in number, and do not often prove troublesome.

Fine-art policies don't cover wear and tear or gradual deterioration; in other words, they don't cover the aging process. In fact, it is rare that an insurance company needs to invoke these exclusions. Most good art increases in value as it ages, and gradual deterioration may not diminish its appreciation. However, damage by light, moisture, or other environmental factors can affect the appearance of the work and reduce its value.

Damage by moths and vermin are normal exclusions, as is *inherent vice*. Insurers are hard put to come up with a good definition of inherent vice. It could be described as the ability of a cake to turn stale. Only time will tell if some of the flotsam and jetsam sometimes used by contemporary artists to liven their canvases will fall victim to the inherent-vice exclusion. Historically, insurers have tried to be extremely reasonable in this regard.

A standard exclusion refers to "damage sustained due to or resulting from any repairing, restoration, or retouching process." The message here is to try always to select top-rated conservators to clean or repair the objects in a collection, because if the process itself results in damage, there is no insurance coverage in the owner's policy. The conservator could of course be held personally liable if it can be proved that such negligence caused the damage, but most conservators request a waiver before commencing their work. It is reassuring, however, that there have been very few instances when mistakes in the conservation process have actually caused damage to a work of art.

Then there are the exclusions that have to do with war and nuclear reaction, radiation, or contamination. The war exclusion includes "insurrection, rebellion, revolutions, civil war, usurped power . . . and confiscation by any government authority, or risks of contraband or illegal transportation or trade." The war exclusion should not include the risks of "strike, riot, or civil commotion," which are normally covered under a fine-art insurance policy.

Some insurers also exclude breakage, mysterious disappearance, and the dishonesty of employees. For obvious reasons, these three exclusions are to be avoided if at all possible.

Most art insurance policies stipulate that the insured property is packed for any shipment and unpacked upon arrival by competent packers. Although there are less than competent art packers, it is extremely rare that an insurer will invoke the "competent packer" warranty, but, by the same token, it is a good rule to always engage the services of an established fine-art packer.

Many policies covering art still contain a rather archaic exclusion with regard to "property on the premises of fair grounds or any national or international exposition." This wording harks back to the days when great concentrations of very valuable works of art were assembled at world's fairs. While it is still not unusual for art to be loaned to a world's fair, it is rare nowadays that these exhibitions challenge in size or value the so-called blockbuster exhibitions that almost routinely visit major museums.

There is also a standard clause warning that if there is in existence "any other valid and collectible insurance covering the property insured," then such other insurance is to be considered primary. In fact, every insurance policy carries with it such a warning, and the result is that in those rare instances when two or three policies may cover a loss to the same object, each of the policies contributes its proportionate share. However, it is not unusual for a collector to lend several objects to a museum exhibition and to request that the museum insure, yet at the same time allowing the personal insurance to remain in force. In such a situation the museum's insurer is considered primary and therefore pays first. As stated, if two brothers own a collection, and each, unbeknownst to the other, obtains insurance on the collection, then each brother's policy would pay its proportionate share of any claim. Insurers see to it that they are never put in a position where they have to pay twice for a single loss.

It goes without saying that anyone purchasing art insurance should be as accurate as possible about any information provided to the insurer. Obviously there may be facts the purchaser doesn't remember or simply has no knowledge of, but any information that could be construed as a deliberate misrepresentation could act to void the insurance "whether before or after a loss."

In the Event of a Claim

It is not unusual for an object to have been misplaced or to simply disappear. Many collectors are certain that the loss is just temporary and that the object will surely turn up. What they don't realize is that there is a requirement in an insurance policy that "the Insured shall as soon as practicable report to the Company or its agent every loss or damage which may become a claim." While insurers generally try to be fair in this regard, the fact is that a late report of a claim could seriously jeopardize the chances of recovery from the insurer. There is a little leeway in the words, "as soon as practicable," but the better part of valor is to file a report as soon as any object turns up missing.

There is also a requirement in these policies that a dated and sworn proof of loss be filed with the insurance company within a certain number of days (usually ninety) from the date of loss. Because it is difficult if not impossible to file such a document until a conservator completes his or her work and a proper assessment of the loss can be made, this requirement is treated rather loosely in a damage claim. In practice, therefore, this requirement is rarely enforced.

Although they do not often enforce it, in the event of a claim, insurers retain the right to examine under oath "all persons interested in the property and members of the household and employees." Insurers feel that when there are several suspects in a theft case, among whom may be two or three servants, an examination under oath can often bring out the truth.

The insurance company generally agrees to make good a claim within thirty days from the day a proof of loss is accepted, and in practice there is no real reluctance on the part of insurers to pay once the paperwork has been accepted and approved.

One of the most misunderstood aspects of an art-insurance policy is its *subrogation* clause. The policy language generally stipulates that once the insurance company has made good its claim to its customer, "the Company shall be subrogated to all the Insured's rights of recovery therefore against any person or organization." This means that if a collector lends a painting to the local museum and elects to insure it personally, in case of loss or damage that is clearly the fault of the museum, the insurer can pay its customer in full and then simply turn around and sue the museum to recover what it had to pay its customer. Most museums will not accept an insured loan unless they are in prior receipt from their lender of a certificate of insurance waiving this right of subrogation.

There is also a clause in most policies which requires a claimant "to sue, labor, and travel for, in and about the defense, safeguard and recovery of the property insured hereunder." This means that a claimant is compelled by contract to journey to another state or jurisdiction if necessary in order to assist the insurer in the recovery of a stolen object.

The vast majority of claims involving art are settled quickly and judiciously, but it is inevitable that from time to time there are disagreements between the insurance company and its customer. When disagreements do occur, there is a predetermined method built into the insurance policy that prescribes the remedy. Referred to as the Appraisal or Arbitration Clause, it stipulates that in the event of a disagreement as to the amount of loss, the customer and the insurance company each elects an appraiser of choice, and the two elected appraisers then agree on an umpire satisfactory to both. Experience has shown that this method of resolving differences works extremely well.

It is comforting to know that damage to insured objects sustained through the efforts of firemen, policemen, or other civil authorities during a conflagration is recoverable from the insurance company. Very often water from fire hoses can do more damage than the fire itself.

An insurance policy may usually be canceled at any time, either at the request of the insured or the insurance company. An insured who elects to cancel does so on the basis of what insurers refer to as the "short-rate table," a formula that provides a penalty equal to something more than the pro-rata credit for the paid premium. If on the other hand cancellation is initiated by the insurer, at least thirty days advance notice must be provided and the premium credit is issued on a straight pro-rata basis.

The intense interest in art, particularly in the last couple of decades, has spawned a whole new group of specialists—insurance brokers who specialize in art, appraisers who specialize in various segments of art, and conservators who specialize in the various disciplines. Collectors are well served by these specialists because they understand art and what can happen to art. For example, a claims adjuster without any particular art background has a difficult time understanding depreciation; an insurance broker who serves construction contractors will not have much knowledge about a Miró; and a paper conservator will shy away from working on a broken statue. It is comforting to do business with people who know what they are talking about, which is why so much art-related activity has gravitated toward the specialists.

There are art-related specialists all across the country. To find them, talk to a respected commercial art dealer, the registrar at your local museum, or another collector. These specialists not only provide very comprehensive art-related policies, but they are generally able to do so at a very competitive price.

DONATING YOUR COLLECTIONS

Leonard L. Silverstein

It cannot be doubted that, at some stage in the lifetime of the collector, the pleasure of accumulating a collection of works of art is matched by the dilemma of the mode of its disposition. Indeed, since the excavations of the tombs of the pharaohs made it abundantly clear that efforts to transport objects of art to the collector's next life did not, in fact, succeed in actually removing them from the planet, this dilemma remains. Nevertheless, today's collector enjoys a variety of options that depend only upon frame of mind and pocketbook. Regretfully, the federal tax laws bear a significant—perhaps too important—impact upon the resolution of a collector's choices, and Congress, in framing tax laws respecting charitable donations, including works of art, has acted in all too idiosyncratic fashion.

In this brief chapter, various forms of disposition of a collection will be outlined with—because of its often cardinal importance—identification of tax effects to collectors and/or their families.

For purposes of this survey, it may be assumed that the collector in question is a person having a charitable inclination with respect to all or part of the collection. Although he or she may have a spouse, children, grandchildren, and/or other descendants who are interested in the collection, it is also assumed that the collector may either sell or donate all or part of the collection to a museum or another independent "qualifying"[1] facility, utilizing other net financial resources for support of his or her family.

Temptations of Sale versus Inducements for Donations

First, it should be noted that if a collector desires to realize current financial gain from a collection (whether for the benefit of family or for any other reason), the combination of the tax laws and long-term appreciation in works of art strongly militate in favor of sale and therefore against donation. Since the maximum federal tax burden on ordinary income is 31 to 33 percent[2] and, conversely, only the same percentage of tax "savings" is realized from a donation, the temptation of sale from a donee institution's standpoint, as many donee institutions have learned, is painfully evident. If, however, in the longer term, gift or estate taxes on the after-tax proceeds of a sale are taken into consideration, the ultimate amount of wealth transmittable to family members, other than a surviving spouse, may not be as great as it first appears.[3]

Donation: A "Life or Death" Decision

Assuming that a collector is motivated less by net financial consequences than by the satisfaction derived from the donation of a fine collection, the potential donor must confront a threshold question respecting the timing of such gifts. Various alternatives include:

> (1) a gift of the complete collection during life;
> (2) a gift of selected works of art during life, with retention of the balance until death;
> (3) a loan of part or all of the entire collection during life with transfer to the donee institution at death; and
> (4) a gift of a partial undivided interest in one or more works of art or of the collection during life with the retained undivided interest transferred at death. A collector's choice among the described alternatives involves factors such as the desire for immediate or deferred public recognition, or, on the other hand, for anonymity, the expense of maintenance of the collection in light of accelerating insurance and other costs, as well as spousal and/or family desires for enjoyment of the collection.

Federal tax laws, as earlier noted, can skew a collector's decision. For example, a transfer of property to a spouse and/or to a qualified charity is not taxable. Hence, if a collector desires only to assure later enjoyment of the collection by the surviving spouse, the latter may receive the collection at the collector's death, enjoy it during his or her lifetime, and make a subsequent bequest to a public museum or other qualified donee institution entirely free of federal (and in all probability state) tax. If, on the other hand, the collector and/or the surviving spouse desire to transmit all or part of a collection during life or at death to children, grandchildren, or other noncharitable entities, such a transfer is, in general, subject to federal, gift, estate, or generation-skipping tax.[4] Further, because the rate of the estate tax can reach 55 percent of the value of the bequest, the collector's cash needed to pay the taxes must be "grossed up" by the amount of the tax. Thus, if a collector in the top 55-percent-estate-tax bracket desires to transmit a painting having an approximate value of $10,000 as a bequest to a child, the collector must have additional funds of $12,000 available to pay the total tax attributable to the value of the painting.[5]

Serious questions regarding valuation of the donated objects of art, as well as other technical statutory limitations needed to calculate the amount of the tax deduction, also complicate lifetime gifts. Unless a collector who debates the question of donating his collection during life or at death has no concern for tax consequences (or has a collection without significant appreciation in value), the present state of the federal tax laws strongly favors a deathtime bequest to a museum or other qualified donee institution. In that instance, the total value of the collection, whatever it may be (and whatever the portion of the donor's estate which it represents), is fully deductible from the federal estate tax, thus rendering moot the often controversial question of valuation of the works of art.[6]

Mechanisms for Lifetime Donations

Notwithstanding the extraordinary bias in the tax laws toward deathtime bequests, circumstances do

Claude Monet. Camille Monet in the Garden at the House in Argenteuil. *1876. Oil on canvas, 32½ x 23⅝". Collection Mr. and Mrs. Walter H. Annenberg. Promised gift to The Metropolitan Museum of Art, New York*

In March 1991 Mr. Annenberg publicly announced his intention to bequeath fifty-three French Impressionist and Post-Impressionist works to the Metropolitan Museum, stating, "I love [the paintings] with a passion and want them to remain together after I am gone." Mr. Annenberg's generosity belies the pessimism reflected in a September 1987 article in the New York Times, *which stated, "In interviews with auctioneers, art dealers, lawyers, and museum officials since the announcement [of the reduced benefit to donors under the 1986 Tax Reform Act], several have said they expected donations to museums to be down this year.*

exist in which a lifetime donation may be desirable, indeed appealing. Much depends upon the financial circumstances of the donor and the extent to which, on the one hand, altruistic motivations can be harmonized with an art market in generally a long-term appreciation mode.

Under these circumstances, an outright lifetime donation of an art collection to a tax-qualified donee—such as a museum or other charitable organization that meets the requirements of Section 501(c)(3) of the Internal Revenue Code—may be very attractive. At a minimum, such a transfer relieves the donor of both gift and estate tax and will generate an income-tax deduction in an amount at least equal to the donor's cost of the donated property.[7]

If, however, income-tax consequences are a significant factor in animating a donation, as is more normally the case, the donor must adhere to a series of complex rules and limitations to achieve maximum income-tax "savings" as a result of the donation.

Under the first limitation, the total amount of all of a taxpayer's annual deductible contributions may not exceed 50 percent of the taxpayer's income[8] for the year in question. This 50-percent limit applies to all cash contributions made by the taxpayer but also includes, to the extent of the donor's cost, art objects as well as other items of property. This rule may well serve the tax and donative motives of a collector whose collection (or the donated property) has little or no appreciation in value. Additionally, even if the donated art object has a value greater than cost, the collector may, through the making of a special election,[9] deduct the amount extent of such cost to the extent of (together with other contributions in such year) the full 50-percent-of-income ceiling amount.[10] When the collector's deductible amount exceeds the 50-percent limit, the excess amount may be "carried over" and deducted against future years' income[11] for each of the five taxable years succeeding the year in which the donation was first made.

In today's high-intensity art market, a much more common situation is presented when a collector holds one or more art objects that have appreciated materially in relation to original cost. In that instance, important additional income-tax constraints apply respecting lifetime donations. Assuming that an art object that has appreciated in value since purchase could have been sold by the collector at a capital gain, the maximum amount of the value of the object that may be deducted cannot exceed 30 percent of the taxpayer's income.[12] Even here, however, if the excess appreciation value exceeds the 30 percent,[13] such excess value may be carried over and deducted against the 30-percent ceiling in each of the five years following the year of the gift. It is to be observed, however, that in this instance any unused carryover deductions, otherwise usable in later taxable years, are eliminated if the collector dies before the carryover period has expired.[14]

Regardless of whether or not a collector's collection has appreciated in value, if the contributed art objects cannot be used in furtherance of the exempt purposes of the donee, the donor's income-tax deduction is also limited to his or her cost for the art objects.[15] For example, in contrast to a museum, whose function is to display art objects, the objectives of a social-welfare organization would not be enhanced by the display of antique Roman coins. In that case, the donor's tax deduction for a gift of the coins is limited to the purchase cost of the articles, even though their value may have risen to many times its value.

The Specter of the Alternate Minimum Tax: But a "Window of Opportunity"

Unfortunately, the aforementioned 30-percent ceiling does not constitute the final constraint on the donation of a work of art (except as noted hereafter for contributions made before July 1, 1992). In concept, the infamous Alternate Minimum Tax (AMT) requires that a donor of an appreciated art work recompute his or her tax under a special AMT regime. Indeed, if (except before July 1, 1992) the appreciation element in an art object is substantial in relation to the donor's total income, it is more likely than not that the AMT will apply,[16] thereby subjecting the deductible portion of the appreciation to the AMT at a rate set for 1991 and later years at 24 percent. As many museum directors and trustees know all too well, these circumstances can often "tip the scales" in favor of sale rather than donation, since the AMT can substantially nullify the tax savings that the collector may otherwise expect to enjoy from the making of a gift.[17]

On the other hand, but again solely with respect to gifts made before July 1, 1992, a different and substantially more favorable rule obtains. Thanks to the eleventh-hour action of the Senate Finance Committee, which was approved by Congress in late October of 1990, charitable contributions of paintings and other tangible personal property such as "collectibles" totally avoid the AMT, *provided, however:*

> (1) that the donated property is neither inventory (for example, artworks held for sale by a dealer), nor short-term capital-gain property (i.e., works held for less than six months); and
> (2) that the use of the donated property is related to the donee's tax-exempt purpose. This latter condition may be satisfied, in the clearest case, where a collector donates a painting, antique furniture, or other comparable art object to a recognized museum whose tax-exempt function is to display the donated objects. It is important to observe also that, notwithstanding this 1991–92 AMT "window of opportunity," the other code rules (such as the 20-, 30-, and 50-percent limitations previously referred to) continue to apply, together with the previously noted limitation on itemized deductions.[18]

The Necessity of Careful Valuation of Donated Property

It cannot be doubted that in past years certain donors were abusing tax laws in claiming exorbitant values for donated items of works of art. This situation became of particular concern in periods when income-tax rates were substantially higher—for example, 70 percent. In that case, the donor of a work of art with an inflated value could reduce taxes on other income by the excessive amount of valuation and in certain situations could actually generate an economic profit from the donation. Because a grossly excessive valuation, even at today's rate of 28 percent, theoretically can produce a comparable result, Congress has taken steps to penalize false and/or excessive valuations of works of art. For example, if the claimed value is 200 percent or more of the amount of the value ultimately determined, a penalty tax is imposed equal to 20 percent of the underpayment of tax attributable to the overvaluation. This penalty rises to 40 percent of the amount of the underpayment in the case of a "gross misstatement" of value, i.e., 400 percent or more of the correct amount. And if fraud is involved, the penalty rises to 70 percent of the portion of the underpayment due to fraud. To avoid penalties, a donor must demonstrate that the excessive valuation was due to "reasonable cause" and that the donor acted in "good faith." To establish good faith, the code requires that a so-called "qualified appraisal" be made by a "qualified appraiser" and that (in some undefined manner) the donor review and/or confirm the work of the appraiser, as well as the quality of the appraisal.

Summary Guidelines for Potential Donors

In light of the foregoing complexities, the following guidelines may assist a collector who is not interested in selling his or her collection and who contemplates making a lifetime or deathtime donation of all or part of the collection:

1. A collector of advanced age, for whom current income-tax deductions are not of concern, should consider either a current gift or a bequest to a museum or other qualified donee institution. If the collector and spouse desire to enjoy the collection during their lifetimes, a bona-fide loan of the collection (which will not generate tax) may be made, with title (as well as physical possession of

the collection) passing to the donee institution at death of the collector and/or his or her spouse.

2. A collector desiring to "benefit" from current income-tax allowances may consider a lifetime donation of one or more paintings from the collection, with a loan of the balance until death. In some instances, a so-called "double benefit" may be obtained if the collector transfers a partial interest in one or more works of art to a donee institution or institutions while retaining (and enjoying through possession) the retained portion of ownership. For example, if a collector spends three summer months at a vacation location, he or she may transfer a 25-percent interest in a painting to a museum for display during the summer months. Upon the collector's return from holiday, the painting can be transferred back to the collector for the remaining nine months of the year. This process may be repeated each year until death.

3. Assuming a collector desires to make a current donation of one or more works of art with maximum tax benefits, careful calculation of tax consequences must be made by a skilled tax professional. These will include assurance that the donation does not generate an Alternate Minimum Tax payment and that the deductible portion of the appreciation of the donated works of art does not exceed 30 percent of the taxpayer's "total reportable" income during the year of the donation. If the value exceeds 30 percent, the collector may be in a position to take a deduction for the excess amount by "carrying over" the excess to later years (assuming that the collector is prepared to assume that he or she will remain alive in future years with income sufficient to absorb the additional deduction). Alternately, the collector may transfer a partial interest in a work of art in the year of donation with additional transfers of partial interests in succeeding taxable years and/or at death.

4. If a work of art has not materially appreciated in value or if the donor does not need a deduction with respect to the appreciation, a collector may take a deduction of the original cost of the work of art to the extent of 50 percent of that year's income if the donation is made to a museum or other qualified public charity, and if the donor has made no other charitable contributions during that taxable year. If the latter is true, or if the amount of the deduction otherwise exceeds 50 percent of income, the excess may be carried over to later taxable years.

5. In rare cases, a collector may achieve certain estate-planning goals through the donation of a collection to a museum or other public institution. For example, a collector who is a principal owner of an incorporated family business with substantial liquid as well as operating assets may make a contribution of substantial shares to a museum or other donee institution. The donor's children may purchase at fair value (or may have otherwise acquired by gift) shares in the company in question. In a separate transaction, the corporation can redeem the shares in the hands of the museum for cash or its equivalent, thereby increasing the percentage ownership of the shares held by the children. The donee institution with the funds now in hand may purchase the collection from the donor at the donor's cost and retain the excess funds to finance the maintenance of the collection. Variations of the foregoing are, of course, possible, but in this and all other cases of significant donations, consultation with a qualified tax professional is essential.

NOTES

1. The tax classification of the donee institution can bear materially on the income-tax effects of the donation, i.e., depending upon whether the institution is categorized as a publicly supported museum (which may receive certain gifts equal to 50 and/or 30 percent of the donor's annual income subject to limitations more fully described in the text); as a "private operating foundation" (to which a donor may give and deduct as much as 50 or 30 percent of income gifts but which is subject to "self-dealing" transactional constraints); or as a "private foundation" (which is also subject to self-dealing transactional constraints, as well as a 30- or 20-percent income limit on deductions).
2. Add to that, where applicable, state and local taxes. To be noted also is the 1990 Tax Act, which increased the maximum marginal income-tax rate from 28 to 31 percent and the alternate minimum tax rate from 21 to 24 percent. In addition, a limitation on so-called itemized deductions is imposed whereby the amount of such items (other than medical expenses, casualty and theft losses, and investment interest) is reduced by an amount equal to 3 percent of the taxpayer's adjusted gross income in excess of $100,000. Although the amount of the reduced deduction may in no event exceed 80

percent of the taxpayer's itemized deductions, the net economic effect (depending upon the taxpayer) approximates an additional 1 percent tax burden. Of course, depending upon the state of the collector's residence, additional state taxes may be payable.

3. In other words, transfer of property to children or other persons may be subject to federal gift, estate, or generation-skipping taxes at rates per generation reaching 55 percent.

4. Part or all of the transfer may be free of tax if it qualifies for the lifetime exclusion ($600,000 per transferor), or for the annual exclusion ($10,000 per transferor).

5.

Gross Funds:	$22,000
Tax (55% x 22,000):	12,100
Residue (value of painting):	$ 9,900

Possible state and generation-skipping taxes are not taken into account. It is also to be observed that, in the case of a lifetime gift, the gift tax is applied without "gross up," assuming that the collector survives the gift by three years. In that situation, the tax generated by the gift is $5,500, making the total cost of the transaction $15,500.

6. The identity of the institution must also be taken into account for estate-tax purposes. To qualify for receipt of a deductible bequest of a collection or a work of art, the donee institution must not (in contrast to the situation, described in note 1, of a lifetime gift) necessarily be a museum or other arts organization, but only an organization whose exemption under Section 501(c)(3) of the Internal Revenue Code has been approved. If the donee institution is a foreign entity, such entity must have purposes that—were the organization operated in the United States—would satisfy the charitable tests of Section 501(c)(3). Accordingly, a museum is more often than not the recipient of a bequest from a collector; any other qualifying "charity" will enable the collector to qualify the donation for an estate- (but not necessarily an income-) tax deduction.

7. The 1990 amendments to the Tax Code permit a deduction equal to the fair-market value of the property, even if greater than cost, if the use of the donated property is related to the donee institution's exempt purpose.

8. Technically, the term utilized is "contribution base," i.e., adjusted gross income without regard to so-called net operating-loss carrybacks.

9. This election assumes that the donor is not a "dealer" in the art objects, i.e., that the objects are otherwise so-called "capital gain" property in hand. If the donor is a dealer (so that the property is inventory), the deduction amount is the donor's cost.

10. If an election to reduce the amount of the deduction to cost is not made, the donor may nevertheless deduct as much as 30 percent of the income-ceiling amount.

11. This can be done each time to the extent of the same 50-percent amount (minus the amount of any other future charitable contributions in those years).

12. This 30-percent ceiling may be reduced further if the donor has made other contributions during the taxable year.

13. This limit could be lower if it is otherwise reduced by other contributions.

14. A similar result obtains with respect to carryover of transfers in excess of the 50-percent limitation. Note also that no estate tax is payable on the previously donated collection.

15. The foregoing assumes that the collector could have sold the art objects and realized a long-term capital gain. If the collector were a dealer, the same result (i.e., deduction for cost) would also obtain.

16. Technically, no tax is imposed on the appreciation, but the taxpayer is denied a deduction otherwise obtainable.

17. Because a gift of appreciated property does not directly generate tax as a result of the donation, this consequence has been viewed as a structural defect in the statute (which, in general, taxes profitable dispositions of property). Countering this is the economic fact that, in donating an appreciated work of art, the donor reduces his or her current net worth, both by the then-current value of the property (minus the tax savings, if any), as well by the loss of the financial opportunity benefit of its potential future growth.

18. Whether and to what extent the reduced itemized deduction rule will apply depends upon the amount of the taxpayer's adjusted gross income in excess of $100,000 and the amount of other itemized deductions (such as state and local income and property taxes) that he or she would otherwise claim. Such other items, so long as they equally exceed 3 percent of adjusted gross income, will bear the burden of the reduced itemized deduction, and the benefit of the charitable contribution will not be affected directly.

At the time of publication, it was not known whether this rule would be extended. Therefore, consult your tax advisor before taking any action based on this article.

OBTAINING PROFESSIONAL CONSERVATION SERVICES

Shelley G. Sturman

Owning or acquiring a work of art immediately leads to the responsibility of preserving the object entrusted to your care. As has been described in the preceding chapters, conservation encompasses all aspects of preservation, be it structural consolidation, cosmetic restoration, scientific analysis, condition examination, or environmental evaluation and control.

Naturally, the maintenance of your art objects, antiquities, and historical artifacts should be entrusted to professional conservators and restorers. But locating and selecting an appropriate professional is not an easy undertaking for the private owner of valuable cultural property. The wrong choice could result in irreparable damage affecting the cost of future conservation treatments as well as the aesthetic and monetary value of the object. Yet the task of selecting a conservator becomes manageable when one is armed with a basic knowledge of the profession, a series of questions to pose, and an idea of what to expect.

A number of questions frequently arise when trying to obtain professional conservation services. These questions and their answers follow.

What is the first step I should take when seeking conservation of a work of art?

Before making contact with a conservator, research the object's history to the best of your ability, including artist, date of execution, materials of manufacture, former exhibitions, and any past treatments. Photographic and written records from the artist, manufacturer, former owners, or previous conservator can provide examples of the original or intended appearance of the object. This

Textile conservator working at a tapestry frame. Courtesy National Gallery of Art, Washington, D.C.

information can prove invaluable in assessing current condition and treatment options.

Can I treat my own objects?

Unfortunately, most "home remedies" and "do it yourself" methods are often harmful. Only a trained conservator has the accumulated knowledge of chemistry, studio art, art history, restorative treatments, and practical experience in the preservation of works of art. Conservators are sometimes compared to physicians; just as you would not diagnose and treat your own illness, you should not try to conserve a valuable work of art. However, this does not preclude the preventive measures that have been described in the foregoing chapters which you can take at home in the housing, handling, and display of your artworks.

Are conservators licensed to practice?

As yet there is no formal professional accreditation or licensing of conservators in the United States according to a universally recognized professional standard. The Canadian Association of Professional Conservators (CAPC) has a registry of professional conservators who have met strict entrance requirements. This accrediting organization provides a mechanism for impartial review of consumer complaints against member conservators.

Do conservators have professional standards?

Perhaps the closest thing to an industry standard is the *Code of Ethics and Standards of Practice,* produced by the American Institute for Conservation of Historic and Artistic Works (AIC), and the *Code of Ethics and Guidance for Practice for Those Involved in the Conservation of Cultural Property in Canada,* produced by the International Institute for Conservation—Canadian Group (IIC-CG) and CAPC. These documents set specific standards for treatment, analysis, and practice for the protection of the work of art and its owner, in addition to reflecting the moral responsibilities of the conservator to the object, the profession, and the public. Professional members of these organizations have agreed in writing to abide by their ethical codes.

Are conservators listed in the Yellow Pages and other advertisements?

A few conservators may be located via telephone directories or magazine and newspaper advertisements but most cannot. Since there is no licensing of art conservators, anyone who wishes may claim to be a restorer or conservator. Some artists and framers believe they are competent to conserve works of art but in reality do not fully understand the properties of art materials, their degradation processes, or the techniques of treatment and ultimate preservation. Far too often an art object can suffer greater damage from improper treatment than when simply neglected.

The AIC *Code of Ethics* has specific guidelines regarding advertisements that must reflect the highest professional standards. Direct solicitation of clients is considered unethical.

Without the aid of advertisements, how do I locate a conservator?

Since there is no "central clearinghouse" for conservators, and relatively few advertise their services, you must develop a list of conservators with expertise in the particular areas needed, such as painting, sculpture, antiquities, paper, rare books and manuscripts, photographs, ethnographic objects, decorative arts, furniture, and other art forms. Referral from individuals or institutions having firsthand experience and knowledge of conservation is ideal. Conservation organizations, museum conservation departments, conservation training programs, university art departments, state arts councils and commissions, gallery owners, historical societies, and other collectors are normally good sources for obtaining names of qualified practitioners, regional conservation centers, and private conservation enterprises.

The Foundation of the American Institute for Conservation of Historic and Artistic Works (FAIC) has a free Conservation Services Referral System for a wide range of specializations and many types of services. In response to public inquiries, a computer-generated list of conservators with appropriate expertise, and who are members of AIC, is provided. Similarly, the Conservation Unit of the Museums and Galleries Commission of the United Kingdom operates a database called the Conservation Register. For a small fee, a list of five suitable conservators who have satisfied specific criteria for entry to the Register can be obtained. The CAPC Registry of Professional Conservators can also be consulted.

How do I evaluate the various conservators on the list?

It is your responsibility to select a conservator who will provide the best possible care for your object or entire collection. Do not be afraid to ask around. If the same conservators are recommended from a number of sources, that speaks favorably for the named practitioners. Ascertain if the recommendation is from someone who has had direct contact with the proposed conservator. Ask for references and names of former clients from the conservator in question. Follow through by contacting references, but remember that this approach is not infallible. Sometimes a cosmetically attractive, but technically flawed, treatment may not be detected.

Some of the selection criteria to consider include a conservator's training, practical experience, ethical orientation, and professional involvement. These credentials, combined with an evaluation of prior work and recommendations, should establish the conservator's professional reputation and abilities.

What credentials should I look for when choosing a conservator?

A true professional should gladly answer your questions about credentials covering background, current practice, and ethical philosophies. Keep in mind the following:

Training

There are two legitimate routes for training in conservation: apprenticeship with a recognized expert and formal graduate training. Usually, apprenticeship training will take longer than a formal graduate program. In addition to the graduate-training centers associated with North American universities, a number of institutions offer graduate-level internships, courses, and seminars in art conservation. Many major European cities have recognized conservation-training programs, though most do not offer a graduate degree. (For more information refer to the section on training in the comprehensive bibliography.)

A conservator well trained by any method should have an understanding of the chemical and physical properties of artists' materials, the ability to analyze and identify changes, familiarity with the art history within a defined area, and the skills to successfully preserve the object for the future.

No diploma or certificate can guarantee competence. You must weigh a number of factors when judging a conservator's suitability.

Practical Experience

Apprenticeships and internships beyond graduate training with respected conservators in established laboratories are vital to the conservator's professional development. Naturally, a number of years of experience beyond graduate or apprenticeship training (much like a medical residency) is highly recommended before a conservator claims sufficient experience to work alone. Subspecialties generally require even longer training with more specific practical experience. Be wary of the generalist who claims expertise in restoring works of art fashioned from any type of material.

You may also wish to observe examples of completed treatments or objects currently undergoing conservation to help in your evaluation of the practitioner. Visit the conservation facility. Is it in order? Is there adequate storage? Are the objects treated respectfully and handled carefully?

Ethical Orientation

The professional conservation organizations have been instrumental in developing a codified ethical standard for their members. Although not all qualified conservators are members of a professional organization, these principles and philosophical ideals provide a framework for formulating your own expectations of the conservator. Many municipalities, state arts councils, museums, granting agencies, and large contractors include adherence to the *Code* as a stipulation of employment or contract.

Professional Involvement

An individual's membership and status in the conservation organizations demonstrate a commitment to the field and its continued development. By attending annual conferences and reading professional publications, one is kept abreast of new materials, newly discovered treatments, and the latest applications of scientific analysis. Although a conservator's membership in professional organizations is no assurance of competence, it does indicate an interest in sharing in the latest research and thinking in conservation. (For more information refer to the source list on professional conservation organizations.)

What if no one on the list is near me?

You need not limit your search to a specific geographic area, especially if your object has unique problems. Many conservators are willing to travel for lengthy projects, and they certainly can advise you on the best way to pack and ship the work of art if necessary.

It is definitely worth spending a little more time on shipping the object a farther distance in order to obtain the most appropriate services. If your recommendations lead you to a conservator who is farther away than an individual who is physically closer but for whom you could not obtain reliable references, you should not be restricted by limited boundaries.

What is involved once I have selected a conservator from the list?

Establish a relationship with the conservator who will be treating your works of art; avoid dealing with a third-party consultant or office personnel. Use this opportunity to discuss the type of treatment desired. Treatments for structural, chemical, and functional problems differ from cosmetic work. Discuss potential risks of alternative treatment options. At some point the conservator will also need to know the future environmental conditions for the conserved objects since these may affect the choice of materials.

Do not expect an estimate from your telephone description of the problem. The work of art will have to be examined. A conservator may be willing to provide an estimate based on examination of high-quality photographs. It is wise to keep a photograph of the object in the event that you need to consult with the conservator once the work of art has left your premises. An examination report and proposal for treatment should follow.

What is a treatment proposal?

Following the initial examination, a conservator should provide the owner with a written report describing the object, the materials of manufacture, and the present state of preservation. A proposal outlining recommended conservation treatment may be included in this report or written as a

Painting conservator examining Leonardo da Vinci's Ginevra de' Benci. *Courtesy National Gallery of Art, Washington, D.C.*

separate document. In unusual circumstances, a recommendation against any treatment may follow the initial examination.

The treatment proposal should address the actual procedures and materials planned, expected results of the treatment, a cost estimate, and estimated completion date.

The owner's written approval of the proposal is required prior to treatment by the conservator. If new information is discovered during treatment that necessitates a serious deviation from the agreed-upon proposal, you may be asked to sign a revised proposal. A clause allowing modifications to the proposal due to unforeseen developments may be part of the original agreement. The conservator may wish to contact a living artist before establishing a treatment plan for a contemporary work of art.

Until a contract is signed and the treatment proposal approved, you are under no obligation to have work done by the conservator. If you have any doubts, you may wish to seek a second opinion. Speak to a number of conservators until you are able to make a comfortable decision.

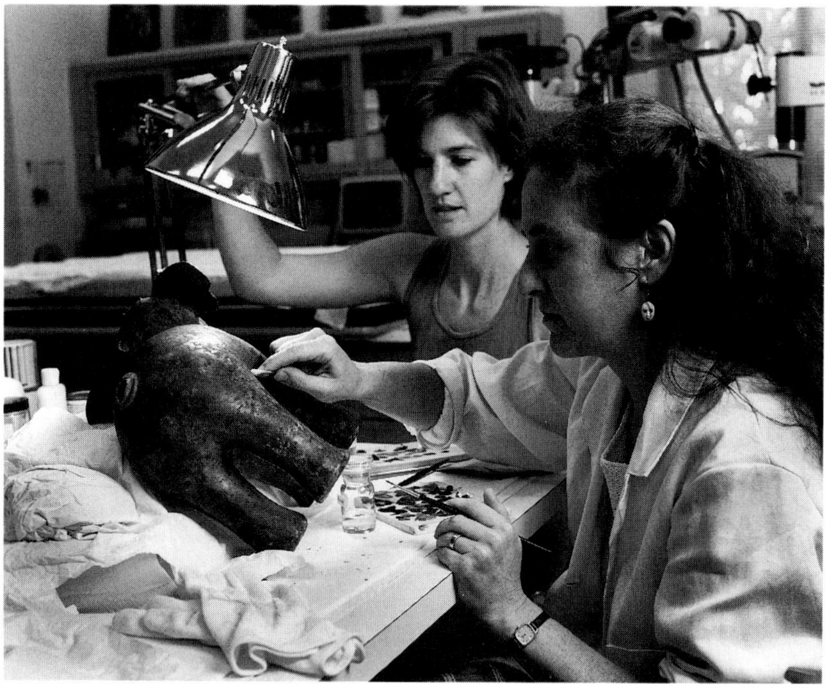

Filling and inpainting losses on a bronze sculpture. Courtesy National Gallery of Art, Washington, D.C.

What about the costs?

Before approving any proposal, discuss the scope of the work and the charges with the conservator. Determine in advance if the initial exam and follow-up report with treatment proposal are billed separately and if they are deductible from subsequent contracts. Ask how the conservator charges for individual treatments and what is included in the fees. For example, the proposal should clearly state whether costs for packing, shipping, storage, insurance, photographs, materials, and taxes have been covered in the estimate.

Conservation work is often very time and labor intensive and may be fairly expensive. Costs are based on the time and materials required to perform and document the treatment, not on the value of the object. In fact, the ethical codes forbid involvement of a conservator in financial gain from dealing, appraising, and speculating. Avoid a conservator whose charges are based on an appraised or market value of the work of art or historical property or who offers different qualities of service at variable prices.

Although a conservator can put forth an opinion regarding urgency or priority of a treatment, you, the owner, must determine if the work of art is worth the cost of conservation.

How long should treatment take?

It has been stated previously that conservation is a very time-consuming business. The projected completion date is usually based on an estimate of the number of hours required to perform each step of the treatment. In some cases, testing and evaluation of materials or scientific analyses may be necessary before work begins. These factors add to the actual time required for a conservation treatment.

Competent conservators may have a backlog of work and there may be a waiting period. The added time to secure the most qualified professional, and to ensure that your object is properly treated, is certainly worthwhile.

What happens after I approve the proposal?

The conservator will schedule the work at a mutually agreeable time, and then treatment can begin. If it is convenient, you may wish to observe the object during different stages of the treatment. The conservator should have nothing to hide and should not discourage your presence. On the other hand, do not expect to be welcome in the laboratory on a daily basis where your presence could present a safety hazard or monopolize too much of the conservator's time.

When the conservation work is complete, the object should be returned or recovered by you together with a written report describing the treatment and including the names of the materials employed. Written and photographic documentation (before, during, and after treatment) are essential components of the finished work and should accompany any future disposition of the object. Recommendations about ongoing care and maintenance also should be provided in the package.

What if problems arise?

If you are not satisfied with the outcome or have questions about the report or the treatment, you should discuss it with the conservator. A professional conservator will try to resolve issues while respecting your concerns. Contact between conservator and client throughout the course of the treatment should eliminate most causes for misunderstandings.

It is also valuable to point out that conservators do not always agree. Some forms of treatment may be considered too invasive by some yet perfectly appropriate by others. If a proposal appears questionable to you, it is probably best to select the more conservative treatment. Additional conservation can always be performed at a later time if you learn more or change your mind.

Are there other practical considerations?

Ask about the security of the laboratory where the treatment will be carried out, and, if possible, view the premises and satisfy yourself regarding its suitability. Determine in advance packing and shipping responsibilities. Consider insurance options. Does your carrier cover conservation, transit to and from the laboratory, and include time while on deposit with the conservator? If not, the conservator's insurance may be sufficient, or you may be able to purchase additional coverage through the conservator.

If you have a number of objects in need of conservation and this is your first time employing a particular conservator, you may wish to have only one work of art treated initially. After evaluating the treatment, you can decide whether to proceed with the rest of your collection.

In Summary: Points to Consider When Obtaining Conservation Services

Learn about conservation and research the object

Seek advice from a number of sources

Develop a list of conservators

Ask questions about a conservator's
- training
- length and scope of practice
- references
- ethical philosophies
- professional affiliations

Expect to find in the examination report
- description of the object
- discussion of method of its manufacture
- present condition

Expect to find in the treatment proposal
- recommendations for correcting the problem
- procedures and materials to be used
- intended results
- cost estimate
- time estimate for completion

Expect to find in the treatment report
- description of actual treatment carried out
- names of materials employed
- photographic documentation of the work
- recommendations for future care

Practical considerations
- packing
- shipping
- security
- insurance

CONSERVATION RESOURCES

There are numerous professional and public-service organizations in the various fields of conservation. A few of the larger organizations are listed below, with a guide to specific subgroups included where appropriate. Also included are names of manufacturers for more difficult to find archival storage containers and other materials.

Organizations

American Association for State and Local History
172 Second Avenue North, Suite 202
Nashville, Tenn. 37201

American Association of Museums
1225 Eye Street, N.W.
Washington, D.C. 20005

American Institute for Conservation of Historic and Artistic Works
1400 16th Street, N.W., Suite 340
Washington, D.C. 20036
Conservation Services Referral System

American Library Association
50 East Huron Street
Chicago, Ill. 60611
Association for Library Collections and Technical Services

American Society for Industrial Security
1655 North Fort Myer Drive, Suite 1200
Arlington, Va. 22209
Museum, Library, and Cultural Property National Standing Committee

American Society of Appraisers
535 Herndon Parkway, Suite 150
Herndon, Va. 22070

Art Dealers Association of America
575 Madison Avenue, 16th Floor
New York, N.Y. 10022

Association for Preservation Technology International
P. O. Box 8178
Fredericksburg, Va. 22404

Canadian Conservation Institute
1030 Innes Road
Ottawa, Ontario, Canada K1A 0C8

The Conservation Unit
Museums & Galleries Commission
16 Queen Anne's Gate
London SW1H 9AA, England

International Centre for the Study of Preservation and Restoration of Cultural Property
13 Via di San Michele
1-00153 Rome, Italy

International Foundation for Art Research
46 East 70th Street
New York, N.Y. 10021

International Institute for Conservation of Historic and Artistic Works—Canadian Group
P.O. Box 9195
Ottawa, Ontario, Canada K1G 3T9

National Conference of State Historic Preservation Officers
444 North Capitol Street, N.W.
Washington, D.C. 20001

National Fire Protection Association
1 Battery March Park
Quincy, Mass. 02269
Committee on Protection of Cultural Resources

National Institute for the Conservation of Cultural Property
3299 K Street, N.W., Suite 403
Washington, D.C. 20007

National Park Service
P. O. Box 37127
Washington, D.C. 20013-7127
Preservation Assistance Division

National Trust for Historic Preservation
1785 Massachusetts Avenue, N.W.
Washington, D.C. 20036

Society of American Archivists
600 South Federal Street, Suite 504
Chicago, Ill. 60605

Southeastern Library Network
Plaza Level, 400 Colony Square
1201 Peachtree Street, N.E.
Atlanta, Ga. 30361

United Kingdom Institute for Conservation
37 Upper Addison Gardens
London W14 8AJ, England

Manufacturers

Conservation Materials, Ltd.
P.O. Box 2884
1165 Marietta Way
Sparks, Nev. 89431
(702) 331-0582

Hollinger Corp.
P.O. Box 8360
Fredericksburg, Va. 22404
(800) 634-0491

Light Impressions Corp.
439 Monroe Avenue
Rochester, N.Y. 14603
(716) 271-8960

Nielsen & Bainbridge
17 South Middlesex Avenue
Cranbury, N.J. 08512
(609) 395-5550

Paper Technologies, Inc.
25801 Obrero #4
Mission Viejo, Calif. 92691
(714) 768-7497

Rising Paper Company
295 Park Street
Housatonic, Mass. 01236-0565
(413) 274-3345

TALAS Division of Technical Library Service
213 West 35th Street, 7th Floor
New York, N.Y. 10001
(212) 736-7744

University Products, Inc.
P. O. Box 101
Holyoke, Mass. 01041
(413) 532-3372

FURTHER READING

As indicated, many of the resource organizations listed previously offer technical publications, a few of which are included here. The various listings of the Art and Archaeological Technical Abstracts, found in the local library, also contain a great deal of specific technical advice.

General

Buck, Richard. "Inspecting and Describing the Condition of Art Objects." In *Museum Registration Methods.* Edited by Dorothy Dudley, Irma Bezold Wilkinson, and others, 237–44. Washington D.C.: American Association of Museums, 1979.

———. "On Conservation: What Is Condition?" *Museum News* 52, no. 2 (Oct. 1973): 15–16.

———. "On Conservation: What Is Conservation?" *Museum News* 52, no. 1 (Sept. 1973): 15–16.

Horne, Stephen A. *Way to Go: Crating Artwork for Travel.* Hamilton, N.Y.: Gallery Association of New York State, 1985.

Housekeeping Our Heritage: Practical Advice for Alberta Collections. Edmonton: Provincial Museum of Alberta, 1984.

Johnson, E. Verner, and Joanne C. Horgan. *Museum Collection Storage, Protection of the Cultural Heritage Technical Handbooks for Museums and Monuments* No. 2. Paris: UNESCO, 1979.

Levenstein, Mary Kerney, and Cordelia Frances Biddle. *Caring for Your Cherished Possessions: The Experts' Guide to Cleaning, Preserving, and Protecting Your China, Silver, Furniture, Clothing, Paintings, and More.* New York: Crown, 1989.

The Museums Association. *Manual of Curatorship.* Edited by John M. A. Thompson. London: Butterworths, 1984.

The National Trust. *The National Trust Manual of Housekeeping.* Compiled by Hermione Sandwith and Sheila Stainton. London: Penguin Books, 1985.

Rose, Carolyn L. "An Introduction to Museum Conservation." *American Indian Art Magazine* 3, no. 1 (1977): 30–31, 83, 104.

Shelley, Marjorie. *The Care and Handling of Art Objects: Practices in The Metropolitan Museum of Art.* New York: The Metropolitan Museum of Art, 1987.

Snyder, Jill. *Caring for Your Art.* New York: Allworth Press, 1990.

Stolow, Nathan. *Conservation and Exhibitions: Packing, Transport, Storage and Environmental Considerations.* London and Boston: Butterworths, 1987.

Stoner, Joyce Hill. "A Look at Art Conservation." *Art Dealer and Framer* (March 1978): 14–18.

Environment

Black, Jim. *Preventive Conservation in Museums: Lighting/Climate.* London: ICCROM and The Institute of Archaeology, 1983.

Canadian Conservation Institute. *Controlling Museum Fungal Problems.* Technical Bulletin No. 12. Ottawa: Canadian Conservation Institute, n.d.

———. *Examining for Insect Infestations.* CCI Notes 3/1. Ottawa: Canadian Conservation Institute, 1983.

———. *Recognizing Active Corrosion.* CCI Notes 9/1. Ottawa: Canadian Conservation Institute, 1989.

———. *Track Lighting.* CCI Notes 2/3. Ottawa: Canadian Conservation Institute, 1988.

Hillary, Nancy. *Prevention of Mildew: General Guidelines.* National Park Service Conserve-O-Gram 3/6. Washington, D.C.: National Park Service, 1978.

Knapp, Tony. *Arsenic Health and Safety Update.* National Park Service Conserve-O-Gram 2/6. Washington, D.C.: National Park Service, 1989.

Nero, Anthony V., Jr. "Controlling Indoor Air Pollution." *Scientific American* 258 (1988): 42–48.

Raphael, Toby, and Diana Pardue. *Basic Steps to Follow for Insect Infestations.* National Park Service Conserve-O-Gram 3/10. Washington, D.C.: National Park Service, 1981.

Stolow, Nathan. "The Action of Environment on Museum Objects, Part 1: Humidity, Temperature, Atmospheric Pollution." *Curator* 9, no. 3 (September 1966).

———. "The Micro Climate: A Localized Solution." *Museum News* 56 (1977): 52–63.

Thomson, Garry. *The Museum Environment.* 2nd ed. London and Boston: Butterworths, in association with the International Institute for Conservation of Historic and Artistic Works, 1986.

Painting

Canadian Conservation Institute. *Keying Out of Paintings.* CCI Notes 10/9. Ottawa: Canadian Conservation Institute, 1988.

Keck, Caroline K. A *Handbook on the Care of Painting.* Nashville: American Association for State and Local History, 1970.

———. *How to Take Care of Your Paintings.* New York: Charles Scribner's Sons, 1978.

———. *How to Take Care of Your Pictures.* New York: The Museum of Modern Art and The Brooklyn Museum, 1954.

Works of Art on Paper

Clapp, Anne F. *Curatorial Care of Works of Art on Paper: Basic Procedures for Paper Preservation.* 4th rev. ed. New York: Nick Lyons Books, 1987.
Ellis, Margaret Holben. *The Care of Prints and Drawings.* Nashville: American Association for State and Local History, 1987.
Goldman, Paul. *Looking at Prints, Drawings and Watercolours: A Guide to Technical Terms.* London: The British Museum, 1988.
Hunter, Dard. *Papermaking: The History and Technique of an Ancient Craft.* New York: Dover, 1978.
Reed, Ronald. *Ancient Skins, Parchments, and Leathers.* London: Seminar Press, 1972.
Smith, Merrily. *Matting and Hinging Works of Art on Paper.* Washington, D.C.: Library of Congress, 1981.

Library and Archival Collections

Baumann, Roland M., ed. *A Manual of Archival Techniques.* Rev. ed. Harrisburg: Pennsylvania Historical and Museum Commission, 1982.
Collings, T. J., and R. F. Schoolley-West. *The Care and Preservation of Philatelic Materials.* State College, Pa.: American Philatelic Society, 1989.
Cunha, George D. M., and Dorothy G. Cunha. *Library and Archives Conservation: 1980's and Beyond.* 2 vols. Metuchen, N.J.: Scarecrow Press, 1983.
Greenfield, Jane. *Books, Their Care and Repair.* New York: H. W. Wilson Co., 1983.
———. *The Care of Fine Books.* New York: Nick Lyons Books, 1988.
Morrow, Carolyn Clark. *The Preservation Challenge: A Guide to Conserving Library Materials.* White Plains, N.Y.: Knowledge Industry Publications, Inc., 1983.
Ritzenthaler, Mary Lynn. *Archives and Manuscripts: Conservation, A Manual on Physical Care and Management.* Society of American Archivists Basic Manual Series. Chicago: Society of American Archivists, 1983.
Roberts, Matt T., and Don Etherington. *Bookbinding and the Conservation of Books: A Dictionary of Descriptive Terminology.* Washington, D.C.: Library of Congress, 1975.
Waters, Peter. *Procedures for Salvage of Water-Damaged Library Materials.* Washington, D.C.: Library of Congress, 1975.

Photographs

Albright, Gary. "Photographs." In *Conservation in the Library: A Handbook of Use and Care of Traditional and Nontraditional Materials.* Edited by Susan Garretson Swartzburg. Westport, Conn.: Greenwood Press, 1983.
Canadian Conservation Institute. *Care of Black-and-White Photographic Prints.* CCI Notes 16/4. Ottawa: Canadian Conservation Institute.
Coe, B., and M. Haworth-Booth. *A Guide to Early Photographic Processes.* London: Victoria and Albert Museum, 1983.
Eastman Kodak Company. *Conservation of Photographs.* Kodak Publication F-40. Rochester, N.Y.: Eastman Kodak Company, 1985.
———. *Copying and Duplication in Black-and-White and Color.* Kodak Publication M-1. Rochester, N.Y.: Eastman Kodak Company, 1984.
Hendriks, Klaus. "The Stability and Preservation of Recorded Images." In *Imaging Processes and Materials, Niblette's Eighth Edition.* Edited by John Sturge, Vivian Walworth, and Allan Shepp, 637–84. New York: Van Nostrand Reinhold, 1989.
———. *Storage and Care of Photographs.* Bulletin No. 16. New York State Conservation Consultancy, n.d.
———, and A. Whitehurst. *Conservation of Photographic Materials: A Basic Reading List.* National Archives of Canada, 1988.
Keefe, L., and D. Inch. *The Life of a Photograph: Archival Processing, Matting, Framing and Storage.* Stoneham, Mass.: Butterworths, 1983.
Reilly, James. *Care and Identification of 19th Century Photographic Prints.* Kodak Publication G-28. Rochester, N.Y.: Eastman Kodak Company.
Ritzenthaler, Mary Lynn, G. Munoff, and M. Long. *Archives and Manuscripts: Administration of Photographic Collections.* SAA Basic Manual Series. Chicago: Society of American Archivists, 1984.
Schwalberg, B., H. Wilhelm, and C. Brower. "Going! Going!! Gone!!!" *Popular Photography* 97, no. 6 (June 1990): 37–60.

Furniture

Brommelle, N. S., J. A. Darrah, and A. J. Moncrieff. *Papers on the Conservation and Technology of Wood.* Madrid: The International Council of Museums, Committee on Conservation, October 1972.
Canadian Conservation Institute. *Proceedings of the Furniture and Wooden Objects Symposium, July 2–3, 1980/Canadian Conservation Institute, National Museums of Canada.* Ottawa: Canadian Conservation Institute, 1980.
Guldbeck, Per E. *The Care of Antiques and Historical Collections.* 2nd ed. Nashville: American Association for State and Local History, 1985.
Kirk, John T. *Early American Furniture: How to Recognize, Evaluate, Buy & Care for the Most Beautiful*

Pieces—High-style, Country, Primitive, & Rustic. 1st ed. New York: Alfred A. Knopf, 1970.
McGiffin, Robert F. *Furniture Care and Conservation.* Nashville: American Association for State and Local History, 1983.
Williams, Marc A. *Keeping It All Together: The Preservation and Care of Historic Furniture.* 1st ed. Worthington: Ohio Antique Review, 1988.

Decorative Arts

Atterbury, Paul. *The History of Porcelain.* New York: William Morrow, 1982.
Evetts, Echo. *China Mending.* London: Faber & Faber, 1978.
Fleming, John, and Hugh Honour. *Dictionary of the Decorative Arts.* New York: Harper & Row, 1986.
Fournier, Robert. *Illustrated Dictionary of Practical Pottery.* New York: Van Nostrand Reinhold, 1977.
Gardner, Paul Vickers. *Glass.* The Smithsonian Illustrated Library of Antiques. New York: Cooper-Hewitt Museum, 1979.
Gilchrist, Brenda, gen. ed. *Pottery.* The Smithsonian Illustrated Library of Antiques. New York: Cooper-Hewitt Museum, 1981.
Hodges, Henry. *Artifacts, An Introduction to Early Materials and Technology.* London: John Baker Publishers, Ltd., 1976.
Kingery, W. D., and P. B. Vandiver. *Ceramic Masterpieces—Art, Structure, Technology.* New York: Macmillan, 1986.
Lawrence, W. G. *Ceramic Science for the Potter.* Philadelphia: Chilton Book Company, 1972.
MacLeish, A. Bruce. *The Care of Antiques and Historical Collections.* Nashville: AASLH Press, 1985.
Newton, Roy, and Sandra Davison. *Conservation of Glass.* London: Butterworths, 1989.
Rhodes, Daniel. *Stoneware and Porcelain, the Art of High-Fired Pottery.* Philadelphia: Chilton Book Company, 1959.
Rice, Prudence M. *Pottery Analysis, a Sourcebook.* Chicago: The University of Chicago Press, 1987.
Valenstein, Suzanne G. *A Handbook of Chinese Ceramics.* New York: The Metropolitan Museum of Art, 1975.
Williams, Nigel. *Porcelain Repair and Restoration.* London: British Museum Publications, Ltd., 1983.
Zerwick, Chloe. *A Short History of Glass.* Corning, N.Y.: The Corning Museum of Glass, 1980.

Textiles

Finch, Karen, and Greta Putnam. *Caring for Textiles.* New York: Watson-Guptill, 1977.
Kajitani, Nobuko. "Care of Fabrics in the Museum." In *Preservation of Paper and Textiles.* Edited by J. C. Williams. Washington, D.C.: American Chemical Society, 1977.
Mailand, Harold F. *Considerations in the Care of Textiles and Costumes.* Indianapolis: Indianapolis Museum of Art, 1980.
Ordonez, Margaret T. *Cleaning and Storing Your Wedding Gown.* University of Maryland Cooperative Extension Service Fact Sheet 360. College Park: University of Maryland, 1983–84.
Textile Conservation Center. *Technical Bibliographies.* Andover, Mass.: Museum of American Textile History, n.d.

Metal Objects

Canadian Conservation Institute. *The Cleaning, Polishing, and Protective Waxing of Brass and Copper Objects.* CCI Notes 9/3. Ottawa: Canadian Conservation Institute, 1988.
Drayman-Weisser, Terry, ed. *Dialogue 89: The Conservation of Bronze Sculpture in the Outdoor Environment.* National Association of Corrosion Engineers, in preparation.
Heller, Don B. "Conserving Metal Objects." *Museum News* 55, no. 5 (May/June 1977).
Maryon, Herbert. *Metalwork and Enamelling.* 5th ed. New York: Dover, 1971.
Naude, Virginia Norton, ed. *Sculptural Monuments in an Outdoor Environment.* Philadelphia: Pennsylvania Academy of Fine Arts, 1983.
Untracht, Oppi. *Metal Techniques for Craftsmen.* Garden City, N.Y.: Doubleday, 1975.

Stone Objects

Amoroso, Giovanni G., and Vasco Fassina. *Stone Decay and Conservation.* Amsterdam: Elsevier, 1983.
Cooper-Hewitt Museum and New York State Conservation Association. *Storage of Stone, Ceramic, Glass, and Metal.* Bulletin No. 5. New York: Smithsonian Institution's National Museum of Design, n.d.
Mitchell, Richard S. *Dictionary of Rocks.* New York: Van Nostrand Reinhold, 1985.

Musical Instruments

Barclay, R. L. *Care of Musical Instruments in Canadian Collections.* Technical Bulletin No. 4. Ottawa: Canadian Conservation Institute, 1978.
Eliason, Robert E., and Friedemann Hellwig, eds. "Musical Instrument Collections in Scandinavia—Report of the Conservation and Security Working Group."

International Committee for Musical Instrument Collections Newsletter: 69–87.

McKean, James N. *Strings Magazine Guide to Common Sense Instrument Care*. San Anselmo, Calif.: Strings Magazine, 1990.

Ethnographic Materials

Byrne, Greg. *Ceramics and Glass, Preventative Conservation*. National Park Service Conserve-O-Gram 8/1. Washington, D.C.: National Park Service, 1978.

Canadian Conservation Institute. *Care of Basketry*. CCI Notes 6/2. Ottawa: Canadian Conservation Institute, 1983.

———. *Care of Ivory, Bone, Horn, Antler*. CCI Notes 6/1. Ottawa: Canadian Conservation Institute, 1983.

———. *Care of Quillwork*. CCI Notes 6/5. Ottawa: Canadian Conservation Institute, 1991.

———. *Care of Rawhide and Semi-Tanned Leather*. CCI Notes 8/4. Ottawa: Canadian Conservation Institute, 1983.

Clark, Thurid. *Storage Supports for Basket Collections*. National Park Service Conserve-O-Gram 5/5. Washington, D.C.: National Park Service, 1989.

Hoveman, Alice. *Conservation-Wise Guide, Manual on Basic Care for Alaskan Artifacts*. 1985.

Lougheed, Sandra. "The Deterioration of Glass Beads on Ethnographic Objects." *Symposium 86: The Care of Ethnological Materials*. Getty Canadian Conservation Institute, 1986.

Odegaard, Nancy, and Dale Kronkright. "Giving Your Baskets a Long, Healthy Life: A Basic Guide to Basketry Conservation." *Fiberarts Magazine* 11, no. 1 (1984): 43–49.

Pacific Regional Conservation Center. *The Care of Tapa*. Bulletin no. 7, 3 pp. Honolulu: Pacific Regional Conservation Center.

Rose, Carolyn L. "Ethical and Practical Considerations in Conserving Ethnographic Museum Objects." In *The Museum Conservation of Ethnographic Objects*, Senri Ethnological Studies 23, edited by T. Morita and C. Pearson. Osaka, Japan: National Museum of Ethnology, 1988.

———, and A. R. Torres. *Workbook for the Storage of Natural History Collections*. Pittsburgh: Society for the Preservation of Natural History Collections, 1992.

Snow, Carol E., and Terry Drayman-Weisser. "The Examination and Treatment of Ivory and Related Materials." In *Adhesives and Consolidants, IIC Paris Congress Papers*, 141–45. London: International Institute for Conservation, 1984.

Sturtevant. William C. *Guide to Field Collecting of Ethnographic Specimens*. Smithsonian Information Leaflet 503. Washington, D.C.: Smithsonian Institution Press, 1977.

Thomsen, Fonda. *Storing Baskets in Polyethylene Bags*. National Park Service Conserve-O-Gram 5/4. Washington, D.C.: National Park Service, 1976.

Walston, S. "A Mounting System for Paintings on Bark." In *Symposium 86: The Care of Ethnological Materials*. Getty Canadian Conservation Institute, 1986.

Warthen, David. *Packing Specimens for Shipment*. National Park Service Conserve-O-Gram 17/2. Washington, D.C.: National Park Service.

Wolf, Sara J. "Feathers." *American Indian Art Magazine* 3, no. 4 (1978): 77–81.

———. "Preserving Navajo Textiles." *Four Winds* 3, no. 1 (1982): 44–46.

———, and Lynn Denton. "Labeling Museum Specimens." *Conservation Notes* no. 11 (1985): 1–4. Austin: Texas Memorial Museum, University of Texas at Austin.

Security

American Association for Industrial Security. *Suggested Guidelines in Museum Security*. Arlington: American Association for Industrial Security, 1989.

Association of Art Museum Directors, *Planning for Emergencies: A Guide for Museums*. Washington, D.C.: Association of Art Museum Directors, 1987.

Burke, Robert. *A Manual of Basic Museum Security*. Mount Vernon, N.Y.: Consumers Union of United States, 1988.

Consumers Union of United States, Inc. *Home Security*. Mount Vernon, N.Y.: Consumers Union of United States, 1988.

Faulk, Wilbur. *How the J. Paul Getty Museum Plans and Prepares for Emergencies*. The Hague: ICOM Security Committee, August 1989.

Fennelley, Lawrence J., ed. *Museum, Library, Archives, and Library Security*. London and Boston: Butterworths, 1983.

Morris, John. *Managing the Library Risk*. 2nd ed. Berkeley: University of California Office of Insurance and Risk Management, 1979.

National Fire Protection Association, Inc. *Recommended Practice for the Protection of Museums and Museum Collections*. NFPA 911. National Fire Protection Association, Inc., 1991.

Collecting

Marion, John L., and Christopher Andersen. *The Best of Everything: An Insider's Guide to Collecting—for Every Taste and Every Budget*. New York: Simon and Schuster, 1989.

Reitlinger, Gerald. *The Economics of Taste: The Rise and Fall of Picture Prices from 1760-1960*. 3 vols. New York: Hacker Art Books, 1982.

Rigby, Douglas, and Elizabeth Rigby. *Lock, Stock and Barrel: The Story of Collecting*. Philadelphia: J. P. Lippincott, 1944.

Sack, Harold, and Max Wilk. *American Treasure Hunt*. New York: Ballantine Books, 1986.

Taylor, Francis Henry. *The Taste of Angels: A History of Collecting from Rameses to Napoleon*. Boston: Little, Brown and Co., 1948.

Authentication

Fleming, Stuart J. *Authenticity in Art: The Scientific Detection of Forgery*. New York: Crane, Russack and Co., 1975.

Leute, Ulrich. *Archaeometry: An Introduction to Physical Methods in Archaeology and the History of Art*. New York: VCH Publishers, 1987.

Obtaining Conservation Services

American Institute for Conservation of Historic and Artistic Works (AIC) and the Foundation of the AIC (FAIC). *Guidelines for Selecting a Conservator*. 3rd ed. Washington, D.C.: AIC/FAIC, 1987.

AIC. *Conservation Training in the United States*. Washington, D.C.: AIC, 1989.

Appelbaum, Barbara A., and Kathryn Hebb. "The Ethics of Consulting." *Museologist* 52, no. 181 (Spring/Summer 1989): 31–32.

Conservation Unit, Museums & Galleries Commission. *How to Choose a Conservator or Restorer*. London: Conservation Unit, Museums & Galleries Commission, n.d.

Dillon, Phyllis. "Conservation Planning: Where Can You Find the Help You Need?" *History News* 42, no. 4 (1987): 10–15.

FAIC. *Selecting and Working with a Conservator: Conservation Services Referral System*. Washington, D.C.: FAIC, 1990.

International Centre for the Study of Preservation and Restoration of Cultural Property (ICCROM). *International Index on Training in Conservation*. Rome: ICCROM, 1987.

International Institute for Conservation of Historic and Artistic Works—Canadian Group (IIC-CG), and Canadian Association of Professional Conservators (CAPC). *Selecting and Employing a Conservator in Canada*. Ottawa: IIC-CG and CAPC, n.d.

Keck, Caroline. "On Conservation: Recognizing Qualified Practitioners." *Museum News* 50, no. 6 (1972): 9.

———. "Technical Assistance: Where to Find It, What to Expect." *Curator* 8, no. 3 (1965): 197–211.

National Institute for the Conservation of Cultural Property, Inc. (NIC). *The History and Future Directions of Conservation Training in North America*. Washington, D.C.: NIC, 1984.

Orraca, Jose. "Shopping for a Conservator." *Museum News* 59, no. 4 (1981): 60–66.

United Kingdom Institute for Conservation, Conservation Unit (UKIC-CU). *Training in Conservation—A Guide to Full-time Courses in the United Kingdom*. London: UKIC-CU, 1985.

Walsh, Judith. "Special Conservation Problems for Collectors: Choosing a Conservator." *Drawing* 5, no. 6 (1984): 129–30.

AUTHOR BIOGRAPHIES

Robert McCormick Adams earned his undergraduate and graduate degrees and his Ph.D. at the University of Chicago. He went on to a long and distinguished career there as a professor of anthropology and director of the Oriental Institute, serving two years as provost before becoming The Secretary of the Smithsonian Institution in 1984. Mr. Adams is a member of the National Academy of Sciences, the American Philosophical Society, and the American Academy of Arts and Sciences, and he serves as a trustee for the Russell Sage Foundation, the Santa Fe Institute, George Washington University, Morehouse College, and the American University in Beirut, among other institutions. He has lectured and published widely in his field.

Huntington T. Block is a Chartered Property Casualty Underwriter and the president of the Washington, D.C., insurance firm that bears his name and which is a subsidiary of the international insurance brokerage organization Rollins Burdick Hunter Co. Mr. Block has been involved with fine-art insurance practically since he began his insurance career in 1948, and some 25 people in his 130-person firm work exclusively with collectors, dealers, and museums. He has also lectured extensively on the subject to arts organizations and museum groups. In 1989 he was honored at a luncheon hosted by the Committee of Lloyd's to mark his thirty-five-year association with that prestigious insurance institution. He is a graduate of Princeton University.

Brian Considine graduated from the University of Pennsylvania with a degree in architecture. After first apprenticing with a maker of fine custom Shaker furniture, he ran his own custom furniture and restoration business in Vermont for six years. He worked next in the Department of Furniture Conservation at the Museum of Fine Arts, Boston, on both the European and American furniture collections. Mr. Considine came to the J. Paul Getty Museum in 1983 and was named department head of Decorative Arts and Sculpture Conservation in 1988. He has lectured and published extensively in the field of making and conserving furniture and is coordinator of the Furniture Group of the International Council of Museum's Conservation Committee. He is also a member of the American Institute for the Conservation of Historic and Artistic Works, the International Institute for the Conservation of Historic and Artistic Works and its Canadian group, and the United Kingdom Institute for Conservation.

Meg Craft is a graduate of the University of Delaware/ Winterthur Art Conservation Program. She has worked as an assistant object conservator at the Walters Art Gallery and the Henry Francis du Pont Winterthur Museum. Since 1982 she has been in private practice in Baltimore, Maryland, and specializes in the treatment and care of three-dimensional objects, particularly ceramics.

Terry Drayman-Weisser earned a degree in art history from Swarthmore College, studied metallurgy in the graduate program at Johns Hopkins University, and received a diploma with distinction from the University of London's Institute of Archaeology. She has been director of the Division of Conservation and Technical Research at the Walters Art Gallery since 1977 and has served as president of both the American Institute for Conservation of Historic and Artistic Works (AIC) and its foundation. She is a fellow of the AIC and the International Institute for Conservation of Historic and Artistic Works and is a member of the Advisory Board for the Peabody Archives and Fine Arts. She also serves on the board of the National Institute for the Conservation of Cultural Property and on the National Association of Corrosion Engineers Subcommittee on Conservation of Artistic and Historic Works. Ms. Drayman-Weisser has lectured and published extensively on conservation and preservation, has served as conservator on several archaeological expeditions and excavations in Cyprus, Greece, and England, and has led a group of American conservators across China to meet colleagues and discuss common problems and possible solutions.

Margaret Holben Ellis is chairman of the Conservation Center at the Institute of Fine Arts, New York University, and consulting conservator of prints and drawings for the Metropolitan Museum of Art. She has written extensively about the conservation of works of art on paper, including *The Care of Prints and Drawings*, published in 1987.

Wilbur Faulk was born and raised in Southern California and holds a B.S. degree in business administration as well as an A.A. degree in fire science. He spent fifteen years with the Santa Monica Fire Department and retired as a fire captain/ paramedic after serving in all branches of the department. Mr. Faulk has been director of security for the J. Paul Getty Museum since 1986. His affiliations include: chair of the Security Committee's Disaster Preparedness Sub-Committee for the International Council of Museums; chair of the National Standing Committee on Museums, Libraries, and Cultural Property for the American Society for Industrial Security; and member of the Technical Committee on Protection of Cultural Resources for the National Fire Protection Association. Mr. Faulk has lectured extensively on security and disaster preparedness for cultural institutions.

Doris A. Hamburg heads the Paper Conservation Section of the Library of Congress Conservation Office in Washington, D.C. She has traveled widely to consult and lecture on library, archival, and art conservation and has published a number of articles on related paper- and parchment-conservation subjects. She has been active in the American Institute for Conservation of Historic and Artistic Works, Washington Conservation

Guild, and National Information Standards Organization. Ms. Hamburg holds an M.S. degree and certificates in conservation of art and historic artifacts and in museum studies from the University of Delaware/Winterthur Art Conservation Program and an M.A. degree in art history from Columbia University.

William R. Leisher received his B.A., B.F.A., and M.A. degrees from Michigan State University and studied conservation at the Intermuseum Conservation Laboratory, Oberlin, Ohio. Mr. Leisher was assistant conservator of paintings at the National Gallery of Art, Washington, D.C., and head of conservation at the Los Angeles County Museum of Art before becoming executive director of conservation at the Art Institute of Chicago in 1985. He is an associate member of the American Institute for Conservation of Historic and Artistic Works and chairman of the National Institute for the Conservation of Cultural Property. He has participated in numerous conservation projects and has lectured extensively on environmental controls and disaster planning for museums as well as on conservation care, treatments, and issues.

John L. Marion is widely known for his frequent auction appearances in New York and throughout the country. Chairman of Sotheby's North America since 1975, he has personally auctioned hundreds of millions of dollars worth of fine art, antiques, rare books, and jewelry. A graduate of Fordham University, Mr. Marion served overseas as a lieutenant in the U.S. Navy and studied decorative arts at Columbia University. He is chairman of the Fine Arts Division of the American Cancer Society, a member of the Appraisers Association of America, and is on the board of governors of the Winterthur Corporate Council, the board of trustees of Fordham University, and the board of the International Foundation for Art Research. A frequent lecturer at educational and cultural institutions throughout the country, Mr. Marion has been interviewed often on television and radio and is the author of *The Best of Everything*.

Richard Newman received a B.A. in art history from Western Washington University in 1974 and an M.A. degree in geology from Boston University in 1983. He completed a three-year apprenticeship at the Center for Conservation and Technical Studies at the Harvard University Art Museums in 1980 and served as conservation scientist and object conservator there until 1986. He has been research scientist at the Museum of Fine Arts, Boston, since 1986.

Debbie Hess Norris received an M.S. degree in art conservation with a specialty in photographic conservation from the University of Delaware/Winterthur Art Conservation Program. She now serves as assistant director and professor for the same program. Ms. Norris has consulted on the care and preservation of photographic collections across the United States and lectured widely on this and other related topics.

J. Scott Odell graduated from Middlebury College in 1957 and then trained with William Dowd, maker of harpsichords based on historical models, in Boston. Mr. Odell came to the Smithsonian Institution in 1963 to establish a laboratory for the documentation and conservation of the collection of more than three thousand musical instruments at the then newly constructed National Museum of History and Technology (now National Museum of American History). In 1978 he was appointed head conservator there and charged with planning and managing a central conservation program for the museum's collections of more than two and a half million artifacts documenting American material culture. He is a past president of the Washington Conservation Guild and a fellow and former director of the American Institute for Conservation of Historic and Artistic Works. Active as a consultant and lecturer on collection care and conservation, his publications include articles, technical drawings of musical instruments, and a book on historical musical wire.

Carolyn L. Rose became senior research conservator for the Smithsonian Institution's National Museum of Natural History after serving as director of anthropology conservation there for more than a decade. She is an adjunct professor in the departments of anthropology and art history at George Washington University in Washington, D.C. A member of the board of directors of the Society for the Preservation of Natural History Collections, Ms. Rose is also chairman of the society's Conservation Committee, and she serves on the editorial board of the International Biodeterioration Society. During the past four years, she has been chairman of the National Institute for the Conservation of Cultural Property, chairman of the membership committee of the American Institute for Conservation of Historic and Artistic Works, and president of the Washington Conservation Guild.

Arthur W. Schultz is the retired chairman and chief executive officer of Foote, Cone & Belding Communications. A graduate of the University of Chicago, Mr. Schultz is a life trustee and former chairman of the Visiting Committee to the Division of the Humanities. He is a director of Springs Industries, Zenith Radio Corporation, Chicago Sun-Times Co., Schwinn Bicycle Co., The Folger Adams Co., and life trustee and former chairman of the board of trustees of the Art Institute of Chicago. Mr. Schultz is a member of the President's Committee on the Arts and Humanities and chairman of the National Committee to Save America's Cultural Collections. He is president of the Santa Barbara Museum of Art and director of the National Institute for Conservation of Cultural Property.

Leonard L. Silverstein received his B.A. degree from Yale University and his law degree from Harvard University. He is a member of the District of Columbia Bar and American Bar Associations, Bar Association of the District of Columbia, and the American Law Institute. His many appointments and affiliations have included attorney in the Office of Chief Counsel, Internal Revenue Service; member, Advisory Group, House Ways and Means Committee; and adjunct professor, Georgetown University Law Center. Currently he serves as chief editor and technical director of Tax Management, Inc.; member, Board of Directors (and past president), National Symphony Orchestra Association; vice chairman, board of trustees, John F. Kennedy Center for the Performing Arts; president, Alliance Française de Washington; and member, board of directors, White House Historical Association.

Joyce Hill Stoner graduated from the New York University Conservation Center and was later a visiting scholar in paintings conservation at the Metropolitan Museum of Art and at the J. Paul Getty Museum. She has taught for the Art Conservation Program at the University of Delaware/ Winterthur for fifteen years and is currently director of the program and chair of the department of conservation. Mrs. Stoner recently was instrumental in establishing at the University of Delaware the first Ph.D. program in North America devoted to research in art conservation materials and methods. She served as managing editor for *Art and Archaeology Technical Abstracts* for seventeen years and has published numerous articles in other professional journals. She has served on panels for the Institute of Museum Services, the National Institute for Conservation of Cultural Property, the American Association for Museums, and the National Museum Act. Mrs. Stoner was executive director of the Foundation of the American Institute for Conservation and still coordinates its oral-history project.

Shelley G. Sturman is head of the Object Conservation Department at the National Gallery of Art in Washington, D.C. Ms. Sturman received her B.A. and M.A. degrees in Mediterranean Studies from Brandeis University and holds her M.S. degree in conservation from the University of Delaware/Winterthur Art Conservation Program. She is a fellow of the American Institute for Conservation and the International Institute for Conservation. Ms. Sturman has published and lectured widely and is actively involved in the International Council of Museums Committee for Conservation, the American Institute for Conservation, of which she is a former director, and in the Washington Conservation Guild, of which she is a past president.

Steven Weintraub is an art conservator specializing in the environmental protection of museum collections. After completing graduate work at the Conservation Center, part of New York University's Institute of Fine Arts, he was employed at the Metropolitan Museum of Art. He went on to work with the Getty Conservation Institute's Scientific Research Department as head of the Conservation Processes Group. In 1989 he founded Art Preservation Services, a company specializing in products and consultation services dealing with monitoring and controlling the environment in order to preserve important artifacts for museums, archives, and private collections. Mr. Weintraub has been active in developing new methods for climate control and holds a patent on a system utilizing silica gel for humidity control in museum exhibition cases.

George Segan Wheeler is research chemist in the Objects Conservation Department of the Metropolitan Museum of Art and specializes in the care and preservation of stone objects and monuments. Dr. Wheeler received a diploma in conservation from the Conservation Center at New York University's Institute of Fine Arts, an M.A. in art history from Hunter College, and a Ph.D. in chemistry from New York University. He is the author of more than twenty-five articles on the preservation of stone.

Sara J. Wolf is head of the Conservation Department at the Textile Museum in Washington, D.C., with a specialization in the conservation of ethnographic and archaeological textiles. Ms. Wolf is very active in the field of conservation; she serves on the board of the American Institute for Conservation of Historic and Artistic Works and has produced more than twenty-five publications on conservation treatment and ethics.

INDEX

Numbers following entries refer to page numbers. Page numbers in *italic* type refer to illustrations.

PHOTOGRAPH CREDITS

The publisher would like to thank the institutions and individuals named in the captions—and especially the authors—for supplying the necessary photographs. Additional photograph credits are listed below.

Courtesy The Art Institute of Chicago Photography and Conservation Departments, copyright 1991. All Rights Reserved. Museum number 1938.310: 31; museum number 1927.4, Friends of the American Art Collection: 2, 30
Leslie Tate Boles: 86, 92, 94, 95
Phil Charles: 200
Thurid Clark, 1988. Courtesy of the University of California at Davis, Department of Anthropology Museum, C. Hart Merriam Ethnographic Collection. Based upon work supported by the National Science Foundation under Grant Nos. BNS-8305981 and 8606469 to the University of California, Davis, Department of Anthropology, D.L. True and Suzanne Griset, Co-Principal Investigators: 154–55
Sheldan Collins: 43
Courtesy of Cooper-Hewitt, National Museum of Design, Smithsonian Institution/Art Resource, N.Y.: Evaristo Baschenis, Italy, 1617–1677. *Still Life with Musical Instruments.* Oil on canvas, 126.3 × 153.1 cm. Gift of Adam G. Norrie, 1921–32–6: 7
Herbert L. Crossan: 17; courtesy Debbie Hess Norris: 64, 66, 67, 69, 70, 74
Nancy Demyttenaere: 144
Terry Drayman-Weisser: 121 left
Wayne Gibson: 10
Doris A. Hamburg: 56, 59 above, 61
Greta Hansen: 153
Harvard University News Office: 121 right
Lizzie Himmel: 18
William R. Leisher: 33, 34, 35, 36, 39
Courtesy of the Library of Congress Conservation Office: 52, 53, 54
Laurie Minor-Penland: 129, 133, 137
Courtesy Museum of Fine Arts, Boston, 1988-484. University Museum of Philadelpha and MFA Persian Expedition, MFA Expedition, Theodora Wilbour Fund in Memory of Zoe Wilbour, Gift of the John Goelet Foundation, Arthur Mason Knapp Fund, Gift of the Estate of William F. Whittemore, Gift of Ananda K. Coomaraswamy, Gift of the Honorable Lady Hood, Bequest of Dona Luisa Coomaraswamy, Gift of Mrs. Henry Lyman, General Funds, Gift of Abdul Farag Shaer, Anonymous Gift, Gift of Reginald Jenney, Gift of N. M. Heeramaneck, Gift of W. O. Comstock, by exchange, and William Francis Warden Fund: 172, 173
W. Ng: 49 left, 50
Jane Norman: 138, 149
Courtesy the Textile Conservation Workshop, Inc., South Salem, New York: 87
The Walters Art Gallery, Harry Connolly, Jr.: 114; Susan Tobin: 108, 113, 115 above, 119
Courtesy Winterthur Museum Conservation Division: 11, 14
Courtesy Winterthur Museum and Gardens: 22